SPORT IN THE MAKING OF CELTIC CULTURES

Sport and Nation

Series Editor: Stephen Wragg

Books in this series concentrate on individual countries or, where appropriate, groups of countries, and focus on the historical, sociological and political aspects of sport. They consider issues of class, gender, ethnicity and globalization in the context of attempts to define national identity through sport, and cover both theoretical issues and case studies.

Also published in the series

John Nauright, *Sport, Cultures and Identities in South Africa*

SPORT IN THE MAKING OF CELTIC CULTURES

EDITED BY

GRANT JARVIE

Leicester University Press
London and New York

Leicester University Press

A Cassell imprint
Wellington House, 125 Strand, London WC2R 0BB
370 Lexington Avenue, New York, NY 10017-6550

First published 1999

British Library Cataloguing-in-Publication Data
A catalogue record for this book is available from the British Library.

ISBN 0-7185-0129-2

Library of Congress Cataloging-in-Publication Data
Sport in the making of Celtic cultures/edited by Grant Jarvie.
    p. cm. — (Sport and nation)
    Includes bibliographical references and index.
    ISBN 0-7185-0129-2
    1. Nationalism and sports—Scotland. 2. Nationalism and sports—Ireland. 3. Nationalism and sports—Wales. 4. Nationalism and sports—France—Brittany. 5. Sports—Scotland—Sociological aspects. 6. Sports—Ireland—Sociological aspects. 7. Sports—Wales—Sociological aspects. 8. Sports—France—Brittany—Sociological aspects. I. Jarvie, Grant, 1955— . II. Series.
GV706.34.S64   1999
306.4'83'094—dc21

98-42299
CIP

Typeset by BookEns Ltd, Royston, Herts.
Printed and bound in Great Britain by Biddles Ltd, Guildford and Kings Lynn

CONTENTS

ACKNOWLEDGEMENTS

A number of people have to be thanked for the intellectual and practical support that has produced *Sport in the Making of Celtic Cultures*. I am grateful to Donald Meek for his detailed and humorous comments on an earlier draft of this book. I am indebted to Janet Joyce of Cassell for her sensible management of the project. Numerous colleagues and friends have continually reminded me how much a book of this nature is needed. Lorna Jackson's eye for detail was invaluable. I consider it a privilege to have worked with so many Celtic scholars who have taken sport seriously enough to contribute their work, or comment upon the journey that has been the making of this book. Hugh Dan MacLennan's humour, knowledge and friendship has been invaluable. Lindsay Paterson's interventions on culture and Scottish politics have been, as ever, stimulating. Finally, a big thank you to Elza Stewart and Grace Smith, who have been so helpful and supportive of this and of other projects at the University of Stirling.

THE CONTRIBUTORS

Alan Bairner teaches at the University of Ulster at Jordanstown. He has contributed numerous articles on various aspects of sport and politics in Northern Ireland, and is co-author (with John Sugden) of *Sport, Sectarianism and Society in a Divided Ireland* (Leicester University Press) and joint editor of *Sport in Divided Societies* (Meyer and Meyer).

Di Bass is a course tutor at Loughborough University. She is currently researching the relationships between physical education and the development of children's attitudes towards self and others.

Joseph M. Bradley teaches at the University of Stirling. He has written extensively on Irish–Scottish relations, and is author of *Ethnic and Religious Identity in Modern Scotland* (Avebury Press) and *Sport, Culture, Politics and Scottish Society: Irish Immigrants and the Gaelic Athletic Association* (John Donald).

Brian Davies teaches at Cardiff University. He is author of *Education and Social Control* and co-editor with Paul Atkinson and Sara Delamont of *Discourse and Re-Production: Essays in Honour of Basil Bernstein* (Hampton Press).

Marcus de Búrca lives in Dublin and is the author of numerous texts on the history and politics of the Gaelic Athletic Association. These include *The Gaelic Athletic Association: A History* (Cumann Lúthchleas Gael) and *Michael Cusack and the Gaelic Athletic Association* (Anvil Books).

Philip Dine teaches at Loughborough University and is author of numerous articles on the history and politics of sport in France.

John Evans teaches at Loughborough University. He is author of *Teaching in Transition: The Challenge of Mixed Ability Groupings* and editor of *PE, Sport and Schooling: Studies in the Sociology of PE* and *Equality,*

Education and Physical Education. His current research interests involve aspects of physical education and nationalism in England and Wales.

Lorna Jackson teaches at the University of Edinburgh. Her research interests include the social history of sport and popular pastimes in the former county of Argyll. She is currently researching the place of sport in the lives of the Argyllshire aristocracy.

Grant Jarvie teaches at the University of Stirling. He is author of *Highland Games: The Making of the Myth* (Edinburgh University Press) and co-editor of *Scottish Sport in the Making of the Nation* (Leicester University Press).

Michel Lagrée teaches contemporary history at the University of Rennes. His research interests include the diffusion of football in Breton culture.

Hugh Dan MacLennan is Scotland's leading authority on the social history of shinty. His current research provides much more than just the focus for a doctoral thesis at the University of Aberdeen. The recipient of numerous press awards, he is the author of numerous books including *Shinty!* (Balnain Press) and *Not an Orchid* (Kessock Communications, Inverness).

Art Ó Maolfabhail was Chief Placenames Officer of the Irish national mapping agency, Ordnance Survey, Dublin, from 1976 to 1997 and during the same period he was Secretary of the Irish Government's Placenames Commission. He is a recognized poet and authority on the history of hurling.

Michel Raspaud is a Professor at Lille 2 University. He has recently been a research fellow at De Montfort University and has written extensively on the cultural history of mountaineering and football as a social element of Breton identity.

Gareth Williams teaches history at the University of Wales, Aberystwyth. He is author of *1905 and All That* (Gomer Press), co-author of *Fields of Praise: the Official History of Welsh Rugby Union, 1881–1981* (University of Wales Press) and co-editor of *Heart and Soul – the Character of Welsh Rugby* (Univeristy of Wales Press). He has written numerous articles on the social and economic history of sport in Wales.

1

SPORT IN THE MAKING OF CELTIC CULTURES

Grant Jarvie

HIGHLAND GAMES, TRADITION AND CELTIC FUNDAMENTALISM

During the 1930s and 1940s, the writer, novelist and Scottish Nationalist Neil Gunn (1891–1973) continually probed the relationship between symbolism, tradition, nationalism and culture (Gunn and Murray, 1991; McCulloch, 1987). Born in the small coastal town of Dunbeath in Caithness, Gunn continually asserted that nationalism could only be interpreted out of an awareness of tradition. Tradition for Gunn was the essence of nationalism, which in turn would lead to an outward appreciation of internationalism. This was a specific awareness of tradition which was rooted in Highland culture. Indeed, Gunn continually wrestled with the tension that existed between forms of Celtic fundamentalism and the pragmatism that was involved in winning nationalist votes for the Scottish National Party (Finlay, 1994: 117). Tradition for Gunn was essentially a Highland tradition, which was often informed by the aristocratic political Celticism associated with Erskine of Mar and C. M. Grieve. It was not football and its place within male working-class culture that Gunn chose to comment upon in his essays on tradition, nationalism and culture, but the changing nature of the Scottish Highland Games during the 1930s.

The importance of sport within a changing way of life did not escape his attention and he questioned not only the notion of the Highlands as a sporting playground for the rich, in particular the nouveau riche from the South, but also the commercialization of Scottish Highland Games and the spectacle of the professional athlete travelling from village to village collecting any money that local labour and patronage could gather (Gunn, 1931). Commenting upon one particular incident, Gunn recalls an occasion when the dancers were called together and the prize piper, who had carried off all the money that day, appeared not in the traditional

Highland dress but in a blue suit and bowler hat. The judge, obviously astonished, called the piper over and asked him to explain what the rig-out meant. Not recognizing the importance of the blue ribbon tradition of the best piper having the honour of playing for the dancers at the last event, the piper explained that he had wanted to catch an early train and therefore he had jettisoned his borrowed kilt so that he could beat it at the earliest moment (Gunn, 1931: 413). At one level, the incident may seem humorous and insignificant, yet the writer's point is a serious one, since what Gunn was commenting on was the decline of a Highland way of life in the 1930s and the inroads being made by a more urban, commercialized and, at times, Anglicized culture, which took little cognizance of Celtic tradition, local people and customs. What seems clear about Gunn's writings on tradition, including sporting traditions and nationalism, is the view that they were both inextricably linked and that the life and death of one was the life and death of the other (Gunn, 1931).

The above is but one illustrative example of the way in which sport in all its forms both contributes to and is constitutive of the social, cultural and historical milieu in which it moves. *Sport in the Making of Celtic Cultures* is the first text to draw leading sociological and historical writers together in a thorough examination of the unique and specific ways in which sport figures in those European borderlands often mistakenly referred to as the Celtic Nations. It is commonplace in the post-modern world to talk of Celtic art, Celtic mythology, Celtic law and Celtic spirituality, yet *Sport in the Making of Celtic Cultures* is the first attempt to explore the place, meaning and content of Celtic sport.

Any research agenda that has at its heart the notion of sport in Celtic cultures might ask why so many of the peripheral borderlands of Europe struggling for assertiveness and elements of autonomy tend to be passionate about national and regional forms of culture. It is clear that there is no intrinsic 'Celtic' European unity and that when examined critically the idea of being Celtic needs to be specifically unpacked in terms of time, space and culture. It might also be that historical sociological studies of sport organized around notions of Celtic nationalism, Celtic identity, Celtic revivalism, Celtic mythology, Celtic romanticism and Celtic cultures may provide a useful critique of centre nationalisms, be they British or Scottish, French or Spanish. There is a useful reminder to the plethora of writers who have claimed to produce definitive texts on the relationship between sport, culture and forms of civic and state sponsored nationalism, that the old world is still active in the new (see Art Ó Maolfabhail's account of hurling in the old world and the new, in Chapter 11); that the past figures in the present, that residual sporting cultures are never dead but dormant and that in a post-modern world of sporting values and mass commercialization the ancient and the classical have much to say about the contemporary sporting world (see Alan Bairner's discussion of the Celtic vision in Irish sport, in Chapter 2). There is a reminder also that, for example, in Scotland various regional cultures and identities are neither fixed nor immutable, and that representations of Scottishness or Welshness or Irishness were never homogeneous in the sense that the idea of Scotland was never wholly Catholic or Protestant; Williamite or Jacobite; Celtic or Non-Celtic; Nationalist or Unionist; Irish Scot or Scottish Gael or British Scot (Kellas, 1996).

CELTIC REVIVALISM IN EUROPE?

It is always exciting and sometimes a little confusing to live through a revival of any kind, when something long forgotten rises from oblivion, and gains a fresh and potent currency (Meek, 1992). Given the current interest in all things Celtic it is not surprising that during 1996 one of the focal points of the Edinburgh International Festival was an ensemble of artists who performed under the banner of the Edinburgh Celtic Gathering: a three-week cultural extravaganza of music, art and dance which, according to the organizers, promoted both 'the rhythms of the Celts and a Celtic dance spectacular'. During 1997 the city of Glasgow heralded in its fourth Celtic Connections festival – itself part of a worldwide boom in enthusiasm for Celtic culture. In this particular instance the generic term Celtic referred to singers, dancers and artists from Ireland, Scotland and Wales: a small event in comparison to the Inter-Celtic Festival held in the port of Lorient on Brittany's south coast. The Festival Interceltique de Lorient attracts well over 100,000 spectators a year in comparison to the 65,000 who attend Glasgow's Celtic Connections and the 40,000 who regularly attend the annual Falun Festival in Denmark.

For the linguist, the Celts are the people who spoke, and still speak, languages of great antiquity and of Indo-European origin (Ross, 1986: 8). Of course the borderlands covered by the Celtic languages have included vast areas of Europe, including most of France, much of Germany, and parts of Spain and Italy. In the late twentieth century they are now mainly confined to Britain and Ireland with the exception of Breton, spoken in Brittany (see Chapters 6 and 9). These languages have often been categorized within two main divisions: (i) Brythonic (P-Celts), which includes Welsh, Breton and Cornish and (ii) Goedelic (Q-Celts), which includes Scottish Gaelic, Irish and Manx. For the archaeologist the Celts are the people who are recognizable as such on account of a distinctive material culture which gives meaning to the term Celtic, and for Celtic nationalists the term has been appropriated to take on the specific political values and ideologies associated with various Celtic political movements of the various social and historical milieux which have supported Celtic nationalism in its various disguises. In a more generic sense the term Celtic culture as it is used in this text is deliberately open and inclusive of the fact that all of these meanings and others have contributed to and have been constitutive of Celtic cultures in the making. *Sport in the Making of Celtic Cultures* is inclusive of the linguistic, material and political values which have accompanied the term Celtic, an approach accommodating both the classical and the post-modern, Cù'Chulainn and the GAA in late twentieth-century Scotland. It is clear that subsumed within the term Celtic is a wide range of social and political structures which are as much about the present as they are about the past. All of the authors in this book are critical of monolithic constructions and caricatures of the Celt, which marginalize and simplify the diverse multiplicity of that which encompasses *Sport in the Making of Celtic Cultures*.

In Scotland alone the popularity of musical groups such as Run-Rig and Capercaille; the repopulation of areas such as Skye, where depopulation has been the trend for centuries; the upsurge in interest in Gaelic poets such as the late Sorley Maclean, Donald MacAuley, Catriona NicGumaraid, Mary Montgomery and Norman MacCaig; the establishment of the Gaelic Television fund in 1991; the much increased quota of Gaelic TV programmes since 1993; a debate about the relationship between Celtic spirituality and New Age religious movements; the number of recently published popular histories of shinty clubs and football clubs with an affinity to some real or mythical Celtic identity; and the offer by the Scottish Office to hand back land to the crofting communities – all might in some small way be a testament to a revival of interest in Scottish Gaelic history and culture, if not to a broader Celtic revivalism. Concussed by many battles, the Celts who were down and out in the eyes of many are suddenly permitted to make a staggering comeback to the stage of world history, and for a glorious moment when the stagger becomes a stand the Celts are up and in (Meek, 1992). The eyes of all knowledgeable people are upon them as yet another Celtic revival gathers momentum and the Celts are even told that they definitely have something that other cultures do not (Meek, 1992).

The Celts hold an unusual place in the mythology of modern Europe (Graves-Brown, Jones and Gamble, 1996). At one and the same time they are taken as a symbol of European unity and a symbol of separateness, of regional identity and of diversity. Exhibitions such as *I Celti* in Venice are meant to symbolize the common cultural roots of an area from Eire to Turkey, from Portugal to Poland. This influential exhibition, which originated at the Palazzo Grassi in Venice and was supported by the European Union, developed the argument that the Celts of the fifth and sixth centuries BC in fact created the first pan-European culture, one which still, at a deep level, unites Europe today, from Prague and Milan in the south and east to Galicia and Galway in the west. Excavations at Mount Beuvray also have an overt political aim of European cooperation, with teams from more than a dozen countries working together and with an exhibition at the Centre Archéologique Européen. At the same time the Celts are used as a symbol of regional diversity and national identity, as in the case of the Irish and Welsh Celts and the establishment of, for example, the National Eisteddfod and other organizations which are aimed at preserving the Welsh language. The previously mentioned festival of Lorient in Brittany attempts to contribute to a celebration of Celtic cultures and identities.

Whatever the definition of the Celt, the concept and the peoples have had a role to play in the imagining of a modern Europe. According to European Common Market historiography, European identity is something organic and rooted in the past: a history of selective forgetting as much as remembering. In evoking the idea of European heritage the idea of European cultural unity is often framed within classical antiquity. Critical anthropologists and others have long since questioned the notion of cultures as homogenous, discrete, bounded wholes, and yet European Council history tends to construct European history as a series of evolutionary stages drawing on classical images in an attempt to identify essential elements of European culture. The choice of SOCRATES, ERASMUS and TEMPUS as acronyms for major education exchange programmes is but one small example of the appeal to the ancient roots of an alleged common European ancestry. President Mitterand during the early 1990s appealed to the ancient Celtic past as a basis for a form of pan-European unity, a unity which showed little sensitivity to post-colonial criticisms of the orientalist and supremacist ideologies of Western cultures. In so far as Celtic cultures have been suppressed and partly destroyed by the structures of the big European states, any modern Celtic revivalism is itself somewhat ironic, a triumph of popular memory over the kind of forgetting that suits the powerful.

Of course until recently, there has been little need to ask complex questions about the Celtic cultures of Europe's Western seaboard and their continuing struggle for survival. Punished, excluded and systematically oppressed in many of the great nation states – despised and forbidden in Castilian Spain, banned in metropolitan France and marginalized within an inch of their lives in the state school system of Britain – Celtic culture, including sporting culture, was spiralling rapidly towards extinction by the beginning of the twentieth century. (See, for example, Chapters 3 and 7 for a discussion of the way in which shinty and the Scottish Gael struggled to survive against the more dominant metropolitan nationalism of the British state.) The cultural history of how the Celts clung on to the ledge, fought back, learned how to build onto fragments of a threatened culture eventually to win through to a late twentieth-century revival, is a tremendous testament to the power of human memory, oral history, tradition and community to outlast the most powerful structures of state bullying and control. In this sense *Sport in the Making of Celtic Cultures* is but a critical celebration of the way in which sport has contributed to the conviviality and solidarity, resistance and struggle, and sheer accessibility within and between the configuration and development of Celtic cultures.

The term critical celebration is deliberately active in the sense that the writers in this book are all too familiar with the dangers of accepting uncritically the cultural baggage that accompanies the Celt in her travels through history. In so far as Celtic cultures have been suppressed and partly destroyed by the structures of the big European states, their recovery is somewhat ironic, as mentioned above: a triumph of popular memory over the kind of forgetting that suits the powerful. But in the context of continental Europe, where folkloric movements have often had unfortunate political associations, there is also the danger of attracting reactionary nostalgists who dislike the progressive multiracial face of Europe and would like to seen themselves as white sturdy Europeans rebelling against the metropolitan decadence of Paris, Madrid or London. A reversion to a 2,000-year-old Celtic identity of settlements like Milan has the danger of becoming a code word for rich, white north Europeanism.

SPORT IN THE MAKING OF CELTIC CULTURES

Any reading of this book would support some or all of the following general ways in which sport has contributed to the making of Celtic cultures:

1. that all nations, be they stateless or otherwise, use sport to further certain ends, but this is not to suggest that all nations and all nationalisms are the same (see Alan Bairner's discussion of civic and ethnic nationalism(s) in Chapter 2);

2. that an examination of the unique and specific ways in which sport figures in those European borderlands often mistakenly referred to as the Celtic Nations serves as a timely reminder that the relationship between core and peripheral nationalisms is but a two-way process and that sport both contributes to and is constitutive of the cultures in which it moves (see, for example, the work of Michel Lagrée in Chapter 4 and Michel Raspaud in Chapter 6);

3. that sport can be an instrument of national unity, can help to consolidate cultural nationalism and national consciousness, and can contribute to the search for cultural identity (see, for example, the contributions by Gareth Williams (Chapter 5), Marcus de Búrca (Chapter 8) and John Evans *et al.* (Chapter 10));

4. that sport can contribute to community sentiment and mythology (see, for example, the contributions by Hugh Dan MacLennan (Chapter 7) and Philip Dine (Chapter 9); and

5. that the obvious presence of nationalism in many social histories of the Celts needs to be specifically unpacked in terms of content, symbolism and place (for example, refer to Lorna Jackson's discussion in Chapter 3 and the research of Joseph Bradley in Chapter 12).

In *Sport and the British: a Modern History* it is suggested that although the term Celtic nationalism provides a convenient general term for the sense of possessing a distinct territory, culture and history, there are two quite distinct elements within it (Holt, 1989: 237). The first and most dramatic arose from a root-and-branch rejection of British sports by Irish cultural nationalists, which led to the setting up of an alternative tradition of Gaelic games with its own administration, funding and regulations. The study of Gaelic Athletic Association and Irish Nationalist politics during the period 1880–1920 has been the subject of authoritative studies by some of the contributors to this book (see the chapters by de Búrca and Ó Maolfabhail on particular aspects of GAA activity in Ireland). Yet the specific links between the Irish and Scottish GAA organizations and the attitude of the Scottish communities in Ireland during the high period of Irish nationalism has been a forgotten link in the politics of not only Irish nationalism but Celtic revivalism of the late nineteenth and late twentieth centuries (see Joseph Bradley's discussion of GAA activity in modern Scotland and de Búrca's commentary on the politics of the Scots in relation to Michael Cusack and the GAA in Ireland).

The other element of Celtic nationalism alluded to by Holt took less extreme forms. He suggests the cultural identity of the modern Scots and Welsh was not so much a question of kilts and Eisteddfods but of football at Hampden Park and Rugby at Cardiff Arms Park (see the chapters by Williams and by Evans, Davies and Bass for the specific role which sport has played in the making of Welsh cultural identity in both the past and the present). Indeed Holt is absolutely right when he argues that sport in this sense both contributed to but was also part of a broader cultural history and identity which was associated with Celtic nationalism.

Such discussion of sport, nationalism and cultures whose identity is in part caught up with what it means to be a Celt must itself be specifically unpacked in terms of content, history and place. Indeed the writers in this book all recognize that any meaningful understanding of the contribution which sport makes to a whole host of concepts associated with nationhood and cultural identities must acknowledge that the particular and specific will take us further than the general and the abstract.

SHINTY, CELTIC RADICALISM AND LAND REFORM

This chapter started with illustrative examples drawn from the Scottish context and it shall draw towards a conclusion with a second illustrative example, namely, shinty, Celtic radicalism and land reform. (For a further examination of shinty's living tradition in the Celtic New Year, see Chapter 7.) One of the leading figures in both the Highland and Irish land reform movements of the late nineteenth century was John Murdoch, a gentleman who perhaps held a mythical sense of Pan-Celticism. Murdoch above all ensured that the Celtic influence and land reform issues would have a considerable influence upon an emerging Scottish nationalism of the early twentieth century. Davitt (1904) described him as one of the true Celts, an opinion shared by William Gilles, founder of the Scots National League in the 1920s. Gilles (1920) wrote of his great work in reviving Celtic ideas and a Celtic communal spirit. The term Celtic radicalism as used in this context specifically in the sense recognized by late nineteenth-century land reformers: to refer to the cross-fertilization of ideas, politics and people who supported a form of Celtic revivalism at that time and which gave rise to the formation of organizations, for example, such as the Federation of Celtic Societies in 1878.

It was not football or rugby that land reformers such as John Murdoch saw as an essential element of Celtic identity but shinty. Shinty, land reform and Irish nationalism regularly filled the pages of the *Inverness Courier, Celtic Monthly, Celtic Review* and *The Highlander* during the high period of Irish nationalism and Gaelic radicalism between 1880 and about 1920. For many Land League agitators in Scotland the politics of land reform, Gaelic affairs, Celtic radicalism and shinty were often inextricably linked. The breaking up of many large farms or estates, meant the breaking up of communities from which generations of shinty players emerged. For instance, in the 1890s the fact that once thriving communities such as Kilchiaran on the Island of Islay could not sustain a cohort of shinty players was often linked, by land reformers, to the fact that many west coast communities were being broken up. Shinty therefore was not just a casual pursuit for land reformers such as John Murdoch, Michael Davitt, the Skye Bardess Mary Macpherson, Archibald Chisholm, and John Gunn Mackay. The success or failure of shinty was often seen to be inextricably linked to a broader Celtic radicalism, land politics and Gaelic affairs of late Victorian Scotland. Many land agitators held prominent positions within the early shinty clubs.

Born in Strathglass in 1825, Archibald Chisholm was the founder of Strathglass Shinty Club and author of the first set of printed shinty rules in the Highlands (Hutchinson, 1989). A practising Roman Catholic and committed Gaelic speaker, he expressed a great deal of sympathy with Highland radicals and land reformers of the nineteenth century (Hutchinson, 1989). On a number of occasions he offered financial assistance to *The Highlander*. John Murdoch, editor of that newspaper, and founding member of the Highland Land League Reform Association, was often an honoured guest at Strathglass Highland Gathering days. In July 1881 Archibald Chisholm not only invited John Murdoch to the Strathglass Highland Gathering but the prizes on the day consisted of six-month subscriptions to *The Highlander*. Like Murdoch, Archibald Chisholm disliked tobacco and strong drink, and on more than one occasion warned the Strathglass shinty players that 'Ach chan ionan fear air mhisg is fear an uisg – the drunken man and the drinker of water are not alike' (Hutchinson, 1989).

John Gunn Mackay, a founding member of both Skye Camanachd and the first Glasgow Skye shinty club, was one of the most forthright and effective of the Land League activists (Macdonald, 1992). He was born in 1849 in Lochalsh, where his Sutherland-born father was a schoolmaster, and brought up in Skye, his mother being from Bracadale. He learned the draper's trade in Glasgow, but was sacked in 1881 for making a pro-Irish Land League speech at a rally. Having set up business in Portree in 1885, in the appropriately named Gladstone Buildings, he immediately became embroiled in land politics, shinty and Gaelic affairs – being elected as Land League councillor for Portree on the then recently formed Inverness City Council.

One of the most prominent women in the land agitations of the late 1880s was the Skye bardess Mary Macpherson, more popularly known as

Mairi Mhor nan Oran (Big Mary of the Songs). Mairi Mhor was born in 1821 near Skeabost where her father John Macdonald was a crofter. Through her songs and her poetry she took an active part in the crofters' cause during the 1880s, regularly appearing on Land League platforms throughout the Highlands (Macdonald, 1992). Like John Gunn Mackay, Mairi Mhor also commented upon the relationship between Highland social and economic history and the development of shinty (Macdonald, 1992: 3):

> Bho'n chaill sinn am fearann
> Gun chaill sinn an iomain
> S cha mhor gu bheil duin' ann tha eolach oirr

> Since we lost our land
> We lost shinty as well
> And there are few men left who are skilful now

Much more could be said about the social and political significance of Celtic sport during the Victorian period and yet it is perhaps more insightful at this point to draw upon one further example as a means of illustrating the power of the past in the present. Landscape was but one strong influence in the work of modern Gaelic poets like Norman MacCaig (1910–96) and Sorley Maclean (1911–96), writers who were also ever mindful of the past in the present, and that the use of land, the physical environment and community often blended together with what they knew of Highland social history. For Raasay-born Sorley Maclean locality, community, physical environment and the past are forever intermingled aspects of Celtic identity. Assessing the influence of late twentieth century poems such as 'Hallaig', John MacInnes has asserted that the earliest Gaels would certainly have recognized the link between people and locality. Community and place have always been believed by Celtic scholars to be an integral aspect of changing historical identities in the Highlands. An inescapable fact of that history was the clearances that took place on Raasay in the 1850s. It was the implications of the clearances that the poet wrestled with in 'Hallaig' (1958) – the name is that of one of the twelve Raasay townships cleared. In this poem, as in the most ancient Gaelic poetry, trees, so long regarded with reverence by Celts, are much in evidence. But Maclean's trees are symbols as well as simple objects of affection. The trees represent the township's former occupants – its ghosts and presences, its living past in the present. In the same sense it might be argued that the vast tracts of land and empty spaces preserved for sporting estates and other sporting purposes in the 1990s are but reminders and symbols of a time when the Highlands were thickly populated and culturally, socially and economically capable of sustaining thriving local communities.

THE PRESENT AS HISTORY

Since at least the 1800s Celtic revival movements have almost been commonplace. For instance, primarily concerned with linguistic and cultural matters, the Gaelic movement of the late nineteenth century acquired something of the status of a political pressure group by conducting campaigns for a Chair of Celtic Studies at Edinburgh University and the enhancement of Gaelic language teaching in Highland schools. Perhaps the notion of Celtic culture is more at home in the nineteenth century, or even a Celtic Iron Age? As mentioned earlier, it might also be commonplace in the 1990s to talk of Celtic art, Celtic mythology, Celtic spirituality, Celtic law, Gaelic music, Gaelic coffee, Celtic Studies and so on. Yet the specific place of sport in Celtic history and culture has perhaps been a notable absence from the research which has begun to reveal the extent to which social and historical studies of sport have contributed to notions of, for example, nationhood, multiple identities and community. *Sport in the Making of Celtic Cultures* not only adds to this body of knowledge but serves as a reminder and intervention to those historical, sociological and cultural authorities on sport that *identity history is not enough*. Perhaps more importantly it serves to illustrate the power of the past in the present.

2

CIVIC AND ETHNIC NATIONALISM IN THE CELTIC VISION OF IRISH SPORT

Alan Bairner

The important links between sport and national identity have been increasingly recognized both by sport sociologists and by students of nationalism (Bairner, 1996a; Hargreaves, 1992; Hoberman, 1993; Jarvie, 1993; Kellas, 1991; Mangan, 1996). The extent to which these two communities of scholars have learned from each other, however, is altogether less certain. Specifically, the discussion of nationalism within the sociology of sport discipline has seldom drawn upon those typologies of nationalism which are so dear to the hearts of political scientists. Instead sport sociologists have preferred to focus on categorizing the different ways in which nations and nationalist movements seek to use sport without exploring the degree to which the resultant categories may relate to more general propositions about the varieties of nationalism. Thus, we learn that nations use sport to develop and maintain a sense of identity, to foster internal unity and to enhance international standing. But these are all essentially pragmatic concerns. They tell us little or nothing about the precise character of the nation or nationalism involved in the manipulation of sport for political purposes. All nations use sport to further certain ends but this is not to reveal that all nations and all nationalisms are the same. Nor should their manipulation of sport be regarded as problematic in the sense that it prevents people from recognizing the differences which exist. In fact, as is argued in this chapter, it is precisely through an examination of the approach to sport in particular nationalist settings that we can begin to appreciate more fully the various types of nationalism as well as the constant evolution of nationalist politics.

In terms of typologies of nationalism, the chapter concentrates on what has become arguably the best known distinction, namely that between civic and ethnic nationalism. In his study of nations and nationalism in the global era, Anthony Smith argues that it is inappropriate to suggest that there exists in practice a clear separation between these two forms of nationalism. According to Smith, 'modern nations are simultaneously and necessarily civic and ethnic' (Smith, 1996: 99). He observes that 'it is often assumed that the intrusion of ethnic elements and sentiments of collective belonging into the life of the nation inevitably breeds exclusiveness and intolerance, and that ethnic closure is the chief basis of many of the current national conflicts that afflict the world' (ibid.: 100). For Smith, however, 'not only ethnic but also civic nationalisms may demand the eradication of minority cultures and communities qua communities, on the common assumption, shared by Marxists and liberals, not just of equality through uniformity, but that "high cultures" and "great nations" are necessarily of greater value than "low" cultures and small nations or *ethnies*' (ibid.: 101). It is important, therefore, to avoid falling into the trap of regarding the civic nationalists as the good guys of the history of nationalism and ethnic nationalists as the men or women in black hats. On the other hand, it is perfectly reasonable to explore the issue of nationalism in terms of a distinction between those practical expressions of the doctrine which seek to unify people within a particular political context (civic nationalism) and those which emphasize the unity of the ethnic group (ethnic nationalism) (Kellas, 1991: 51–71).

In order to explore this distinction with reference to a real expression of nationalism, this chapter examines the emergence and subsequent development of a Celtic vision of sport in Ireland within the context of the broader development of Irish nationalism – an approach which is fundamentally different from that adopted by Marcus de Búrca and Art Ó Maolfabhail in Chapters 8 and 11. It is argued that because this vision of sport emerged in the nineteenth century as part of a more general upsurge of political and cultural romantic nationalism, it was always likely to lean towards exclusivistic interpretations of the nation. The sports and pastimes being promoted were for the enjoyment and self-betterment of specific people and, by implication, and, on occasion, even by edict, were denied to others. As the twentieth century progressed, the situation changed somewhat. With the partition of Ireland and the establishment of the Irish Free State, the Celtic vision of sport initially played an important part in providing cultural support to the goal of a Gaelic Ireland as proposed by Eamon De Valera. More recently, however, as the Irish Republic has endeavoured to become a more culturally diverse and pluralistic democracy, the role of Gaelic sport has become more symbolic. Specifically, it has operated alongside the Irish language as an indicator that Ireland is a separate place. To perform this function, however, it has been less necessary than in the past to promote exclusivistic, ethnic nationalism. In the six counties of Northern Ireland which have remained an integral part of the United Kingdom, on the other hand, there is evidence that the Celtic vision of sport is still closely linked to ethnic nationalism or, at the very least, that this is how it is perceived by the political opponents of Irish nationalism. As a consequence, it is difficult to see how Gaelic sports can become more inclusive in the north in the absence of any political settlement to the problems which beset that part of the island.

The history of sport in Ireland is the story of the difficult relationship which exists between the people who live on the island and their more powerful neighbour. At least in its modern form, sport came to Ireland as a direct result of the close ties with Britain. Games which had been codified in England in the nineteenth century were quickly taken up in what was, in effect, the closest component of an otherwise far-flung empire (Bairner, 1996b). Naturally, they were played with great enthusiasm by members of the military garrisons which were scattered throughout the country, and also by civil servants charged with the administration of British rule in Ireland. British games, such as association football (soccer), cricket, rugby and hockey, were also played by members of the native population, although for the most part only by those who had studied in England or at educational institutions modelled on the English system. But with the exception of association football, which rapidly won support amongst the Protestant working class of Belfast, these games tended to appeal mostly to the middle classes and the fact that most of them were regarded both as elitist as well as fundamentally linked to British rule in Ireland made them doubly unpopular with the more nationalistic and radical sections of the native Catholic population. Out of this resentment emerged the Gaelic Athletic Association (GAA) which was formally established on 1 November 1884, at the Commercial Hotel in Thurles, Co. Tipperary. The formation of the GAA can be seen as just one element in a broader cultural struggle which also included the Irish language movement (Mandle, 1997). Its founding fathers, however, drew upon a Celtic vision of sport, partly real and partly imagined, thereby giving the Association its own perspective on physical activity.

Although it involved itself in the early days in a wide range of sports, including cycling and track and field, together with certain cultural activities, the GAA increasingly concentrated its attention on what were seen by its leaders as distinctively Irish games – hurling, Gaelic football, handball and camogie. Above all others, hurling was taken to be peculiar to the Irish, although stick and ball games of some sort or another had existed throughout the world virtually since the beginnings of time. Certainly, a game resembling the modern sport of hurling had been played in Ireland for more than 2000 years (Mandle, 1987: 15). In Irish legend, it is depicted as an aristocratic or even a royal game and many of the main legendary heroes, King Labhraidh Loinsech, Diarmuid, Cahir the Great together with Cuchulain and Fionn Mac Cumhaill are associated with hurling exploits. This legendary hurling, as W. F. Mandle points out, was to play no small part in the nationalist mystique of the GAA (Mandle, 1987: 16). From the Norman invasion of the twelfth century onwards, moreover, successive attempts were made to control or even prohibit traditional Irish pastimes, creating a sea of resentment out of which the GAA was able to make significant populist capital (De Búrca, 1980: 2). As T. S. C. Dagg observes, the game became so popular that it was proscribed both by the statutes of Kilkenny (1366) and the Galway Statutes (1527) (Dagg, 1944: 19–20). Nevertheless, the eighteenth century witnessed the rapid growth of organized hurling, with gentry and landowners fielding teams made up of tenants (Mandle, 1987: 16). Hurling games began to attract large attendances together with a significant amount of wagering on their outcome. From the beginning of the nineteenth century, however, this expansion was arrested temporarily. According to Mandle, 'as with English cricket, the Napoleonic wars and, in the case of Ireland, the consequences of the 1798 rising, caused a noticeable lull in the development of hurling in the early years of the nineteenth century' (ibid.). In addition, the Famine and emigration each had a detrimental effect on hurling as well as on other sports and pastimes. So serious was the situation that some were moved to lament the passing of hurling completely (ibid. 2).

Traditional forms of football, which had never enjoyed the same mythical status as hurling, were also undermined by events of the early nineteenth century. The oldest recorded form of football to have been played in Ireland was *caid* or cad, which was also popular with other Celtic peoples and resembled the rough-and-tumble ball games played through-out Europe. It is thought to have been first played in Ireland at least 1000 years ago (Sugden and Bairner, 1993: 71). Like hurling, forms of football grew in popularity in Ireland during the eighteenth century and, although frowned upon by members of the aristocracy, it was played regularly at College Park in Dublin by students of Trinity College. The game which was now evolving, however, owed more to the influence of the English sporting revolution than to native traditions and, when football managed to negotiate the difficulties of the nineteenth century, it did so in the form of rugby union and soccer, both of which were associated initially with the British presence in Ireland. To all intents and purposes, Gaelic football had to be more or less invented by the GAA. Moreover, it can be argued that the potential to revitalize the game of hurling also owed much to the Anglo-Irish connection inasmuch as it was members of Trinity College, which was modelled along similar lines to England's ancient universities and which drew its students from the ranks of an Anglo-Irish, Protestant ascendancy class, who were largely responsible for resurrecting the northern form of the game after its decline in popularity during the first half of the nineteenth century (West, 1991: 35–6).

By the last quarter of the nineteenth century, the possibility of British sporting hegemony in Ireland had become very real indeed. Irish nationalists, therefore, became increasingly concerned that this development both paralleled and complemented similar trends in other areas of activity, resulting in a diminished sense of distinctive Irish identity and a weakened desire for political independence (Bairner, 1996b: 64). Archbishop Croke, who was to be one of the GAA's original patrons, made clear his feelings about these developments.

> Ball playing, hurling, foot-ball kicking, according to Irish rules, casting, leaping in various ways, wrestling, handy-grips, top-pegging, leap-frog, rounders, tip-in-the-hat and all such favourite exercises and amusements amongst men and boys, may now be said to be not only dead and buried but in several locations to be entirely forgotten and unknown.... If we continue travelling for the next score years in the same direction that we have taken for some time past, condemning the sports that were practised by our forefathers, effacing our national features as though we were ashamed of them, and putting on, with England's stuff and broadcloths, her mashier habits and other effeminate follies as she may recommend, we had better at once and publicly abjure our nationality, clap hands for joy at the sight of the Union Jack, and place 'England's bloody red' exultantly above the green. (Puirseal, 1982: 50)

Despite his distinctly florid language, Croke spoke for many when he denounced what he and other nationalists regarded as British cultural imperialism, carried out with support from members of the ruling Anglo-Irish elite and increasingly also from the working-class Protestant community in the province of Ulster, whose love of the imported game of soccer was to be matched by the fervour of their support for the continuation of the political union of Britain and Ireland. It was against this background that the GAA emerged.

From the outset, the GAA committed its members to the cause of Irish nationalism and, more than one hundred years later, it remains true to the same aspirations which inspired its founders.

The Association is a National Organisation which has, as its basic aims, the strengthening of the National Identity in a 32 county Ireland through the preservation and promotion of Gaelic Games and pastimes. The Association further seeks to achieve its objectives through the active support of Irish Culture, with a constant emphasis on the importance of the preservation of the Irish language and its greater use in the life of the Nation; and in the development of a community spirit, to foster an awareness and love of the national ideals in the people of Ireland. (Gaelic Athletic Association, Rule Book, 1991)

As Michael Mullan argues, 'the formation of the GAA in the 1880s represented something different in the development of Western sport; eschewing an integrationist approach, it organized its Gaelic revival around what would become a permanent state of conflict with established British bourgeois sport forms' (Mullan, 1995: 275). Yet, in spite of its avowed nationalist aims, the Association started out as a relatively broad social movement, embracing not only former players of British games but also Protestant nationalists like Douglas Hyde and even political unionists such as the Reverend Maxwell Close (Mandle, 1987: 8). By operating a ban on the playing of 'foreign' games, however, the GAA made it difficult for non-nationalists, and by implication, Protestants, to play Gaelic games. An accompanying ban prevented members of the Crown forces, recognized by nationalists as the defenders of British interests, from GAA involvement. In this way, according to Mullan, the Association 'consolidated its position within Ireland, especially in the rural districts, through appeals to Catholic nationalisms and the implementation of creative techniques of counterclosure, such as the athletic and political bans on British games and those who played them' (Mullan, 1995: 275). Indeed, in a very short period of time, the Association became not only a political football, kicked around by the various strands of Irish nationalism, but also a significant element in the life of rural Catholic Ireland. Furthermore, the Gaelic games movement made an important contribution to a conception of Irishness which was founded upon ethnic exclusivism and which expressed itself, on occasion, in racist rhetoric. Emphasis was put on the ethnic purity of Irish Gaels and their supposed intellectual and physical superiority to the English, a view clearly expressed in an article in the *Gaelic Annual* of 1907–8:

The Irish Celt is distinguished among the races for height and strength, manly vigour and womanly grace; despite wars and domestic disabilities, the stamina of the race has survived in almost pristine perfection. The ideal Gael is a matchless athlete, sober, pure in mind, speech and deed, self-possessed,

self-reliant, self-respecting, loving his religion and his country with a deep
and restless love, earnest in thought and effective in action. (Cited in Corry,
1989: 87)

Whilst the manifest hyperbole, not to mention downright self-deception,
might make a statement like this seem laughable, the message is serious
and, arguably, sinister when viewed in relation to the less endearing
characteristics of ethnic nationalism.

Given the persistence of such potentially exclusive sentiments throughout the history of the GAA, it is interesting to note that when the ancient
Tailteann Games were reconvened in 1924, genuine attempts were made to
transform Aonach Tailteann, first held in the pre-Christian era, into an
international gathering. Ironically, indeed, in the light of the GAA's
opposition to English games, two of the most famous delegates were the
cricketers, C. B. Fry and Ranjitsinhji (His Highness the Maharajah Jam
Sahib of Nawangar) (Mandle, 1987: 216). The games themselves were used
by the government to celebrate Ireland's recently acquired independent
status. They were held again in 1928 and 1932 and, according to one
commentator, not only were they a great success but much of that success
was owed to the involvement of the GAA. As de Búrca (1980: 167) points
out:

> As a cultural exhibition with mass appeal they may be regarded as one of the
> early (and now largely forgotten) successes of the new state. That they were
> so successful was due largely to the leading role in the festival played by the
> GAA, in providing the main stadium and in lending some of its leading
> officials to the various organising committees.

A more sober assessment of the GAA's role, however, is offered by
Mandle, who reveals the antipathy of many of its members to the new state
which had been forged out of a bitter civil war and which represented an
acceptance, albeit temporary, of the partition of Ireland, with six Ulster
counties remaining under British jurisdiction. 'By 1924,' he writes
(Mandle, 1987: 218), 'the GAA had shed its athletics component and,
apart from the provision of the major venue for the Games, the selection of
hurling and football teams, and the personal representation on many of
the organizing committees of a number of its prominent officials, it was
not directly responsible for Aonach Tailteann.' In modern times, nevertheless, and despite continued misgivings on the part of its more
republican-oriented members, the GAA has played an important part in
providing the Republic of Ireland with a distinctive cultural identity and,
thereby, consolidating its political position. Paradoxically, the Association

has also been deeply involved in fuelling nationalist sentiments amongst the Catholic community in Northern Ireland, most members of which desire the political unification of Ireland. In neither role, moreover, has the GAA succeeded fully in freeing itself from its exclusivistic past, although it has had greater success in helping with the development of civic nationalism in the Irish Republic than in Northern Ireland.

It has been argued that there are indications, in the Irish Republic at least, that there has emerged a more pluralist sporting culture, centred around the growth in soccer's popularity. According to Michael Holmes, 'to some extent, the success of the Irish football team mirrors the advance of pluralism and liberalism in Irish society in general' (Holmes, 1994: 97). In particular, its players represent a variety of ethnic backgrounds. A similar argument is put forward by Mike Cronin, who claims that 'soccer can adapt to the wider transformations in the nature of Irishness' (Cronin, 1994: 16). As it does so, Cronin suggests, the GAA will come to play an increasingly less influential role in the construction of the national identity (ibid.: 17). Yet, it can be argued that even the GAA is capable of responding positively to social and cultural change and of helping to create a more inclusive sense of what it means to be Irish.

Three examples serve to illustrate the extent to which the GAA has been implicated in the formation of a more pluralist Republic of Ireland. First, the appointment in 1994 of a southern Protestant, Jack Boothman, as President of the Association was clearly an important development, even if only at the symbolic level, in terms of proving that Gaelic sports need not be exclusive to Irish Catholics. On his appointment, Mr Boothman was quick to deny that the GAA is a sectarian body, claiming that he himself was living proof of this fact (*Irish News*, 12 March 1994). Second, the apparent weakening of interest in hurling in the Irish Republic may also be significant since that game, far more than Gaelic football which continues to thrive despite the challenge of soccer, seems more resonant of Gaelic Ireland and less user-friendly for non-Gaels (*Sunday Tribune*, 17 April 1994). Finally, even global forces have had an impact on the traditionally conservative leadership of the GAA. On 2 November 1996, Croke Park played host to a foreign game in the form of American football. In an interesting example of 'glocalization', the game was foreign but not British and one of the competing teams was Notre Dame University – the so-called 'Fighting Irish' (*Guardian*, 4 November 1996). Nevertheless, the event did mark a significant step away from the sporting insularity which has long characterized GAA decision-making. It should also be noted that, in the recent past, games between Gaelic and Australian Rules footballers and between hurlers and Scottish shinty players have been staged using compromise rules. In addition, Gaelic sport continues to be played beyond the shores of Ireland – for example in England, Scotland, the United States of America and Australia – albeit usually by members of the Irish diaspora, thereby encouraging the belief that the Gaelic games movement is implicated in the perpetuation of ethnic nationalist ideas. One can only speculate as to which other global forces may yet impact on the world of Gaelic sport. But it seems inevitable that professionalism will become an acknowledged fact of GAA life, and with that will come pressure to recruit the best possible players from whatever sporting and, more significantly, ethnic background. The speed of any such change, however, even in the Irish Republic, may yet depend on what is happening in Northern Ireland. Whilst part of the island is still politically tied to Britain, it remains incumbent on the GAA as a nationalist body to continue to make some contribution to the idea of the ethnic unity of the Irish people. In addition, the resolve of members to fulfil this role has been strengthened at various times both by attacks on them and their facilities by loyalist paramilitaries and by what has been perceived to be a systematic policy of harassment by the security forces.

The murder of Séan Brown on 13 May 1997 was the result of an appalling act of violence directed towards a man who was widely regarded as having an inclusive approach to sport and to his local community despite his deep involvement in Gaelic games. His work had been described by officials of the Sports Council for Northern Ireland as a model for all sports administrators in the province (*Irish News*, 14 May 1997). Mr Brown was the chairman of the Wolfe Tones GAA Club in Bellaghy, Co. Derry. His death was the latest in a series of such incidents involving GAA members. A senior footballer, William Strathearn, a member of the same club as Mr Brown, was shot dead in April 1977. Jack Kielty, chairman of the Dundrum Gaelic Club in Co. Down was killed by the Ulster Freedom Fighters (UFF) in January 1988. Séan Fox, a former Co. Antrim board official and the president of St Enda's Club in Glengormley, Co. Antrim had been targeted by loyalist paramilitaries on a number of occasions before being murdered at the age of 72 in October 1993. In addition, dozens of members and guests of St Enda's have been injured over the years in gun and bomb attacks on the club's premises. In 1995, several GAA clubs in the Ards Peninsula in Co. Down were subject to arson attacks and the loyalist paramilitary organization, the Red Hand Commando, issued a death threat to all GAA members (*Irish News*, 14 May 1997). These (and other more recent) incidents can only be understood if one recognizes the extent to which the GAA is perceived to espouse an exclusive brand of ethnic nationalism in the six counties of Northern Ireland.

Perhaps the most important reason for this is the fact that the GAA (using its Rule 21) continues to ban members of the British security forces from membership and from participating in Gaelic games. Naturally, this is of particular relevance to Northern Ireland. It should be stated immediately that very few British soldiers or members of the Royal Ulster Constabulary (RUC) would wish to become involved in the Gaelic sports movement even if the ban were to be lifted. In Northern Ireland, as in many other places, people tend to acquire sporting preferences, particularly as regards team games, during their school years. The Northern Irish education system is divided, with separate Catholic schools operating alongside a state sector which caters primarily but not exclusively for Protestant children. Post-primary education is divided into grammar schools and secondary schools through a process of selection. There is also a high level of division in terms of the sports which are played in the two systems, with Gaelic games having pride of place in the Catholic sector, especially in grammar schools, and British sports such as rugby union, cricket and field hockey being dominant in the state sector, again particularly in grammar schools. Secondary schools in the two systems are more likely to share a sporting culture, with soccer having a high profile in each. As the overwhelming majority of locally recruited security forces personnel in Northern Ireland are from the Protestant community, it is inevitable that they have grown up without any involvement in Gaelic games. Furthermore, they are unlikely to have any motivation to alter this situation in adulthood (Sugden and Bairner, 1993: 97–100).

However, politics play as important a role as sporting preference in determining Protestant attitudes to the GAA. Gaelic games are regarded within the Protestant community and by many functionaries of the British state, security personnel included, as not only different but also potentially threatening to the political order. There is widespread suspicion that the GAA has been supportive, in some way or another, of the armed struggle of the Irish Republican Army (IRA) and Sinn Féin's complementary political campaign (Sugden and Bairner, 1993: 37–40). But how well founded are these fears?

It is undeniable and, indeed, inevitable, given its political and cultural aspirations, that the GAA has maintained close links throughout its history with the various strands of Irish nationalism and, for a short time at least during its formative period, it was virtually under the control of the Irish Republican Brotherhood, an organization committed to physical force tactics and, thus, a forerunner of the IRA (Mandle, 1987: 37–45). For most of its history, however, the Association has been more closely linked to constitutional nationalism. For that reason, some supporters of armed republicanism have actually viewed it with a certain degree of suspicion. Ironically, too, given the fear which the IRA and its forerunners have instilled in the Protestant community in Northern Ireland, many of these republicans would argue that their brand of nationalism is far less exclusivistic than that which can be identified with the GAA and, indeed, with constitutional nationalists in general. Above all, republicans deny that they are sectarian and claim that they want Protestants to feel welcome in the united Ireland which remains their political objective. It is understandable, however, that Protestants themselves are sceptical about this invitation and continue to resist any moves which would appear to them to be bringing the prospect of Irish unity a little closer. A significant element in their resistance is an ongoing refusal to become involved in or even supportive of Gaelic games. As a result, the exclusive character of the GAA's sporting nationalism as perceived by unionists in Northern Ireland becomes a self-fulfilling prophecy, with nationalists wishing to exclude Protestants from their sporting culture and Protestants, for the most part, excluding themselves. Thus, it cannot be denied that the GAA, by far the largest sporting body in Ireland, continues to be inextricably bound up with ethnic nationalism (Bairner, 1996a: 327).

Although GAA administrators deny that their organization is political, they cannot refute the claim that it is nationalist. The Irish national anthem is played before games and the Irish tricolour is flown. Both stadia and clubs have been called after nationalist and republican heroes. Even a Jesuit priest from Dublin has described the Association as politically sectarian and has commented on what he regards as an ambivalent attitude towards the IRA. According to Father Seamus Murphy, 'the GAA does not support the IRA, but when it comes to the crunch its policy implies a preference for an IRA victory over a "Crown forces" victory . . . the GAA is politically motivated and its political sectarianism lends indirect support to the IRA' (*Spotlight*, 16 September 1993). Although this is a harsh judgement, particularly on the many men and women who are involved in the GAA for purely sporting reasons, it is reasonable to point out that, in a divided society, any individual or group of individuals who engage, even if for innocent reasons, in practices which are sectarian become implicated in the process whereby division is maintained and strengthened. In the GAA's defence, officials argue that their membership has suffered at the hands both of the security forces and of sectarian elements from the loyalist community. As a consequence, the GAA has arguably become even more determined to promote its games and pursue its legitimate cultural interests. But it is others who have deemed these to be political and not the GAA itself.

In the north in particular, but throughout Ireland, there is resistance to the idea that the GAA's nationalist credentials should be weakened. Rule 21 has still not been removed and, in the last major survey of Gaelic fans in the north, there was still a majority in favour of its retention (*Irish News*, 1 March 1994). In the context of the ongoing unrest in Northern Ireland, however, this attitude is scarcely surprising. Many northern nationalists would argue that the security forces have been almost as guilty as loyalist paramilitaries in their hostility to the GAA. Indeed, they would even suggest that there has been collusion between the two in their treatment of the Association's members. For example, the Bellaghy footballer, William Strathearn, was killed by a serving RUC sergeant. In 1988, another Gaelic footballer, Aidan McAnespie, was shot dead at a border checkpoint whilst on his way to play in a match. His killer was a British soldier manning a border checkpoint. Moreover, since the early 1970s, part of the grounds used by Crossmaglen Rangers Gaelic Club, all-Ireland club champions in 1997, has been occupied by the British Army. Meanwhile players and fans speak of being stopped on their way to Gaelic games by members of the security forces for no other reason than the fact that they are associated with the GAA. Furthermore, in addition to the unwelcome attention of the Army, the RUC and loyalist paramilitary organizations, the GAA has had to contend with the suspicion and, in some instances, the downright hostility of the political representatives of the unionist community.

The most celebrated example of unionist opposition to the GAA was the long-term refusal of Craigavon Borough Council to allow St Peter's Gaelic Club to develop a complex for Gaelic sports and pastimes. The club eventually took its case to the High Court. Finding in favour of St Peter's, Lord Chief Justice Lowry argued that, in his view, the council members who had obstructed the development of the sports complex had been motivated by sectarian bitterness (Knox, 1989). Less dramatically but no less significantly at the symbolic level, Unionist councils have frequently been unwilling to give civic receptions to successful Gaelic teams (Sugden and Bairner, 1993: 39).

Against this backdrop of British and Unionist hostility towards the Gaelic games movement, Gaels have been suspicious of initiatives from what they would see as the same ruling elite to alter the Association's character in the interests of improved community relations. Far from seeing such proposals, including the removal of Rule 21, as being innocent contributions to the peace process, many GAA members regard them as nothing more than subtle attempts to continue a historic struggle to undermine their activities and destroy an important element in the construction of Irish national identity (Bairner and Darby, 1999). It is impossible to deny that there may be some truth in this interpretation. Less convincing, however, is the GAA's attempt to respond to those who accuse it of promoting a narrow and exclusive nationalism. The GAA, according to one spokesperson, 'excludes no-one but some exclude themselves by their activities and by upholding a state which denies parity of treatment to Irish culture' (*Irish News*, 10 March 1992). The fact is that one would need to have some feeling for the Irish nationalist cause to be happy to become involved in Gaelic games. Thus, the overwhelming majority of northern Protestants are excluded or exclude themselves. There is, of course, no written rule which prevents most of them from taking part. It is disingenuous, however, to suggest that the absence of a written ban is indicative of inclusiveness. At the same time, in defence of the GAA, one must recognize that it is a cultural as well as a sporting organization and it operates on behalf of Irish nationalists, of whatever complexion, in the first instance. To that extent, it is difficult to see how it could become more inclusive without losing its very reason for being. This is particularly true with reference to the Association's activities in Northern Ireland but it applies also, if to a lesser extent, in the rest of Ireland as well.

Despite the emergence of a more pluralist sporting culture in the Irish Republic, the Celtic vision of sport as portrayed by the GAA remains insular and exclusivistic, because of what Irish nationalists regard as unfinished business in the north. It is undeniable, of course, that the resilience of this vision of sport has been largely facilitated by a set of political circumstances which lie beyond the direct influence of sports people. Nevertheless, given the persistence of those issues which originally gave rise to the GAA, it is unlikely in the foreseeable future that the Celtic vision can rid itself of its close association with ethnic nationalism. Yet it would be slightly misleading to conclude by simply equating the sporting nationalism of the GAA with ethnic nationalism. There are occasional signs, at least in the Irish Republic, that the Gaelic games movement can also play a role in the construction of a more civic-minded sense of Irishness. The fact that it is able to do so whilst at the same time continuing to promote ethnic nationalist feelings tells us much about attempts to categorize the forms of nationalism which seek to simplify what are, in fact, very complex issues. The nationalism promoted by the GAA is neither wholly ethnic nor wholly civic, although it has traditionally been closer to the former. We should not be surprised at this apparent ambiguity because arguably the same holds true for Irish nationalism more generally. Neither wholly ethnic nor wholly civic, it has been involved in a constant struggle between the dark forces of the former and the enlightened outlook of the latter. It is doubtful if it can ever escape fully from its ethnic past and it will be equally difficult for the GAA to free itself from exclusivist ideas about what it means to be Irish. As the comparison between the Association's role in the two parts of Ireland reveals, however, the extent to which it is able to distance itself from its ethnic vision of sport will depend ultimately on political developments over which it has little or no control.

ACKNOWLEDGEMENTS

An earlier version of this chapter was presented as a paper at the annual conference of the North American Society for the Sociology of Sport which was held on 13–16 November, 1996 in Birmingham, Alabama. The author is grateful to Bill Morgan, who organized the session on Sport and Nationalism, and to Grant Jarvie and John Sugden, who presented papers at the session, for their thoughtful and supportive comments. He also wishes to thank Jean Harvey for sharing his ideas on the relationship between ethnic and civic nationalism and Paul Darby for his insights into current attitudes within the Gaelic Athletic Association.

3

SPORT AND SCOTTISH GAELDOM IN ARGYLLSHIRE 1790–1900

Lorna Jackson

We the subscribers hereof, Considering the utility, promotion of friendship and amusement likely to arise from the establishment of a club to be held at Campbeltown for the purpose of bringing together at one time a number of the natives of Argyle and to keep up and foster the ancient customs and manners of Caledonia have therefore resolved to unite and associate ourselves into a club or society for that purpose ... by the name of the Gathering of the Dalrudinians.

(Constitution and Rules, no date but watermark 1824)

While the timing of this may be connected with George IV's visit of 1822, why the location? Argyll – *Earraghaidheal*, coastland of the Gael, in the language of its best known settlers (Thomson, 1994: 50) – is the cradle of Celtic culture in Scotland: the enduring heartland as it has been called (Campbell, 1995). Argyll has historic links with the Ireland of the Dalriadic people and from that era through to the modern period has used the sea as the common means of transport and communication. The Argyll of St Columba's Iona and of *An Comunn Gaidhealach*'s founding is an appropriate setting in which to examine the locus of sport in the making or maintaining of Celtic culture. This study focuses on Argyll in the period from the end of the eighteenth century to the end of the nineteenth – a time of significant and complex change for the whole of Scotland, not just the Highlands (Lynch, 1991; Fraser and Morris, 1990; Devine, 1988; Smout, 1986; Mitchison, 1982). Using a range of documentary and literary sources, it unravels some of the strands connecting history, culture and sport in a very specific context and considers the following questions: What is the significance of Celtic culture in Argyll's history? How did Celtic culture manifest itself in the Argyll of the late eighteenth century and how did it change over the nineteenth century? How significant were Celtic sports vis-à-vis other recreations in the life of the community?

The chapter will thus outline Argyll's history; examine the place of the Gaelic language in culture and the changes over the period in question; consider the occurrence of traditional or Celtic sports as distinct from non-Celtic sports; and outline the other cultural pursuits for which there is contemporary evidence. How Celtic culture was sustained or represented in the sporting lives of the peoples of Argyll in the nineteenth century can be adduced from examination of contemporary evidence, albeit with the proviso that the oral nature of the Gaelic culture and the systematic efforts to extirpate culture and language from mid-eighteenth century on inevitably biases the surviving evidence in favour of non-Gaelic pursuits.

THE CONTEXT

Physically the county is part of the Highlands – 'hills, rocks and mountains rise upon each other in stupendous and fearful disorder. Glencoe is, perhaps, amongst the most awfully picturesque valleys that can be contemplated' (Pigot and Company, 1837), and only in Kintyre were there extensive arable areas, some of which had been formed by the draining of shallow lochs (Smith, 1798: 9). Only eight parishes in south/mid Argyll were not designated as 'crofting' by the Crofting Commission of 1912 (Hunter, 1976: 3).

Historically, Argyll provided the nucleus for the kingdom of Scotland. Movement of population from the coastal area of northern Ireland culminated in the settlement of the royal dynasty of Dalriada permanently in Scotland (Bannerman, 1974: 71) – it was 'from their contemporary designation *Scotti*, or Scots, that Scotland itself was ultimately named' (Thomson, 1994: 54). The union of Scots and Picts in mid-ninth century under Kenneth mac Alpin, King of Dalriada (Lynch, 1991: 24) saw the locus of power of the new kingdom shift to a more central position and Argyll was left as a minor appendage of the new Scotland (MacDonald, 1961: 19). Like much of western Scotland, Argyll felt the influence of Norse raiders from the eighth to the eleventh centuries, but here the traces are slighter than in more northerly counties, being only an influence on place names as a result of the mixing of the Norse and Gaelic languages (MacDonald, 1950: 56). After a period of Macdonald influence (Lynch, 1991: 67), the Campbell dynasty came to power by the early decades of the seventeenth century. Campbeltown was planted as a burgh c.1609 and successively during that century settlers from Cumbria, Ayrshire and Renfrewshire were brought in as tenants in Kintyre (McKerral, 1948: 28). In the eighteenth century further planned villages and fishing villages followed, e.g. in Islay and Mull, and Inveraray, the Ducal seat, was redeveloped (Cregeen, 1970: 10; Smout, 1970: 92). One traveller of 1815 found the new town 'bore no faint resemblance to a scene upon the Italian lakes (Como more particularly)' (Southey, 1929: 241). The new steam ships and the opening of the Crinan Canal led to the development of tourism and by the 1780s Oban was being feued (*Oban Times*, 20 January 1883). By 1848, one of the early tourists commented that Lochgilphead 'is becoming so very Lowland in its appearance' (Stewart, 1848: 43).

The traditional way of life had been mainly pastoral, with the multiple-tenancy farm and sheiling system widely practised. Physical remnants are visible to this day (Fenton, 1980: 93; Turnock, 1995: 204). By the nineteenth century, the crofters 'live mostly on potatoes' (Smith, 1798: 79) and reared the sturdy native black cattle, fattening them up for sale in the Lowlands (ibid.: 226). Black-faced sheep were a recent introduction (Orr, 1982: 3), for which the Duke and his tenants were beginning to clear the land. That was followed towards the end of the century by evictions to make deer-forests (Macinnes, 1994: 1; *Campbeltown Courier*, 29 November 1873; *Oban Times*, 26 July 1890). The economics of famine and clearances over the century are too well narrated elsewhere to need detailing here (Devine, 1988; Orr, 1982; Richards, 1982; Hunter, 1976).

The natural resources of the land were exploited at a few sites: charcoal-making and iron-smelting at Bonawe and Furnace; gunpowder-making at Furnace and Melfort; naphtha from wood distillation at Ardrishaig; granite production at Bonawe and Cruachan; slate production in the vicinity of Easdale and the islands, and at Ballachulish. Cloth was produced at Inveraray and Connel; whisky was a major product from Campbeltown, labelled 'Whiskyopolis' (*Oban Times,* 1 February 1879) from its 43 distilleries (*New Statistical Account (NSA)*, 1845, vol. VII: 464), and Kintyre cheese was regularly exported to Glasgow. However, by the nineteenth century the principal export from Argyll was its people – to the Lowlands for work (seasonal or permanently), or further afield as part of the widespread emigration to North America or Australia.

GAELIC IN CULTURE

Despite Argyll being the source of the first Gaelic books to be published, John Carswell of Carnasserie's translation of the Book of Common Order 1567, and the Synod of Argyll's seventeenth-century translations of the scriptures into Gaelic (Thomson, 1994: 37; MacDonald, 1961: 91), the declining use of the Gaelic language and a corresponding rise in the use of English is evident from the parish reports of the first *Statistical Account* of the late eighteenth century (*Statistical Account (OSA)*, 1983, vol. VIII). 21

out of the 35 Argyllshire parishes (15 out of 25 mainland parishes and 6 out of 10 island parishes) comment on Gaelic as the native language of the common people. The influence of schools in introducing English is noted in several parishes: for example, Dunoon (*OSA*: 92), Kilfinichen (ibid.: 318), Kilchoman (395), as is the effect of 'intercourse with the low country': Glassary (106), South Knapdale (325), Strachur (414), Kilmore and Kilbride (284). The purity of the language is seen as relating to remoteness: for example, Dunoon (92) and Lochgoilhead (357) acknowledge the corruption of the Gaelic with English phrases; Gigha and Cara's report (441) indicates the vicinity of Ireland coarsens it, while Kilfinichen's (318) 'is reckoned very pure, by its vicinity to I' (Iona). Comment on the Gaelic origin of place names is made in 11 of the 21 parishes noted above. It is significant that the parish of Inveraray draws a clear distinction between 'the English [which is] the prevailing language in the town, and the Gaelic in the country part of the parish' (153).

By the time of the second *Statistical Account* (*NSA*, 1845) there appears to have been an increased interest in Gaelic in that 27 out of the 35 parishes offer comment, in the majority of cases identifying the decline of Gaelic through English gaining ground. Few of the authors, however, took the attitude of the minister of Kilcalmonell and Kilberry in mid-Argyll, who acknowledged English as displacing the vernacular Gaelic 'and the sooner it overmasters it the better' (*NSA*: 410). On this occasion a greater interest in Gaelic etymology is evident in that 27 out of the 35 parish accounts now offer some derivations of local place names. In Campbeltown it is noted that there are 'two parish churches, in one of which Gaelic is preached and in the other English' (*NSA*: 465) but that business transactions are carried on in English. The minister of Kilbrandon and Kilchattan in south Lorn acknowledged that the people 'understand and can speak English tolerably well' yet the engineer of the slate works delivered a course of lectures on mechanics and other scientific subjects to the Young Men's Mutual Improvement Association 'communicating ... to the Highlanders in their own language' (*NSA*: 75).

What might have produced this change? Some of the support for the language came through religious and educative agencies: in 1821 Inveraray Presbytery rejected applicants for the post of schoolmaster if they were ignorant of the Gaelic language. Following Patrick Butter's 1824 tour of inspection of the schools of the Society for the Propagation of Christian Knowledge and his critical comments on pedagogy, the Society made it a rule that children should be taught to read in Gaelic first before being taught English. The General Assembly of the Church of Scotland in 1826 were printing suitable books for its schools studying Gaelic, but over a twenty-year period saw a sharp drop in the proportions of scholars of Gaelic from 62 per cent of all scholars in 1831 to 26 per cent in 1852 (Jackson, 1969: 70–2). In 1867 the *Oban Times* editorial denigrated the teaching of Gaelic in schools (28 September 1867 and 19 October 1867) yet by 1879 it was acknowledging Gaelic as one of the most ancient of languages (13 September 1879) and by 1886 was denouncing the lack of support for Gaelic by the Committee for Education as 'another conspiracy against Gaelic' (13 March 1886). The change may not be unrelated to the wider recognition that Gaelic had 'favour in high places', indeed of Queen Victoria herself (*Campbeltown Journal*, 29 March 1851).

The lack of support for Gaelic among education officials may be attributed to its association with a 'political movement' to quote HMI Ross (*Oban Times*, 29 July 1879), but locally the support for Gaelic was evident. Thus the Ardrishaig correspondent of the *Oban Times* boasted of the first Penny Readings in Gaelic (*Oban Times*, 30 March 1869); businesses advertised for Gaelic speakers, e.g. an Ardrishaig baker (ibid., 7 May 1870) and a Campbeltown draper (*Argyllshire Herald*, 28 February 1876); and the trustees of the Islay poorhouse ensured that the governor and matron were Gaelic speaking (*Oban Times*, 24 April 1886). The language was still used to ensure clear understanding: there was a Gaelic lecture on New Zealand in Ballachulish (ibid., 4 January 1868); descriptions of magic lantern slides in a lecture in Coll 'to the great appreciation of those who are not sufficiently familiar with English' (ibid., 17 January 1885); the translation of Sankey's hymns for the Ross of Mull (ibid., 6 October 1883); and the sale of books of Gaelic hymns by the minister of Glenorchy (*Argyllshire Herald*, 24 October 1868). Recognition of the language was also made in legal cases where witnesses' grasp of English was less than sure, and interpreters had to be provided (*Campbeltown Courier*, 29 November 1873 and 29 October 1898).

Another indicator of the strength of Gaelic culture may come from the persistence of old customs in celebrating traditional occasions. Hogmanay and New Year's Day (for a detailed discussion of this custom see Chapter 7) continued to be held with the customary rituals well through the century – Captain Stewart of Fasnacloich requiring his workers to 'circle the house three times ... and recite the *Duan*, which entitled [each] to enter the hospitality of the house' (*Oban Times*, 8 January 1870). The 'Old Style' calendar was most frequently observed at New Year – twelve days after the New Style, i.e. on 13 January according to one description (ibid.), and also at Halloween, e.g. at North Ballachulish (*Oban Times*, 21 November 1891). Even at relatively close distances, communities differed in the timing of their celebrations, e.g. Inveraray (New Style) and Furnace (Old Style)

(*Oban Times*, 15 January 1870), Glenforsa and Salen on Mull (ibid., 21 January 1882); and only towards the end of the century did the more remote communities vote for the 1st of January, e.g. Lochaweside (ibid., 9 December 1876); Kilmartin (ibid., 10 January 1880); Furnace (ibid., 15 January 1887); and Lochaline (ibid., 10 January 1891). In Appin the residents as late as 1889 were celebrating both (*Oban Times*, 5 and 19 January 1889), while Iona on one occasion held three celebrations (ibid., 26 January 1884). Kilberry under its laird John Campbell consistently supported the Old New Year's Day celebration – a custom which persisted through to this century (MacLennan, 1995: 135).

Campbeltown had the unique celebration of burning tar-barrels at the Cross after carrying these 'through the principal streets of the burgh' (*Oban Times*, 12 January 1878, also 9 January 1869; 1 January 1870; *Argyllshire Herald*, 4 January 1873), but after a Sheriff Court case in 1880 there are no further reports (*Campbeltown Courier*, 10 January 1880). Evidence also exists of the gentry having a personal piper – not only the Duke of Argyll, but also John Macdougall Esq. of Lunga, who had insisted on the house-circling tradition the Hogmanay before his death (*Oban Times*, 4 March 1871); the lairds of Ardkinglas (ibid., 11 September 1875), Poltalloch (ibid., 19 September 1879), Dunach (ibid., 5 April 1884), Kilberry and Ormsary (ibid., 31 January 1885), Melfort (ibid., 15 January 1887) and a Major Allanby of Alt-na-Craig, Ardrishaig (ibid., 27 June 1891). Highland dress was supported by a smaller number of non-Campbells, Colonel Gardyne of Glenforsa being specifically identified as a supporter (*Oban Times*, 17 January 1874), while Lord Archibald Campbell, a son of the Duke of Argyll, only accepted the captaincy of the local Volunteer Rifles 'on condition of (their) taking off the trews' and wearing the kilt (ibid., 11 May 1867).

As a counterpoint to the slow erosion of traditional Old New Year customs, there is from the 1870s on an increasing attention to Gaelic matters as reported in the local press. The *Oban Times* began publishing Gaelic poetry in 1871 (16 September 1871) and later proudly commented on the fame of Mr Evan Maccoll the Lochfyne bard – lesser known than his Argyllshire compatriot Duncan Ban Macintyre (Donnchadh Ban) – as 'a gentleman who has contributed to our own poet's corner' (31 May 1873). Gaelic readings (22 February 1879) and Celtic songs (10 January 1880) followed under the guidance of Henry White (Fionn), who later edited the 'Celtic Notes and Queries' column introduced in 1882 (*Oban Times*, 2 September 1882) and continued through the century. The *Oban Times* even ran a series of 21 articles, 'How to learn Gaelic' (July–December 1882). Societies were reported, the aims of which were to cultivate or preserve Gaelic, e.g. the Lorn Ossianic Society (*Oban Times*, 14 December 1872) of which further later; Tobermory Ossianic Society (ibid., 1 February 1873); Kintyre Ossianic Society (ibid., 2 December 1876); Ross of Mull Celtic Society (ibid., 6 October 1883); Salen Celtic Society (ibid., 26 March 1887); Campbeltown Celtic Society (*Argyllshire Herald*, 17 March 1888); and the Tiree Ossianic Society (*Oban Times*, 8 February 1890). The groundswell supporting Gaelic bore fruit in the decision, taken at a meeting in Oban in 1890, to institute a Highland Eisteddfod (reported *Oban Times*, 15 October 1890), the outcome being the formation of *An Comunn Gaidhealach* in Oban in 1891 (ibid., 2 May 1891) 'to promote the culture of Highland music, literature and home industries, as well as to hold an annual gathering at which the several competitions shall take place' (ibid., 17 January 1891).

This increased interest led Robert MacLagan to undertake in 1893 an investigation into the traditional 'games and diversions of Argyleshire' (MacLagan, 1901). He recorded his correspondents' accounts of games played up to seventy years previously: imitative games, ball games, partner games 'played indoors usually ... for practical purposes, "waulking songs"' (ibid.: 48). The children's games and counting-out rhymes in English identified therein were still current in Kintyre school playgrounds in the 1950s. MacLagan notes, 'There seems to have been more unpremeditated dancing in older times than is at present the custom' (ibid.: 102) and while he links that with certain kinds of work, contemporary evidence certainly records incidents of spontaneous dancing on workmen's excursions, e.g. Easdale (*Oban Times*, 26 August 1876) and Furnace (ibid., 13 July 1878); at Volunteer competitions, e.g. Inveraray (*Oban Times*, 15 August 1868) and Ballachulish (ibid., 7 April 1873); and after shinty matches, e.g. Inveraray (*Argyllshire Herald*, 13 January 1866), Kilberry (*Oban Times*, 26 January 1878), Glenbarr (*Argyllshire Herald*, 3 March 1888) and Ballachulish (*Oban Times*, 7 January 1888). The dangers of dancing during the game were highlighted at Bowmore when players following the ball into the midst of the dancers 'resulted in sending the dancers helter-skelter into an adjoining field' (*Oban Times*, 24 January 1885). Inevitably it is the latter game to which MacLagan devotes much attention, 'undoubtedly the game of the Gael' (MacLagan, 1901: 24) and it is to Celtic sports that we now turn.

CELTIC SPORTS

The classic games of Scotland are said to be golf, curling and shinty (*Inverness Courier*, 12 May 1893, quoted in MacLennan, 1995: 1). While the first is not obviously of Celtic origin, the latter two merit some attention. Shinty is dealt with elsewhere in this volume (see Chapter 7), but it is worth noting in Argyllshire the association of traditional shinty games with the celebration of Old New Year's Day and, by the end of the century, New Year's Day. Some of this persistence of association may be attributed to deliberate preservation of the old tradition, e.g. at Campbeltown under the auspices of Campbeltown Celtic Club (*Argyllshire Herald*, 7 January 1888); on Colonel Gardyne's estate at Glenforsa (*Oban Times*, 15 January 1881); and at Kilberry (ibid., 17 January 1891). The role of individuals in its maintenance may be illustrated by the efforts of John Francis Campbell of Islay (*Ian Ile Og*), who claimed in his personal notebook to have given the tradition a boost by his description (published in the *Glasgow Daily Herald* of 6 January 1868, replicated in the *Times* and the *Oban Times*) of a Grand Shinty Match between Inveraray and Ardkinglas (Campbell, 1868). An equivalent report of an earlier match appeared in the *Argyllshire Herald* of 13 January 1866 of unidentified authorship. MacLagan acknowledged the New Year link (MacLagan, 1901: 35), and there is ample contemporary evidence to support this (*Argyllshire Herald* and *Oban Times*, passim).

What of the roaring game? Although Murray suggests its Highland origins, the stronghold of curling was the Lowlands (Murray, 1981: 54). Curling appears widespread in Argyllshire, though records of its occurrence tend to be dependent on winter conditions: Tobermory's correspondent to the *Oban Times* recorded in 1875 the only season's curling for the last twenty-five years (2 January 1875). Club records exist for Inveraray (1855–64), Campbeltown (1881–6 and 1892–1907), and Ballachulish and Glencoe (1897–1907), but local newspapers testify to their existence outwith these dates and identify at least fourteen other clubs over the second half of the century, from Appin in the west (*Oban Times*, 18 January 1868) to Dunoon in the east (ibid., 7 January 1871). Oban's club, founded in 1842, still had a founder member active in 1887 (*Oban Times*, 12 November 1887). Participants in the sport needed time to play: in Campbeltown it was suggested that 'our friends the farmers have the advantage of longer experience and better practice' (*Argyllshire Herald*, 29 December 1860), and the club's membership records for 1881 certainly reflect a high 'country' membership from farm addresses, though also members who were masons, drapers, merchants and distillers (subscription accounts 1881). A local schoolmaster resigned because he was 'unable to get to the ice. When I have no right to be among you, I may be better able to endure the jolly shouts and laughter which reach me unable to leave my post' (letter of Peters, 1897). Inveraray Curling Club records give no account of members' occupations, but the indication of additional calls for money to defray expenses as well as an admission fee (minute book, 11 November 1857) suggests it was not the ordinary folk of the district who might be sharing the ice with the Marquis of Lorne (*Oban Times*, 4 February 1871) or the Duke himself (ibid., 19 February 1876).

A stronger case can be made in terms of competitive sporting activities of the kind consolidated in Highland Games (Jarvie, 1991). The *Old Statistical Account* for Kilchoman (*OSA*: 395) identifies putting the stone as one of the chief amusements, and 'throwing the stone and leaping' in spontaneous competition was still popular among spectators at ploughing matches later in the century (e.g. *Argyllshire Herald*, 20 January 1860 and 24 January 1874). The Dalrudinians as part of their efforts to keep up ancient manners and customs aimed to 'award prizes to those who may excel in any Game of Amusement ... the Games to be contested at or near Campbeltown' (Dalrudinians, 1824?; Kintyre Club, 1885). The Inveraray festivities for October 1842 under the patronage of the Duke and Duchess of Argyll included not only sweepstakes for 'Riffle Shot' and 'Riding at the Ring' for subscribers and a competition for a Silver Arrow by 'the ARGYLL company of ALBYN ARCHERS' but also 'Foot-Races, Long and Short, and other Gymnastic Exercises, which are Open to all Competitors, and for which Small Prizes will be given' (handbill, 1842).

The contrast between the local informal competitions and the more formal 'arranged' games can be traced through to the second half of the century. Into the former category could be placed events such as Port Askaig Regatta and land sports (*Argyllshire Herald*, 4 September 1863); the Cullipool Gymnastic Games arranged annually in connection with the Easdale slate works (*Oban Times*, 10 July 1869); the Ballachulish regatta 'got up by working men' at the slate quarries, which was accompanied by land sports (ibid., 28 August 1869); the Glenforsa and Killiechronan Games, restricted to tenants on the two estates (ibid., 4 September 1875); the Iona games and regatta (ibid., 26 October 1878); and the Tarbert sports and regatta (ibid., 23 September 1882). At these gatherings the traditional sports – throwing the hammer and the stone (both heavy and light), racing and leaping (high jump and long jump) – were pursued as 'trials of strength, swiftness and agility' (Kilmartin, ibid., 10 October 1868). The caber seldom featured in such games, but the link with water sports was often present – as in the report of the Toberonchy, Luing gathering where the land sports were held 'during the time the boats were sailing' (ibid., 13 September 1890). By the 1880s it was more common for the small communities to hold regattas – for fishing skiffs, sailing boats and rowing races as at Tarbert (*Oban Times*, 1 September 1883) – although the traditional competitions were now appearing as part of New Year celebrations, e.g. at Campbeltown (*Argyllshire Herald,* 3 January 1874; *Campbeltown Courier,* 7 January 1881 and 9 January 1892); Kilberry (*Argyllshire Herald,* 4 January 1873); Dunoon (*Oban Times,* 6 January 1877); Jura (ibid., 26 January 1884); Kilmelford and Kilmartin (ibid., 9 January 1886); Appin and Lochgilphead (ibid., 4 January 1890). The Sandbank correspondent claimed in 1878 that New Year sports had been held on the same ground at Cot House for 26 years (ibid., 12 January 1878), while Coll inaugurated Highland Games in 1882 after its Agricultural Society annual ploughing match (ibid., 18 February 1882). There are reports of the old type of informal competition in connection with the building of railway lines – at Connel in 1879 where Highland sports were held by Skyemen engaged on the railway about to leave to join the herring fishing (ibid., 28 June 1879), and at Bridge of Orchy in 1891 by workmen on the Achallader section of the railway (ibid., 2 May 1891).

A more formal organization is evinced by the rise of the Rifle Volunteer regimental games at the annual camp periodically from 1875 onwards (e.g. *Oban Times,* 14 August 1875; 6 August 1881; 16 August 1884). However, the interest in regular formal games predates this. A letter in the *Oban Times* in 1870 advocated the introduction of a Highland sports to Oban as 'affording our English visitors an opportunity of witnessing the ancient and national sport of the Gael' (*Oban Times,* 21 May 1870), but the royal wedding of the Marquis of Lorne and HRH Princess Louise in 1871 seemed to provide the catalyst. Games were reported in Ardrishaig on the wedding day as part of festivities (reported in the *Oban Times,* 1 April 1871) and celebratory games were held in August in Inveraray to welcome the newlyweds (ibid., 12 August 1871). Since most of the county elite had assembled there in expectation that Queen Victoria would honour the homecoming with her presence, the opportunity was taken to institute 'an Annual Gathering of the Gentry of the County of Argyll for social purposes ... to be called the Argyllshire Gathering' (Malcolm, 1971: 5). The first report in the *Oban Times* of 9 September 1871 indicated that 'other gentlemen desirous of becoming members are requested to be good enough to send their names and subscriptions', but evidently that provoked a response from either too many or from the wrong gentlemen, because the Honorary Secretary, M. G. Maclaine of Lochbuy, had to send out a printed response returning 'subscription, which I inadvertently asked for too soon' until the names had been 'balloted for at the first General Meeting of the Gathering' (Maclaine, 1871).

The Gathering held its first Grand Ball in Oban in 1872, and its first Games there in 1873, but what the official history of the Argyllshire

Gathering (Malcolm, 1971) does not record is that the Lorn Ossianic Society (noted above) also instituted Games in that year, on the day preceding the Gathering Games. It was suggested that the two Highland Games be combined to provide a rival to the Northern Meeting at Inverness (*Oban Times*, 2 August 1873), but while the Lorn Ossianic Society agreed to enter into negotiations (ibid., 9 August 1873), there is no public record of a response from the Gathering and the two events proceeded. There was a similar range of events at both: traditional events in stone, hammer and caber (some closed to natives of the county, some open to all comers); races and jumps; pipe competitions for piobaireachds, marches and reels; and dancing reels, sword dance and Highland Fling (ibid., 23 August 1871). Indeed the *Oban Times* considered this 'has a tendency to make the second day rather notorious on account of its being a repetition of the previous day' (ibid., 13 September 1879). The two Games continued in parallel apparently for different audiences 'Gathering for the County as the gentry of Argyllshire give very little encouragement to the games of the Lorn Ossianic society' (ibid., 15 September 1877); the townspeople saw the Ossianic event as the first day of the Games while 'country people prefer waiting till the second day to come to Oban' (ibid., 13 September 1879). There may have been some hidden rivalry – the Lorn Ossianic Society instituted a Gaelic concert in the same year that the Gathering instituted a regatta (ibid., 19 August 1876), later to be taken over by the Royal Highland Yacht Club from 1882 – but the public record is silent on the demise of the Ossianic Games which 'fell through this year from some unexplained cause' (ibid., 17 September 1891) and were never repeated. It is illuminating to note that from 1884 to 1887, no advertisements for the Gathering Games appeared in the *Oban Times*, an omission attributed by one Glasgow correspondent as a 'boycott' because the newspaper's 'support in the land struggle is not palatable to the Argyllshire gentry' (ibid., 23 August 1871).

The other notable Games of Argyllshire, the Cowal Highland Gathering, also trace their origin to 1871 (Inglis, 1957: 1) with subsequent Games at New Year under the auspices of the Dunoon St Andrew's Society (e.g. *Oban Times*, 6 and 8 January 1887) and later the Town Council (*Cowal Chronicle*, 24 December 1896) but the Cowal Gathering in its present form is said to date from 1900 after some less successful attempts in the 1890s. The Highland Games and Cycle Sports of 1893 and the Gathering of 1894 (Inglis, 1957: 1–5) do not seem to stress their Celtic connections in the same way that pertains to the Campbeltown Celtic Society, which ran Games not only at New Year time, but also for the benefit of Glasgow Fair visitors (e.g. *Oban Times*, 20 July 1890).

Inveraray's Highland Games of 1890 were the first occasion on which all the competitions were open to natives of the county rather than only the community (ibid., 27 July 1890), but their link with traditional patronage is clearly evident from the regular presence of the Argyll family (e.g. ibid., 12 September 1891; Telfer, 1994: 115).

SPORT IN CULTURE

In the early years of its publishing life, 'sport' in the *Oban Times* described the gentlemen's activities on the moors and the waters; by 1888 the paper was acknowledging 'Highland Sports, Games etc' in the season (4 August 1888) and a column headed 'Shinty, Football etc' gathered match reports from March 1888 until the 'Sports' column started in 1890 (7 June 1890). At the opening of Oban Bowling Club in 1870, Professor Blackie spoke warmly of the benefits of activity in the open air – cricketing, bowling, curling, quoits and golf 'with cricketing the very best' (*Oban Times*, 9 July 1870). All of these activities were represented in the sporting life in the second half of the century, but not all were given the same attention in the public record.

Cricketing first appears in Campbeltown in the guise of the Campbeltown Civil Service Cricketing Club, a club for the Inland Revenue Officers – 'excisemen' – associated with the town's distilleries (*Argyllshire Herald*, 24 June 1859). Opening its ranks to the town's gentlemen in the next season, the Campbeltown Cricket Club flourished through to the end of the century. It was early noted for 'foreign' matches – an annual match with Ayr on the day of the Kintyre Agricultural Show in Campbeltown was a fixture from 1868 on (ibid., 27 June 1878). There was regular competition against Clubs from Glasgow (e.g. *Oban Times*, 24 July 1869, 24 July 1875) and Greenock (ibid., 4 September 1869), as well as undertaking tours to play there in 1887 (ibid., 30 April 1887) and 1889 (ibid., 10 August 1889). Oban's cricket club was a less thriving organization, failing and being revived on several occasions from 1867 before it seemed to become established from 1889 for a number of seasons, playing matches against visitors, e.g. Stenhousemuir and Grange in 1891 (ibid., 4 July and 15 August 1891). Elsewhere in the county, cricket was played with local or in-club competition, and tended to have links with the gentry, as at Inveraray where an annual fixture against Ardkinglas mirrored the shinty tradition, but this time Lord Archibald Campbell played for the Ardkinglas side (ibid., 5 September 1885 onward). Patronage helped maintain teams at Kilmartin, the summer home of John Malcolm of Poltalloch (ibid., 24 August 1867); at Carradale when Colonel

Buchanan of Drumpellier had gentlemen visitors shooting on his estates of Carradale and Torrisdale (ibid., 29 August 1885); at Lochbuy in Mull (ibid., 18 September 1880); at Kilberry (ibid., 29 August 1885); at Tarbert where Campbell of Stonefield established a club in 1890 after expressions of interest from the fishermen (ibid., 14 June 1890); and at Largie in Kintyre where the Castle Club was supported by the MacDonald laird (ibid., 25 July 1891).

If cricket was associated with the gentry, quoits was the working man's game (Tranter, 1989: 57), but it received little attention in the local press. Certainly there were clubs in Campbeltown (*Argyllshire Herald*, 8 July 1859, *Campbeltown Courier*, 5 July 1884, *Oban Times*, 5 May 1888), Ardgour (ibid., 12 October 1872), Taynuilt (ibid., 2 August 1889), Lochgilphead (ibid., 28 July 1883), Toward (ibid., 17 May 1884), and Achnamara (ibid., 21 July 1884), most with their own grounds, but little detail is provided and the game may have been more widespread. Football appears to have existed in the county in a traditional form, judging by some of the references to a decline by the 1860s, for example, in Oban it had been in decline 'for the last ten years' (*Oban Times*, 23 November 1872), while in Minard an octogenarian participated in a New Year match 'who has not played football for the last thirty years. He went so heartily into the game on this occasion that what he could not do with his feet, he tried to do with his umbrella' (ibid., 16 January 1886). The games in more remote areas still took an unreconstructed form of prolonged duration, for example, Iona's Old New Year's Day match lasting three hours (ibid., 20 January 1883) or of large numbers of participants, e.g. Benderloch and Lochnell's New Year's Day match of 23-a-side (ibid., 20 January 1877). However, by 1880 the spread of Association Rules was being welcomed – 'the fine game of football has been reduced to a rational modern standard, and divested of its whilom brutality' (ibid., 14 February 1880). As interest developed and the number of sides grew, Argyll formed its own Football Association (ibid., 2 November 1889) which prior to affiliation with the Scottish Football Association ran a County Cup Competition, the final of which in its first two years was played at Ibrox Park, Govan and Cappielow Park, Greenock respectively (ibid., 29 March 1890, 7 March 1891). By this date football was receiving much more reporting coverage than shinty.

It has to be noted that far greater attention was paid in the press to non-sporting cultural pursuits, generally of the improving kind for both middle and working class, though seldom were the objectives as explicitly spelled out as at Drumlemble near Campbeltown, where a reading room was established by the proprietor of the Colliery to aid the cause of

Temperance: 'give the masses intellectual food and amusement, and they will not seek after so much stimulant' (*Oban Times*, 25 November 1882). Nonetheless the rational recreation impulse drove many Mutual Improvement Associations, Debating Societies and Scientific and Literary Associations, not to mention all the musical entertainments which raised funds for worthy causes. The Temperance movement was strong, and from the 1880s the Highland Land Law Reform Association (later locally named the Argyll Reform League) had extensive support. Space does not permit elaboration, but the evidence suggests that non-sporting pursuits played a larger part in the lives of the community than did sporting activity.

SPORT AND GAELDOM

How strongly does Celtic culture feature in the social history of Argyll? The historical roots of the population and the language have been discussed above, and although the decline of Gaelic was noted at the time of the New Statistical Account, it still survived as a native language in mainland areas into this century though was said to be 'dying fast' at the time of the Third Statistical Account (MacDonald, 1961: 170ff). Towards the end of last century certainly there was much more support from the gentry for the language – Lord Archibald Campbell had written a book on Gaelic (*Oban Times*, 6 January 1883) long before he became president of *An Comunn Gaidhealach*, while in 1892 for the first time Colonel Malcolm, MP, sent out Christmas cards to the electorate in Gaelic as well as English (*Campbeltown Courier*, 9 January 1892). There is earlier evidence of an awareness of the significance of the Celtic roots – in 1867 an Argyll Rifle Volunteers' ball in Inveraray used Gaelic language and imagery in the banners decorating the hall: in translation 'Success – the sword and the spear, the kilt and the plaid: the sons of the Highlanders shoulder to shoulder' (*Argyllshire Herald*, 28 December 1867). J. F. Campbell's celebrated account of the 1868 shinty match describes the participants as 'genuine Fenians of the old breed' and emphasizes the traditional link of the Campbells of Argyllshire and elsewhere with 'those ancient Fenians of whose exploits and adventures all Celtic tradition in Scotland and Ireland is full'. The New Year match was claimed by him as direct descendant of 'the game which Cuchullin and Oscar Diarmaid and Fionn used to play in the olden time', the heroes of Gaeldom being invoked to 'revive the Celtic feeling' (Campbell, 1868). The imagery also appears at this time in a description of an otter hunt where 'the otter took to the hills in the true Celtic manner' (*Oban Times*, 19 September 1868).

The place of popular sport in this Celtic consciousness is less clear – it may be facile to identify the success of non-Celtic sports such as cricket and quoits with the parts of the county where there were strong Lowland connections or 'gentry' influences (Campbeltown, Inveraray, Oban) but certainly association football had its earliest impact where proprietors actively supported it (e.g. Barcaldine from the accession of a new absentee laird, *Oban Times*, 4 January 1868). As late as 1890 it was the laird Captain MacNeill of Oronsay who introduced the young men to football 'which is rather a new game in Colonsay' (ibid., 26 April 1890), yet on that occasion the players marched to the field with a piper and danced after the match in the traditional way. John Campbell of Kilberry was the most supportive of the lairds in maintaining the old customs on his estate – using shinty and football as part of the celebrations of Old New Year's Day.

The persistence of such physical traditions as dancing and competitions of skill as outlined earlier indicate their significance in the culture of the Gael. The rise of organized sporting activity may have overshadowed the traditional element of sporting pastimes, but the association with Celtic culture was not lost in shinty nor in Highland games, although the latter were increasingly seen as events to be watched by the majority and participated in by the few (Burnett, 1995: 58). Indeed at the founding meeting of *An Comunn Gaidhealach*, one participant waspishly remarked there had been 'too much of the Highland pine and stone' and too little attention paid to the 'intelligent side of the Highland character' (*Oban Times*, 18 October 1890). If this is taken as a reflection of the significance of Gaelic's oral tradition or an expression of regret for the downplaying of artistic activity, it overlooks the contribution of music and dance in the everyday life of the Gael. On the evidence presented here, sport by itself is not a symbol of Gaeldom in Argyllshire, since the Gaelic identity is multi-faceted, but it can justifiably be seen as a significant element in the way in which Celtic culture was manifest in the specific context, time and place of nineteenth-century Argyllshire.

4

BRITTANY, BETWEEN IRELAND, SCOTLAND AND FRANCE

Michel Lagrée

When we consider the role of sport in Breton cultural identity, we are thinking, as in all Celtic countries, about two distinct realities: Breton games and sports in Brittany. Breton games constitute a patrimony, stemming from ancient civilization, rural and parochial. Their recent destiny, during the nineteenth and twentieth centuries, illustrates the double process – a long erosion and then a reactivation – that has more generally affected Breton culture in the face of modern life, Ireland being another case in point. On the other hand, 'sports in Brittany' is also a generic expression covering all modern athletics and games. Their origins generally lie in Britain and they have penetrated provincial France through the cities, affecting first an urban elite then spreading through the whole society. Football is, by far, the most prominent sport in Brittany, and the reasons for this need explaining; this will lead us to look to Scotland rather than Ireland. Brittany is distinct, however, from its Celtic cousins in having cycling in the spectrum of its regional sports; this irrevocably connects it to France and to French mythologies.

POPULAR TRADITION AND REVIVAL: THE IRISH MODEL?

In the heritage of Breton games, collective games, such as *soule* (street football) which can define the parish community, are usually opposed to athletic games or *pardon* games, which encourage individual excellence and lend themselves well to the Celtic ritual of challenge: '*Piv eo ar mestr?*' (Who is the master?) In the first category, the game of lacrosse or *bazhig kamm*, consisted in attempts to gain possession of a small hard wooden or bone ball and to push it into a hole, with the help of a curved stick. Perhaps a distant ancestor of hockey, the game has now completely disappeared. Yet it was *soule* (*ar vell*) that best incarnated ancient rustic sociability. It was not peculiar to the region, since it could be found elsewhere in France, not to mention its relatives: *hurling* in Cornwall, *knappan* in Wales and street football in England, but it thrived spectacularly in Brittany. The team contest over a leather ball lent itself well to the Breton environment, with its large and sparsely wooded terrain, and a strong sense of local identity within parishes, which welcomed rivalries and confrontations. Much evidence, judicial as well as ethnographic, indicates the passion of the participants and the violence of the packs and races, typical of traditional games, and characteristic too of a society in which violence was more readily tolerated. Civilian and religious authorities eventually united against the violent game of *soule*. Both the bishop of Tréguier in 1440 and the Parliament of Brittany in 1686 took prohibitive measures. After the Revolution, *soule* was played only in Morbihan, the most archaic department in Brittany. When Emile Souvestre, during the 1830s, went in search of the *derniers Bretons*, he described, among other things, a Homeric match of *soule*, near Pontivy. Civil authorities carried on the Ancien Regime's struggle to suppress the game: the sub-prefect of Pontivy in 1819 and the prefect of Morbihan in 1857 passed prohibition orders, which, however, had little effect.

Athletic games survived more easily because they were linked to secular feasts, fairs, and above all the characteristic religious festivals of Lower Brittany, the *pardons*. The *pardons*, as the name indicates, were pilgrimages associated with indulgences. They marked the rhythm of the calendar and would often last several days. The games, which gave way to religious manifestation, were often games of *adpardon*, especially in Trégor, meaning games that followed the day of *pardon*. The most prominent among these games of strength was wrestling or *ar gouren*. Brought across the Channel during the fourth century, it is distinct in two ways from Greco-Roman wrestling: Breton wrestlers are dressed in linen shirts and they wrestle standing up, instead of on the ground. It became a Breton national sport, inseparable from all festivities, to the extent that the notoriety of Breton wrestlers spread far beyond Brittany. At the Field of the Cloth of Gold in 1520, François 1 regretted that he had not brought Breton wrestlers to oppose the Cornwall wrestlers of Henry VIII. On this sport, too, the effects of Catholic reform were felt. During the seventeenth century priests were forbidden to participate in wrestling; during the nineteenth, with increasingly stringent piety, some priests are said to have forbidden their congregations even to attend the matches.

Other strength games elevated everyday activities into performances. For example, *Sevel ar berchenn* (the lifting of a pole) was a game that consisted in lifting the heavy parish banner during processions, a feat which young people vied with each other to perform. Other contests, such as *Ar c'hravazh* (lifting a stretcher loaded with bags of sand or large stones), *wintañ ar sac'h* (snatching the sack), *year ahel-karr* (lifting the cart axle), and *maen-pouez* (launching heavy stones) were purely secular in origin. The rules of these games varied greatly, depending on the narrow geographical communities – parishes, cantons – that played them.

In the modern and contemporary era, traditional games have evolved in a similar way to the Breton language. At first there was a retreat and a loss of support, due to the decline of traditional rural civilization and the competition from modern entertainment, responsible for legitimizing, as it were, the use of French. *Soule* could not withstand this, and the last match was certified in 1912. Wrestling, on the other hand, did not disappear. Familiar throughout the peninsula in the sixteenth and seventeenth centuries, it retreated to the confines of Lower Brittany and became one of the elements of the local landscape, prolifically recorded by painters, from the romantics to the realists, but also by innovative artists, such as Gauguin and Sérusier. The famous *Jacob Wrestling with the Angel* (or *Vision after Church*) by Gauguin (Edinburgh, National Gallery of Scotland) transposed the popular subject into a religious register: Jacob and the angel wrestle in Breton fashion in the centre of a circle, watched by an assembly of women in headdresses. When an active movement of support for the old language developed during the second half of the nineteenth century, some people also sought to revive the ancient athletic games, creating an organization similar to the Gaelic Athletic Association in Ireland. Just as the GAA played an eminent role in Irish nationalism, alongside the Gaelic League, so the enthusiasms of Dr Cotonnec, a doctor in Quimperlé, were connected with the cultural activism in inter-war Brittany. At that point numerous initiatives and movements existed. Regionalism, moderate and traditional, was overlapped by the new Breton nationalism. Dr Cotonnec, fond of Breton wrestling and in touch with his counterparts in Cornwall, organized a successful inter-Celtic wrestling tournament in August 1928. He created the Fédération des Amis des Luttes et Sports Athlétiques Bretons (FALSAB: Friends of Breton Wrestling and Athletics) in the hope of homogenizing the structure and regulations of Breton games and thus modernizing them. In a similar way, and at the same time, linguists were working to create a modern written Breton language out of the mosaic of oral dialects. Just as linguists could not agree among themselves about a norm, Breton sports were plagued by divisive arguments after the death of Dr Cotonnec. In comparison with the situation in Ireland there is one key difference: the patrimonial effort focused on wrestling, while nobody thought to restore and adapt the games of lacrosse or *soule*. The equivalent of Gaelic football cannot be found in Brittany.

In 1941, Catholic *patronages* (youth clubs) went back to competing in 'rural Breton sports'. However, the collaborationist behaviour of some extreme Breton nationalists meant that these activities fell into a decline after World War II, when any initiatives of a Breton nature came to be regarded with suspicion. Breton wrestling competitions began again during the 1950s, especially in Paris. The capital city, indeed, accommodated a very active Breton movement, rich in initiatives of all sorts, as often happens among expatriates. In 1965 a new federation, BRUG, appeared. It later became BAG (*Bodadeg ar Gourenerien*: 'meeting of wrestlers'). In 1974, in step with the dramatic revival of the Breton cultural movement and especially the playing of the bagpipes (BAS: *Bodadeg ar Sonerien*), the work of restructuring Breton sports resumed, with common rules to unify the different trends. Thus, Breton games apart from wrestling appeared in official competitions. This happened at the inter-Celtic festival in Lorient, which was first opened to a Scottish team (1973) and then, since 1977, to teams from all Celtic countries: Scotland, Ireland, Wales, Galicia, Isle of Man, Cornwall. In addition, the games (*C'hoariou Langonned*) held annually since 1974 in Langonnet, a vast rural commune in the middle of the Breton-speaking countryside, became, in 1978, the leading celebration of Breton athletic sports. Here the inspiration of the Highland Games and Irish annual games is obvious.

In relation to the crowds attracted by modern sports today, it is obvious that Breton traditional sports reach only a tiny, although growing, minority. This is particularly true for wrestling. In this field as in others (music, language) the main motivation seems to be the search for a Breton authenticity. The organizers of FALSAB and the *gouren* have a militant vocation, which helps connect diverse participants in the Breton movement. The role of a man like Polig Monjarret, ubiquitous organizer of bagpipe players, in FALSAB as well as in the *Kendalc'h* federation, exemplifies this. The aim is to promote modernized traditional games as an alternative to mass and transnational sport. Supplementary evidence is provided by what has happened in Upper Brittany. Lagging somewhat behind the Breton crusade, there has arisen a movement favouring *gallo*, a generic term covering the Romanic dialects used in the countryside of Upper Brittany. *Gallo* militants likewise do their best to revive games that are typical of their part of the province. *La Jaupitre*, a gallèse federation of games and sports that have a cultural tradition, has existed for several years.

In discussing the increasing popularity of traditional sports, we cannot overlook the current general trend towards 'exotic' games. Promoted by educational officialdom and the media alike, this is encouraging an as yet unquantified exodus from the main track. Due to the disappearance of ancient rural society and the profound transformation of the *pardons*, Breton sports have paradoxically managed to acquire a sense of novelty in the eyes of some young people. Yet it is hard to see how they can resist the overwhelming hegemony of modern sport, especially that of football.

BRITTANY AND FOOTBALL: THE SCOTTISH MODEL?

There are two ways to appreciate the importance of football in Brittany and to see it as a source of provincial identity (for a specific analysis of football in Brittany see Chapter 6). The first is to read the sports pages of regional dailies on Mondays: teams from all levels are spread before the reader, from the first-class clubs to teams with only a district audience. When a Breton team rises to the forefront, all of Brittany cheers, as happened in 1997, for example, with the success of the Guingamp team in the final of the French Cup. A small and modest city, Guincamp was known prior to this for its old half-timbered houses and the traditional pilgrimage to the black Virgin, Our Lady of Succour. The intuitive impression gained from such an informal study is supported by a scholarly cartographic and statistical investigation of football in France. Contrary to expectations based on the traditional British pattern, the highest levels of participation in football are to be found not in urban and industrial northern and eastern France but in rural regions, among which the Armorican west stands out very clearly, forming a dark area of shading on the map. The pattern is even more remarkable if we compare it with that for rugby participation, which expresses a different geographical polarization (see Chapter 9 for a discussion of rugby in Breton cultural history). As is intuitively communicated by the accents of many players and by the location of the main clubs, rugby is the sport of southern France *par excellence*. Above all, it is the sport of the southwest, from Guyenne to Catalonia, from Limousin to the Basque country, while the Amorican west appears to be a rugby desert. The origin of this distribution is obviously to be sought in the history of the different athletic cultures. The question we may ask is how much the regional identity has affected the distribution, since other structures, both social and ideological, also seem to have played a role.

In Brittany, the spread of British sport, especially football, was slower than in other regions in France. At the beginning of the century, Brittany was still very rural (74 per cent rural population against an average of 56 per cent in France), barely touched by industrialization or urbanization. There were few potential inlets for modern sports, and still fewer that could promise them any success. They can be rapidly listed: the British sections of Brittany, especially around the mouth of the Rance, rich in real 'colonies': Saint-Malo, Dinard – where the first tennis club in France was opened in 1878 – and especially Dinan. These places contained nearly 5 per cent of British population at that time, paying ten of its city tolls. As has often occurred in France, British subjects implanted football. The first football club in Brittany was known for a long time as 'the English of Saint-Servan'. Their defeat in front of the Football Club of Rennes (see Chapter 6), in January 1901, permitted the daily *L'Ouest-Éclair* to run the headline: 'Bretons' Victory'. In 1902, it became *L'Union sportive servannaise et malouine* and had just one French player, only in 1913 was it really 'gallicized'. Similarly, the *Stade briochin* (Saint-Brieuc), champion of the west in 1913, was founded by students from Jersey. The spread of the sport thus in some ways recalled earlier migrations, of the fourth and fifth centuries, that had brought both language and saints across the Channel to the French shore.

The second invasive wave, from a sociological point of view, consisted of high school and university students, influenced by the model of the British public schools and colleges. Nevertheless, they constituted only a small elite, aristocratic and bourgeois, totally uncharacterized by the anglophobia that had been a feature of the popular Breton outlook for centuries, especially on the northern coastline. They were the originators of the FC Rennes (1902), followed by the Stade Rennais Université Club in 1904. It was the same for the high schools in Brest, Quimper and Vannes. The history of Breton sport resonates to the names of the brothers Joseph and Edmond Gemain, students of the Jules Simon high school in Vannes and founders of the Stade Vannetais (1898), as well as of a short-lived Breton Sport Federation (1901), which was transformed in 1902 into the regional committee of the new Union des Sociétés Françaises de Sports Athlétiques (USFSA). In a centralized and Jacobinic France, the creation of regional leagues, like those in the United Kingdom, was basically inconceivable.

Brittany did not experience a 'third wave' – that of the working-class involvement that was so decisive in Britain. Large industrial concentrations scarcely existed, except in Nantes, and the rural character of the region allied to its outlying geographical position hindered the spread of athletic sports. They penetrated Upper Brittany more easily, while Lower Brittany suffered because of its remoteness and cultural isolation. The military ports of Brest and Lorient were fairly secluded areas, in contrast to Saint-Malo. As a result, the clubs and, above all, the leading authorities in football, were over-represented in Upper Brittany. Thus, in terms of regional identity, the very region reputed to be less Celtic initially became dominant. In these circumstances, forces for the popularization and the democratization of football in Brittany are discovered to be ideological, inherited from the French Revolution, rather than social class-related. This is where regional identity comes back into the history of sport.

It is known that Brittany was rent by violent antagonisms during the Revolutionary decade, with the *Chouans* and the refractory clergy set against the partisans of the new order. Seen from Paris, this Celtic periphery seemed to be the den of 'fanaticism' and counter-revolution. Protestantism had failed to penetrate the region and the influence of the Catholic clergy, already strong, was further strengthened by the resistance to the Revolution. Brittany, in the nineteenth century, was a sort of Ireland, marked by a strong Catholic particularism within a largely secularized France. The Catholic clergy sought to ensure their dominance and to influence the population by all means. Education was greatly influenced by the clergy. Even today, Catholic private schools remain powerful in Brittany, with hegemony in some areas. Less well-known is the other aspect of the ecclesiastical offensive: the influence exerted on extracurricular leisure activities through *patronages*. These charitable organizations existed before the growth of sports, but sports gave them new life. Indeed, a Fédération Gymnastique et Sportive des Patronages de France (FGSPF) was created in 1902 at the national level. In relation to pre-existing athletic structures, the FGSPF was original for two reasons. Firstly, it displayed a clearly denominational character and sought to separate young Catholics from the influence of official groups like the USFSA, which were marked by Republican ideology and, indeed, anticlericalism. Secondly, it united activities that were generally separated elsewhere: gymnastics and shooting on the one hand, athletic sports on the other. Gymnastics and shooting led to military training; they were considered 'conscriptive' physical activities, cultivated for a long time in Germany (the *Turnvereine* of Jahn) and imitated in central Europe, from Switzerland to Bohemia. This movement was closely linked with national affirmation. After its defeat in 1870, and while contemplating revenge, France welcomed these practices. Gymnastics and shooting companies appeared everywhere, under the leadership of the Union des Sociétés de Gymnastique de France (USGF), while the development of gymnastics and 'school battalions' was attempted in primary schools. This was definitely not a regional phenomenon. In fact, at the time of the great performances, such as the one organized in Rennes in 1914 in the presence of Poincaré, President of the Republic, conscriptive gymnastics created an image of national unity. The uniformed teams, parading and executing perfectly coordinated ensemble movements, metaphorically represented the coming mobilization. Yet the enthusiasm for patriotic gymnastics was more strongly asserted in northern and eastern France than in the west. Furthermore, the aristocratic and anglophile elites felt contempt for it. Behind Pierre de Coubertin and within the scope of the USFSA, they were working in favour of athletic sport and of the performance of the team or individual, to the exclusion of any indoctrination.

Catholic *patronages* tried to join both sides. During the 1890s, they cultivated conscriptive activities, thus testifying the conversion of French Catholicism to patriotism, and indeed to nationalism. As a result, names for clubs with a strong patriotic connotation appeared: Les Jeunes Volontaires (Auray), Les Tricolores (Lochrist), Le Drapeau (Fougères), which was the rival of Les Vigilants (Republican club), and of course there were numerous clubs called Jeanne d'Arc. But the leaders were clearly aware that British sports were much more likely than conscriptive gymnastics to have mass proletarian appeal.

It was at this point that an option presented itself which was to be of great consequence for the future of athletic culture in France. Leaders of the FGSPF, the Fédération Gymnastique et Sportive des Patronages, tended to exclude rugby, for two reasons. The first was its increasingly aristocratic and elitist character. The massive success of football had driven anglophile elites to distinguish themselves by espousing the oval ball. This would not be seen as suitable for *patronages*, which were regarded as a means for the Catholic clergy to get in touch with the working class. The second reason was that rugby, like wrestling, presented opportunities for close body contact and was thus morally dangerous. This precluded the sport from adoption by Catholic *patronages*. Conversely, in the southwest of France, which was strongly marked by a Republican and secular ideology and where the clerical influence was much weaker, the oval ball became the sign of circles rallying for state education and was soon being supported by the network of radical notables. The proliferation of a democratic rugby for the masses in the Aquitanian and Languedocian South, even in the smallest towns, and its role in expressing local identity, is thus explained. Until recently, to play football in this region of France would have amounted to a display of Catholic and right-wing sympathies.

Things are quite different in Brittany, where rugby remained an isolated phenomenon. Though the Stade Nantais Université Club were the French rugby champions in 1917 and in 1933 and a Breton, Yves du Manoir (1904–28), ranks among the great names of French rugby, the Amorican contribution to rugby has remained miniscule in relation to the other Celtic countries. Brittany could never be the Wales of France. In a region that had passionately practised *soule*, this is a source of regret and a kind of enigma. Regrets have been well expressed by the writer Jean Lacouture, who stated the following: 'Imagine what the robust blacksmiths of Hennebont in scrummage with similar guys from Cardiff could have brought to French rugby...'. The enigma is resolved if we reflect that is was football that actually inherited the Breton passion for *soule* and that there were two main reasons for this.

The first was the determined choice of Catholic *patronages* for football. As early as 1896, the journal *Le Patronage* widely distributed its rules. Within the FGSPF, it was not long until football grew in importance, so much so that the supervision of the USFSA was shaken. Indeed the FGSPF, with its history of disagreements with USFSA regarding amateurism and of ideological tensions between the right and left wings, created the Comité Français-Interfédéral (1907). This Comité was soon recognized at an international level and was the ancestor of the Fédération Française de Football (1919). The names of Charles Simon, the general secretary of the FGSPF, killed at the front in 1915, and of Dr Michaux, chairman of the Catholic Federation, have been linked with the French Football Cup since its creation in 1917. This close connection between football and Catholicism obviously stimulated the game's growth in a region such as Brittany. Football was inseparable from the development of *patronages* and from the Catholic youth movements, ACJF (Association Catholique de la Jeunesse Française) and Le Sillon, as well as from Catholic social organizations. Starting in 1904, *La Jeune Bretagne*, a Catholic youth journal, ran a regular athletic column. It was not unusual to see the same individual in the position of right-back, secretary of the Catholic study circle, and the president of the mutual cattle insurance society.

The clericalization of football worried Republican Bretons and organizers of the secular camp, who were heirs of the '*bleus*' of the French Revolution. They also made a significant choice: instead of turning to rugby like their southern counterparts, they preferred to fight on the same turf. This explains the appearance of split terms nearly everywhere in Brittany: that is, Catholics against *laïques* (seculars) and Chouans against Republicans: La Jeanne d'Arc against La Patrie in Tinténiac, or in Guingamp, Le Stade Charles de Blois – named after a fourteenth-century anti-English pretender to the dukedom of Brittany, who had been beatified by the Catholic Church – against En avant, a product of the Advanced Primary School. From the 1920s, UFOLEP (Union des Fédérations des

Oeuvres Laïques de l'Enseignement Public) endeavoured to rise to the Catholic challenge even in the field of education. Schools became a breeding ground for future players.

The existence of this rivalry between clubs and numerous consequences. Everybody had to find fields and equipment, relying on the sympathy of the conservative notables for some and on the support of Republican municipalities for others. La Garde du Vœu, in Hennebont, founded in 1909, only got its first municipal subsidy in 1937. For a long time, it was a case of having to use makeshift and hastily laid out playing fields, until a real public sports policy was drafted, first at the end of the 1930s under the Vichy government, and then again in the 1960s. The main result was fierce competition for the recruitment of players, which may be an explanatory key to the successful penetration of football into Breton society. The issue at stake was each camp's honour, and all forces were mobilized for that purpose. The recruitment generally operated by joining the boundaries between the two types of school and any infringement would be quickly considered as betrayal. A typical example is Gourin, a remote small town in the west of Morbihan, a former *soule* 'paradise'. La Gourinoise, a conscriptive and Republican society (1908), developed a football division in 1919 which became Les Chasseurs de Gourin in 1926. In 1927, L'Etoile sportive of Gourin, a parish club created in 1922, united with the *Jeanne d'Arc patronage*, founded in 1909. The rivalry between the two clubs was eloquently expressed by the newspaper *Le Rappel du Morbihan* in 1950:

> Gourin is one of the many places in Morbihan and the West where two clans are fighting for glory, the Reds and Whites – the Chasseurs on the red side, the JA (Jeanne d'Arc) on the white side. But one characteristic here is that a demarcation line is not clearly defined. Do we not see that, on the latter team (the JA), more than half the members stem from the state school?; from this, the defenders of the so-called liberty of education have the gall to attack the sectarianism of the state school. Would the pupils of the Catholic school be free to play among the Chasseurs? Let us ask that question. Where is the freedom? Our readers will decide themselves. Nevertheless, the shoe pinches when we see Gouriners, who are supposed laïques, hasten to applaud the Patro and mix with those who claim they will bury the Chasseurs.

Football fields could become the place to settle external quarrels and to symbolically offset defeats: the victory of L'Amoricaine of Brest (*patronage*) over the High School of Brest (USFSA) in 1905, the very year of the separation of Church and State, was enthusiastically saluted in the Catholic press. This kind of rivalry in Brittany to some extent reproduced the situation in Glasgow between Rangers and Celtic. However, the competition was by no means ethnic: it followed the ideological fracture line that has marked Brittany since 1789. Only if we consider this line as a constitutive feature of modern Breton identity, can we illustrate the link between modern sport and regional culture. On the other hand, a search for ritual confrontation with the 'auld enemy' (which could have created 'ninety-minute patriots') would be in vain in Brittany, because there is no auld enemy for it. Football structures in France have never permitted the symbolic rewriting of history each year.

BRITTANY AND CYCLING, OR THE FRENCH STAMP

Brittany is irrevocably linked to France, and only a few hundred zealots, from the 1920s to our day, have continued to dream seriously about a real autonomy. The role of cycling in Breton athletic identity is supplementary proof. In the general history of sport, cycling tends to characterize Latin countries (France, Italy) rather than the Anglo-Saxon world; it is a significant aspect of French national identity. The Véloce Club of Rennes ranks among the oldest in France (1869), with Vannes coming close second (1870). The Société Vélocipédique of Quimper was created in 1888, part of the boom in cyclist clubs at the end of the nineteenth century, a time when the bicycle changed its social status and became democratic. Clubs named *Pédale ouvrière* ('Biking for workers') appeared in Brest, Morlaix and Auray. Still today, many local cycling clubs count high numbers of workmen and employees among their members.

Even if the poor and rural character of the region at first limited the spread of cycling in the countryside, Brittany nonetheless became a region noted for this sport, a mechanical, i.e., resolutely modern, one which took two forms: cycling on track and on road. At the beginning of the 1920s, the region provided more than the French average number of velodromes. They were often simple hard-packed rings, attracting large crowds. Today, road races prevail: in 1980 the Breton peninsula hosted 2267 of them. Once more, the network of parish feasts and *pardons* was a preponderant reason. As traditional games feel into disuse, people became accustomed to linking cycling races with religious holy days. The example of Châteaulin, a small town in Finistère, is revealing. The first attempt to organize bicycle races there, on 14 July 1889, to celebrate the centenary of the French Revolution, failed for lack of competitors. It wasn't until 1st September, the day of the pardon of Our Lady, that the races got under way, and have continued to be held ever since. Other *pardon* races proliferated between the world wars – the contestants robust local lads, young peasants used to covering long distances on their bikes when going to school or to the fields, often against the wind, in this undulating region with scattered settlements. The interparochial rivalry, a typical feature of Breton sociability, had found a new outlet.

The multiplicity of these races, with worthwhile prizes to be won, tempted some Breton champions to try their luck in professional ranks. In the 1950s, an adage circulated in sporting circles: 'In Brittany, the *pardon* allows a man to earn his bread' and the colourful mass of riders constituted one of the attractions of the feasts, religious or secular. Local champions were much celebrated. These men often found professional cycling to be unrewarding and returned to the country and to its *pardon* races. Many amateur cyclists earned a better living than some professionals. The greatest Breton rallies (Châteaulin, Callac, Plouay, Camors, etc.) still draw crowds of a national dimension: 100,000 spectators flocked to Châteaulin in 1980, 200,000 to Plouay in 1997. They attract even the most famous international champions, who appreciate the warmth and enthusiasm of the Breton public.

Conversely, Breton cycling, in spite of the local tropism indicated above, has made a contribution to the mythology of French cycling, that vital constituent of the national spirit. The first great French race was Paris–Brest return, first held in 1891, and every year until 1951. This 1200 km rally, organized by the newspaper *Le Petit Journal*, was both an exhausting marathon and a point of contact between the capital city and the tip of Brittany. By the same token Brittany was included from the start (1903) in the route of the Tour de France, the national ritual *par excellence*. It is known that this peregrination, repeated each year before ever-growing crowds, strengthens the popular image of a France united on the one soil, by geography rather than by language and habits. Imitated in Italy – where it fulfils a similar function – this kind of event did not take place in the British Isles. But it was replicated from 1931 in the Circuit de l'Ouest, from 1946 known as the Tour de l'Ouest, then the Tour de Bretagne (1956–8), and recently resuscitated as the Ruban Granitier Breton, in recognition of the typical geology of Brittany.

The Breton riders, by turns, have made their mark in this symbolic ordeal. Fourth in 1906, Lucien Mazan, nicknamed Petit-Breton, was the first to achieve a double victory in the Tour de France, in 1907 and 1908. Apart from Petit-Breton, (who actually spent his youth in Argentina and trained there), there was the Morbihannese Jean Robic (winner of the Tour in 1947), who provided the public with a lasting image of the Breton cyclist: stubborn and stoical: the popular press used to enumerate *ad nauseam* these features of the Breton stereotype. Robic was a former altar boy, trained in innumerable *pardon* races. He opened the way to another giant, Louison Bobet. The son of a baker at Saint-Méen le Grand, toughened by delivering daily 37 kilos (c. 80 lbs) of bread on a bike, Bobet finally provided French cycling with a hero to match the legendary Italians, Bartali and Coppi. After a Norman interregnum (Jacques Anquetil), it fell again to a Breton, Bernard Hinault, to dominate international and national cycling. Additionally, Breton cycling could produce managers of the same breed: Paul Le Drogo (French champion in 1927 and 1928) then, more recently, Cyrille Guimard. Their achievement has substantiated the idea of a Breton schooling for cycling.

Press stereotypes of the Breton cyclist raise a more general point about the influence of local, or national, culture, on the practice of sport. Does there exist some *habitus*, to borrow the Aristotelian concept used by sociologists? Can we notice a kind of Breton athletic behaviour, that would be a product of Celtic tradition? According to columnists, a Breton athlete can be nothing other than stubborn, courageous, resistant to bad weather, just as the Parisian will always be astute and resourceful; the Norman prudent, if not cunning; the Southerner exuberant; the Spanish proud, etc. These qualifiers, which generally reflect a Parisian – that is to say national – press, actually accord with common prejudices in France about the regional diversity whose sum is supposed to produce the national spirit. Thus a supposed Celtic culture is projected onto sport, based on a conventional image current since the nineteenth century.

It would be better to view the issue in the opposite way. Does sport have a role in the creation of community feeling in Brittany? Is it the ultimate refuge of a Breton patriotism that cannot find another outlet? There is no straightforward answer. The extreme popularity of some sports in Brittany (football, to a lower degree cycling) is indisputable and seems to indicate a cultural characteristic. The same thing can be said of the capacity to become impassioned for some team, some champion or other, assigned to embody Brittany for the time being: Rennes the day before yesterday, Nantes yesterday, Guingamp today, and where tomorrow? It is necessary however to relativize for two reasons: Bretons are as quick to become impassioned for French teams or national champions, and to be infected by national enthusiasms, and, second, there is little discernible difference when it comes to attitudes to sport between Lower and Upper Brittany, that is to say between the more or less Celtic inhabitants of the region.

ACKNOWLEDGEMENTS

In writing this chapter I have drawn on several papers on the theme of history of games and entertainment in Brittany in *Mémoires de la Société d'histoire et d'archéologie de Bretagne*, vol. lxxi (1994). My thanks to Dominique Ferré, president of La Jaupitre Society, for his helpful comments.

5

'THE DRAMATIC TURBULENCE OF SOME IRRECOVERABLE FOOTBALL GAME': SPORT, LITERATURE AND WELSH IDENTITY

Gareth Williams

Sport is a rich and rewarding terrain for the historian bent on explaining and connecting notions of local and national identity, social class and popular culture, but the pursuit of these themes via the literary imagination is an activity that has attracted few punters. If the contribution of sport to the making of 'Englishness' or to the construction of a 'British' patriotism has, thanks to a combination of academic conservatism, snobbishness and myopia, been neglected by serious scholars who should (or perhaps do not) know better (Holt, 1996: 231–52), then the literary representation of the multiplex meanings of sport and its heroes is, to historians, an even less tilled field (Harvie, 1994: 43–57).

This is perhaps an even more surprising omission on the part of non-English British scholars, given the late twentieth-century resurgence of Celtic nationalisms and of an awareness by historians of the role of sport in the construction and assertion of the separate identities of the Welsh, Scots and Irish. The unpromisingly titled *Celtic Miscellany* (1951) consisted in fact of the distinguished scholar Kenneth Jackson's translations of prose and poetry from the literature of all six Celtic countries (Breton, Cornish and Manx being the other three), and while it succeeded in dispelling the Celtic twilight romanticism that coloured its precursor, Grace Rhys's *A Celtic Anthology* (1927) – 'in fact the Celtic literatures are about as little given to mysticism and sentimentality as it is possible to be' (Jackson, 1971: 20) – sporting activities, even the 'games and pastimes' so beloved of the antiquarian, are conspicuous by their absence. The purpose of this chapter is to look at the writing on sport in the two literatures of one of the Celtic nations: Wales (Williams, 1997: 37–46).

Before trying to say anything about the sporting Welsh and their literature, some warming up may be in order. Clearly we cannot boast a Norman Mailer, a Joyce Carol Oates or a Roger Kahn. I am thinking here of course of Mailer's presidential paper on the Liston–Patterson bout (Mailer, 1968: 231–89) and his epic account of the Ali–Foreman 'rumble in the jungle', *The Fight* (1977); of Joyce Carol Oates's compelling essay 'On boxing' (1987); and, it goes without saying, *The Boys of Summer* (1972), Roger Kahn's classic then-and-now group portrait of the great Brooklyn Dodgers baseball team of the early 1950s, a marvellous and poignant book about youthful dreams in small American towns and big cities and how some of those dreams were fulfilled, and about what happened to those dreamers after reality and old age arrived. Its title taken from Dylan Thomas's poem (Thomas, 1993: 7), *The Boys of Summer* is a book about ourselves, who have shared and identified with the dreams and glories of our heroes. One only wishes that what Kahn did with Jackie Robinson, Carl Furillo, Roy Campanella and company, an equally gifted writer might do with, say, their Welsh soccer counterparts of the '50s – Trevor Ford, Ivor Allchurch, John Charles, and Cliff Jones; or with a collective biography of the great Welsh rugby stars of the 1970s.

Baseball and boxing, with football and basketball some way behind, are the sports that have given Americans almost all their sports fiction: sport, indeed, plays a central role in the American experience (Messenger, 1981; Oriard, 1982). What then about the Welsh, *their* sport and literature? The Welsh writer of sports fiction, or sports history, is afflicted by a dual prejudice: the idea that sport is play and therefore not serious (*work* is the primary adult concern, the source of values, the measurement of success and personal worth) coupled to an historically conditioned puritan suspicion of it anyway. Gwyn Thomas was not being altogether flippant about rugby when he observed (Thomas, 1985: 22–3) that

> in consideration of Welsh culture one has to conclude that this game, with its magnets of remembrance, has drained off much of the ardour that might have gone into a more sedulous cultivation of the arts.

The Rhondda flyer's own tantalisingly brief playing career was confined to one of those notorious Valleys pitches hewn out of the hillside. With the mountain rearing up on one side and a sharp drop on the other, Gwyn recalled one hapless winger sidestepping the wrong way and disappearing down the mountain. Situated high up between Cymmer and Trebanog, 'it was', he wrote (Thomas, 1964: 12),

> the least level pitch in Christendom. Those who survived it got a diploma from Darwin. It was the only rugby field where the players were allowed to

dip their bits of lemon in adrenalin while sitting in an oxygen tent at half-time ... The Trebanog and Cymmer boys mastered the slope. They were badly defeated but once and then the victors were found to have two Sherpas on the wing on loan from Tibet.

The Rhondda, of course, the novelist Jack Jones's 'revolutionary and riotous; religious and musical; sporting and artistic, coal-bearing Rhondda' (Jones, 1934: 7) is in historical terms a recent invention – writers and historians have been reinventing it ever since – whereas in literary terms the sporting Welsh go much further back. According to Tacitus, in one of his crisper epigrams, where the Romans made a desert they called it peace. In Britain they also made a ball game and called it *harpastum,* and it was played by legionaries at Caerleon in between vigorous jousts with the local Silures, a rough bunch who had acquired a sidestep and stamina in the wooded hills to the north. Sometime later the ninth-century Welsh chronicler Nennius tells us of a ball game between young noblemen. By the twelfth century we wish that Giraldus Cambrensis might have elaborated on the athletic inclinations of his countrymen during his tour of the country in 1188. But their attitude appears to have been purely pragmatic: any attention they paid to sporting pursuits arose entirely from their value in war. In Gerald's only reference to sport he tells us that the men of Venta (Gwent) practised archery not for competition purposes but to kill people (Gerald of Wales, 1984: 112–13).

With the growth of a leisured class the amenities of a cultivated life were also sought, and with them opportunities for the display of physical prowess. These gentlemanly accomplishments can be summed up by the traditional 24 feats of skill to which there are many references by the poets of the Welsh princes (Lile, 1994). Of these 24, a number of cabalistic significance in medieval Welsh literature, half the feats are eisteddfodic (composing poetry and singing to the harp) along with physically undemanding recreations like fishing and falconry; but there is also a category of less sedentary athletic diversions, from fencing and wrestling to running, jumping, and throwing, or putting, the stone. Tudur Aled, one of the greatest poets of the gentry in the late fifteenth century, himself a fine athlete, frequently alludes to throwing. In accordance with the prevailing literary convention, he liked to praise his patrons as formidable champions: no one, for instance, could hurl the stone or throw the bar further than Robert ap Ieuan ab Ithel ('Maen neu farr, mwy ni yrrir') while William ap Sion Edwart was a veritable Daley Thompson when it came to athletic versatility: 'Digwmpar dy gampau wyd' (unrivalled are your feats). Lewys Môn in the early sixteenth century sang the praises of one well-sprung patron because of his unrivalled ability as a jumper: 'Neidio i'th nôd nid aeth neb' (none could jump as far), a facility which earned this late medieval Lynn 'the Leap' many trophies (Gwynn Jones, 1926: 291).

As for the communal mass ball game known as cnapan, George Owen's racy description of it in 1603 has become sufficiently familiar since the Cymmrodorion Society's standard edition of 1892 for us safely to show it the yellow card. From motives as diverse as political calculation and rural nostalgia it was hailed in the late Victorian era as the direct forebear of Welsh rugby, sanctioned, even sanctified, by its British-Welsh Tudor origins. Anthropologists and semioticians can have a field day loading games like cnapan with so much symbolic freight that what is being symbolized becomes lost: these neighbourhood virility tests *were* means by which parishes collectively and territorially defined themselves. With up to 2000 onlookers caught up in the general melée they remind us that spectator sport and violence have always accompanied each other, and the line between merriment and mayhem a fine one: the deeply rooted urge to let off steam is age-old. It is the historical context that changes. As for cnapan, one observer noted in the critical year 1588: 'I could wish the Spaniards were here to see our play; certes, they would be in bodily fear of our war' (Owen, 1892: 270–81).

A century and a half later Theophilus Evans in his history of the Ancient Britons describes a game played on the banks of the River Teifi in west Wales which still resembles cnapan (T. Evans, 1740: 75). A century and a half further on again, by which time the mass spectator sports of the late nineteenth century have been standardized, codified and organized into clubs and leagues, the age-old ritual battles between rival parishes can be seen to have merely shifted their focus.

Two other sporting activities that made the transition to industrial society with only minor adjustments and were the objects of considerable literary attention were pedestrianism and pugilism. The most Welsh famous runner of all, from the parish of Mountain Ash, is Guto Nyth Brân, Griffith Morgan (b. 1700), who died from his exertions and the over-exuberant back slap of his girl friend in 1737. His malodorous pre-match practice was to recline in a particularly pungent compost in order to ensure muscular suppleness and the maximum distance between himself and his pursuers. It is of interest that he did not, despite the existence at that time of a lusty vernacular ballad literature, attract contemporary literary attention. His fame is a posthumous creation of the 1880s, the decade which saw the birth of modern Wales. New nations need new heroes and a democracy lacking an acknowledged elite is, *pace* Brecht, in particular need of heroes, including sports heroes. So it has been left to twentieth-century rhymesters like I. D. Hooson in Welsh and Harri Webb in English to sing Guto's praises. Hooson's lyrics which describe Guto as light of foot and as nimble as a hare, faster than the wind or hawk are, in Wales, familiar to generations of school elocutionists. Hooson's conclusion is that however fast Guto is, he will never be fast enough to escape from Llanwynno cemetery, and there is really no answer to that (Hooson, 1958: 86).

The late Harri Webb was high priest of the poems and pints cult, the prolific author of popular and patriotic ballads, light-hearted as often as not, concerned with the more extrovert and active side of our national history and character. His ode to Guto Nyth Brân is in the same vein as his celebration, 'The Bluebirds', of Fred Keenor's team's triumph at Wembley in 1927. The unabashed gusto of lines like (Webb, 1970: 28)

> When they came back to Cardiff
> The City all went mad
> And even down in Swansea Town
> They said that they were glad.

(sentiments ludicrously inappropriate to the modern habitué of Swansea's Vetch Field) indicate that these are verses to be declaimed rather than deconstructed. A folk poet and people's remembrancer, essentially a communicator, Harri Webb would have prospered very well as a balladeer in an earlier age when this kind of fugitive literature – two-sided broadsheets, four-sided pamphlets – served a significant journalistic purpose. In the first half of the nineteenth century ballads, especially among the monoglot, largely illiterate population of industrial Glamorgan, enjoyed a wider circulation than any newspaper, especially when the Welsh language press of the day viewed sporting activities with intense suspicion. Performed by singers at fairs and other popular gatherings, ballads have been traced to 359 printers in 96 different places in nineteenth-century Wales – not only Aberystwyth, Caernarfon and Carmarthen in the west and north but also urban-industrial Swansea, Aberdare and Merthyr, the latter a particularly prolific centre where thousands of ballads were turned out by over twenty printers. Industrialization and demographic density were the stimulus not the death knell of popular cultural forms and provided new audiences for balladeers like Ywain Meirion, Iolo Mynwy, Edward Jones and countless others (Owen, 1986).

A recurrently popular topic among accounts of colliery disasters, shipwrecks, grisly murders and political crises were the accomplishments of local athletes. A favourite runner was John Davies 'Y Cyw Cloff', (inexplicably – since he clearly was not – 'The Lame Chick'), born in Bryncethin near Bridgend in 1822, later publican of the Upper Boat Inn, near Pontypridd, where he died in 1904. He had several epic confrontations with the English champion John Tetlow of Oldham in front of thousands, including a mile race at Llantwit Faerdre which Davies won in the respectable time of 4 minutes 45 seconds. Another English rival was Tom Maxfield of Sheffield, who beat him in Wales but lost to the 'Cyw Cloff' in Bath in December 1845. These races spawned a substantial ballad literature, which rejoiced in the puncturing of what was seen as English hubris by a son of Morgan, i.e. of Glamorgan (Jones, 1971: 28–30; 1993: 38–42). Other Welsh pedestrians acclaimed by the balladeers are Howell Powell of Cefn, Hywel Richards of Vaynor, Rees Meredith of Aberdare and Thomas Llewelyn of Penderyn, all professional runners from the older, upland, iron-making districts of South Wales, areas which would always be susceptible to professional sport well into the twentieth century, whether in the form of rugby league, association football, boxing or running.

George Ewart Evans, growing up in Abercynon in the 1920s where there was little time for the niceties of the debate between professionalism and amateurism, ran and coached professionally to pay his way through university. Some of his short stories draw on his personal experiences of Powderhall sprinting and the shady practices involved in building up a handicap, like fitting a thin plate of lead in the insole of a pair of spikes (G. Ewart Evans, 1983: 28–30). He vividly conveys the physical stimulus and kinaesthetic exhilaration he observed from sprinting, 'a subjective one-ness of mind and body bound together in harmonious order' so that

> my mind appeared to be as much in my muscles as in my head. It was ... like the image I experienced in my dreams: of running over a flat, unencumbered plain each stride carrying me in spectacular bounds over the landscape almost as if I were flying.

It is entirely fitting that George Ewart Evans's Abercynon is in the parish of Guto Nyth Brân's Llanwynno. Welsh ballad literature testifies also to the popularity of prizefighting, a long established activity that attracted a wide spectrum of support. Several were written about 'Dan Bach Pontypridd', Daniel Thomas (b. 1823), who beat John Brooks the Norwich champion (defeated opponents were always champions) in London in October 1858. Three months later he beat the American champion Charlie Lynch. Dan ran the 'Union' public house in Cardiff near Tabernacle Welsh Baptist church in the Hayes, where he heard C. H. Spurgeon preaching and, like Bendigo before him, underwent a religious conversion. He lived until 1910 by which time Freddie Welsh had sought his advice and Dan warned him off the fight game as unrewarding: 'Give it up, give it up, it doesn't pay. I once did a great deal of it but it didn't pay' (Jones, 1971: 31–2).

Nothing will ever have the immediacy of the solar plexus punch that Hazlitt delivers as he sets the scene for the match between Bill Neate and the Gasman in 1821 – 'Reader, have you ever seen a fight?' (Scannell, 1987: 181–4) – but it is to the American literary experience that, given the centrality of boxing in the popular culture of the industrial Welsh, we cast envious eyes. Would that we had anybody approaching a Schulberg, an Algren or a Leonard Gardner. Budd Schulberg's *The Harder They Fall* (1947) is a loosely fictionalized account of the meteoric rise and fall of Primo Carnera and it remains perhaps the best chronicle there is of the boxing world, its trainers, managers, punchy ex-fighters, small-time chisellers and leech-like hangers-on. Nelson Algren's hard-hitting realist novel of Chicago's north-west side Polish community, *Never Come Morning* (1942), traces the career of Bruno 'Lefty' Bicek, whose life is governed by crude fantasies, specifically of becoming heavyweight champion of the world, but who when the novel ends is being indicted at eighteen years of age for murder. Algren's characters – petty crooks, brothel keepers, washed-up pugs – convince from the bell. They don't fall from anywhere, from grace, or innocence, or respectability, because there is nowhere they can fall: from the beginning they are at the bottom. To that extent Lefty Bicek's fall is less than that of the relatively better-placed former neighbourhood athlete Studs Lonigan, the unforgettable anti-hero of James T. Farrell's disturbing *tour de force* of naturalistic fiction (1932–6) set in the teeming world of Chicago's South Side. Studs, like Bicek, is a victim of his grim urban environment. So too are Billy Tully and Ernie Munger, the two small-time professional boxers of Leonard Gardner's superb *Fat City* (1969). Set in Stockton, California, its boxing scenes are vividly drawn, spare, precise, neither sensationalistic nor sanitized, but containing descriptions of violent action worthy of a Hemingway. Its message is that it is not professionalism so much as the crushing weight of a squalid environment that annihilates any true sense of individuality or freedom.

Equally products of their grim environments are Leslie Norris's Merthyr fighters (Norris, 1967), and Ron Berry's Hector Bebb (Berry, 1970), from a Rhondda far removed from that of Gwyn Thomas. Merthyr, as we know, is the home town of Eddie Thomas, Howard Winstone and Johnny Owen, and Robert Minhinnick's elegy on the death of Johnny Owen echoes Leslie Norris's boxing poems like 'The Ballad of Billy Rose'

(Minhinnick, 1982: 93–6; Norris, 1986: 19–20; Pugh, 1993: 22). Billy Rose is standing outside a football ground, blind and begging. Twenty years before, when a boy on a 'sawdust summer night', the poet had paid threepence to see him box when

> He was top of the bill
> So brisk a fighter, so gallant, so precise!

and in a combination of bravado and innocent cruelty had thrilled to see him 'ripped across both his eyes' by George Morgan of Tirphil. Now, feeling disgust and deep personal guilt, the poet once again throws down 'three treacherous pence', this time into Billy's blind tray, and runs off into the comforting anonymity of the stadium:

> Poor Billy Rose. God, he could fight
> Before my three sharp coins knocked out his sight.

Billy Rose appears again in Norris's 'Elegy for Lyn James' (Norris, 1967: 18), epitomizing a whole generation of pre-war Merthyr fighters 'who never had the class', the exploited second-raters reduced to punch drunkenness or worse, like Jock McAvoy, 'swinging his right/From a wheelchair', by fighting warm-up rounds in shabby halls

> or in tents
> On slum ground ... a few
> Sharp rounds to set the mob aloud
> Before the big men came who *had* the class.

Jock McAvoy, Lyn James and Billy Rose are all inhabitants of Fat City, joyless, oppressive places from which they fruitlessly seek a way out.

This fighting culture pervades several accounts of a South Wales on the cusp of the twentieth century, accounts that are themselves less fiction than autobiography, as in Jack Jones's Merthyr novel *Black Parade* (1935), Wil Jon Edwards' *From the Valley I Came* (1956) and D. J. Williams' *Yn Chwech ar Hugain Oed* (At 26 Years of Age, 1959). But it is not a South Wales preserve. Caradog Prichard's *Un Nos Olau Leuad* (One Moonlit Night) is generally reckoned to be the most remarkable Welsh-language novel of modern times, an autobiographical stream-of-consciousness account of growing up against a background of his mother's increasing insanity (Prichard, 1961). In one scene Johnnie South comes up from South Wales and opens a boxing booth behind the Blue Bell. 'By damn, don't they talk funny Welsh in the South' coughs tubercular, bed-ridden Moi, spitting blood and dust, but the first person narrator secretly hopes Johnnie South will give Owen the local big mouth, a pasting, and he does.

The climax of the fight comes when Johnnie buries his right fist in Owen's stomach who falls on his knees 'with his two hands on the floor as if he was looking for something'. 'By damn, those boys from the South can fight', says Roly the Pant.

For another of those boys, and in real life the genuine article, we turn to Rhondda-born writer Ron Berry, by his own account 'five foot eight inches tall, thick set, pigeon-toed, peasant-fisted', who in his 'big-chested prime' boxed, swam, dived, cycled, and played schoolboy rugby and amateur soccer (Berry, 1960: 9). This is no Rhondda Roundabout (Jack Jones) or Meadow Prospect (Gwyn Thomas) but a relatively more prosperous yet still uncompromising 1950s world of flashy clubs, hairdressing salons, pop music, fish and chip shops, mean corners and empty hillsides. If we follow Irving Howe's description of the political novel (Howe, 1961: 17) and define the sports novel as simply one in which sport plays a dominant role or in which the sports milieu is the dominant setting, then Ron Berry's *So Long Hector Bebb* (1970) is the *only* Welsh sports novel. It is *sui generis*. It comes from nowhere and leads nowhere, and bears closer resemblance to William McIlvanney's *The Big Man* (1985) than anything else. It tells, in a series of monologues and in a prose style as sensory and tactile as a left hook from its pugilistic protagonist, the story of Hector Bebb. Tough, truculent, physical, very much his own man, we can regret that he was never played on the wide screen by the young Stanley Baker. As a result it is Richard Harris's portrayal of the inarticulate rugby league player Frank Machin that is the next best thing in the film version of David Storey's *This Sporting Life*. Just as Storey actually signed professional forms for Leeds to pay his way through the Slade School of Fine Art (one of the unlikeliest conjunctions in the history of sport, or art) (Moorhouse, 1989: 91), Ron Berry too writes as an insider. By day Hector Bebb drives a brewery lorry, but every morning he is out early for roadwork, and every evening he trains in the gym at the White Hart. Like Terry Molloy in *On the Waterfront*, he could have been a contender. His trainer is confident, except for one reservation, and Hector Bebb lives up to that reservation and unintentionally becomes a killer. On the run he falls to his death down the mountain, a young life wasted like Studs Lonigan's or Lefty Bicek's.

Berry knows too that the eastern valleys of Glamorgan are primarily soccer-loving communities, as a glance at the addresses of arrested Cardiff City supporters will rapidly confirm. The comedic *The Full-time Amateur* (1966), is a picaresque chronicle of the young manhood of Hugh Davies whose father used to be a great footballer and also won medals for cycling and – a surprising but authentic touch – waterpolo for Glamorgan.

Nothing is more uncompromising than valley soccer, especially when playing against Galed Blues. 'Galed' means 'hard', and Galed 'had the awkwardest right winger you'll ever see. He ran like a man with a stalk on.' The inside right takes 'a spew-maker in the taters from the full back' while Hugh's friend Dilwyn heads the false teeth of the opposing centre forward 'whose upper dentures fell into his cupped hands like broken dominoes' (Berry, 1964: 179–80).

Football is Dannie Abse's game too, for 'though I liked rugby I loved soccer', perhaps because he broke his collar bone in a school rugby game one cold February morning (Abse, 1974: 37–8). 'Throughout the game I was aware of a girl in a yellow skirt sitting some three hundred yards behind the goal posts all on her own, reading a book. Her presence seemed quite incongruous because it was too cold really just to sit there as if at a picnic.' As the stricken Abse is helped to the touchline after falling awkwardly in a tackle by a swarthy Canton lad called Nigger Rees she is still there 'sitting in her yellow skirt, oblivious to the game, not belonging to anybody'. A Jew in a Catholic grammar school in Cardiff, Abse's outsider's view of the South Wales scene has itself something of the detachment of that girl in the yellow dress. His Wales is the Cardiff where he grew up, circumscribed to the east by the bridge that crossed Newport Road.

> This side of the bridge was Wales where dark-haired men were human size 5 feet 8 ½ inches like I am now, whereas over there, the wrong side of that significant bridge, strode flaxen-haired Englishmen affected with pituitary trouble.

To the south lived monsters, of a sort, in Splott and Tiger Bay, 'where people got knifed' his mother warned him, though it was none too safe north of where he lived in Albany Road, either, because that was where Philip Griffiths lurked, ready to bash the young Abse simply for being younger, for preferring Eldorado ice cream to Wall's, or for considering Glamorgan's J. C. Clay a better bowler than Verity.

But west was best: towards the sea, Sunday trips and summer holidays: Penarth, Barry, Porthcawl and Ystalyfera in the Swansea Valley where his mother came from. West was also the direction of religion, in both senses: the Windsor Place synagogue 'and that piece of holy ground near the River Taff where even tries were converted', Cardiff Arms Park (Abse, 1983: 11–12). Dannie Abse's own preference was for Ninian Park, even when Cardiff City were bottom of Division 3 (South) and the brass band played 'Happy Days are here again' – Abse's poem 'The Game' has found its way into many anthologies – but for a sense of occasion he and his friend Keith Thomas would go to the big rugby internationals, when the kind Welsh crowd would pass us down over their heads ... and they sang the Welsh songs that floated sadly but joyfully into the air ... as little dark-haired men invaded the field in an attempt to climb the goal-posts and hang there the all-important leek ... England came out in their white shirts and the crowd clapped politely, but the real applause was reserved for the men in red shirts as they strutted out cocky and clever. Somebody said, 'Jawch, England 'ave an 'efty team, much bigger than ours, mun'. The whistle blew and soon after England scored ...

Eventually Wales scored, too, to great excitement: 'And we shouted too, oh how we shouted ... When the noise was loudest we swore and nobody could hear us' (Abse, 1954: 18–19).

The roar of the crowd can be heard throughout the best-known Welsh-language verse description of a rugby match, Cynan's 'Y Dyrfa' ('The Crowd'), the crown-winning long poem at the National Eisteddfod of 1931. Something of a sensation at the time – one of the adjudicators denounced the writer for prostituting his muse and conflating the spiritual and the secular – the poem describes a Welsh win at Twickenham (something at that time unachieved), its style that of Noyes, Newbolt and Masefield, its matter based on Sir John Squire's long poem 'The Rugger Match'. The excitement of the spectators and ecstasy of the narrator who scores the winning try are vividly described. His fervour then becomes a prayer for still greater delight in the service of God and the poem ends with his vigour being channelled into missionary work in China (Jones, 1959: 170–7). It was apparent even to North Walians that this was a loosely-based verse biography of the Revd John Roberts, who had won thirteen caps for Wales in the 1920s and then quit the game for the mission field. It called to mind too the career of another former rugby international, the fiery charioteer Eric Liddell. What enhanced the poem's popularity subsequently was its prophetic quality: in 1931 Wales had never won at Twickenham, but on their next visit to 'HQ' in 1933 the long-awaited victory was achieved, the winning – in fact all – the points coming from Barry's Ronnie Boon, one of Abse's 'cocky and clever' men in red to whom Cynan's poem was as Chinese as any distant mission field.

While 'Y Dyrfa', rollicking, rhythmic and accessible, has proved more durable in the long term, the most recited because unashamedly populist Welsh language poet between the wars was Crwys, the bardic name of William Crwys Williams. His 'Morgannwg' (Glamorgan) describes an international at the Arms Park with the full trimmings of leeks, sospans and singing. The Welsh XV are all from Glamorgan and in his five short stanzas there's not much room for development except that Wales secure a last-minute try to win the match – a win, Crwys is anxious to point up, among defeats, a victory for 'a wounded nation', bloodied, beaten but unbowed (Jones, 1994: 113):

> A dyna dy ffawd erioed, Forgannwg wen
> Llawer ysgarmes a thithau'n ennill y dydd
> Aml i gwymp ac eilwaith codi dy ben
> I ymladd a chware'r gem a craith ar dy rudd.

> (You have emerged victorious from many a conflict,
> dear Glamorgan, you have been beaten down too, and
> risen again to fight and play the game with your
> face scarred.)

That 'craith' – a scar or wound – is particularly significant in the context of inter-war South Wales, buffeted and battered but still on its feet and hanging on, a groggy, gutsy society for whom, as Dai Smith has suggested, Tommy Farr is the fighting symbol, never gutsier than in defeat that August night in 1937 in New York against Joe Louis (Smith, 1990: 198–217).

The convergence of the international and the specifically local is subtly brought out by a far greater poet from the Swansea Valley than Crwys, and that is D. Gwenallt Jones ('Gwenallt'). He recalls when the hamlet of Alltwen was not a village on the map of Wales and the working class recognized no national or territorial frontiers; they worshipped the flame atop the stack, the flame of universal justice, the brotherhood of man, and work (Jones, 1951: 11). Yet when Saturday came it was resolutely patriotic feelings that surfaced as Wales faced England at St Helen's, when 'Bancroft kicked his Welsh goal and Dicky Owen scored his national try'; clearly the proletariat too had a country. This is also a rueful reflection on a lost era of economic security and not unconnected rugby victories over England, both commodities in short supply in the inter-war period. Gwenallt says more in eight lines than Cynan in eight pages.

In contrast the rugby successes of the 1970s generated quite a different response. Dic Jones a farmer poet from Blaenannerch on the Cardiganshire coast writes a ballad about the 1971 Lions which refers only to the Welsh contingent in it (D. Jones, 1978a: 48–50). In a burst of triumphalist topophilia (Bale, 1994: 120–21) he crafts a *cywydd* about an Arms Park that is more verdant than any valley, and dedicates an *englyn* to the memory of Carwyn James in which Amsterdam and Stradey Park are conjoined in *cynghanedd* (D. Jones, 1978b: 52–3).[1]

Some Welsh language poets were determined that Welsh rugby success should fan the flame of explicitly political aspirations. From Denbighshire the nationalist poet and newspaper editor Gwilym R. Jones, who had probably never seen a live rugby game, pens a eulogy that is positively medieval in its lavish praise of Barry John ('pass master of the national art') (J. Davies, 1991: 71). The themes interwoven around brief action snapshots are of a resurgent Welsh national consciousness, of settling old scores (always against England) and of removing old scars. This is no longer a much-buffeted people scarred by depression but a more assertive, self-confident nation inspired by the new Welsh wizard to cast off the bonds of servility and subjection (G. R. Jones, 1975: 50–4).

> Y glew o Gefneithin
> Dilea graith cenedl grin
>
> (The warrior from Cefneithin
> will eradicate the scar
> of a shrivelled people)
>
> [He leads]
>
> Teigrod i ladd taeogrwydd (Tigers to kill servility)
>
> Mae cyffro'n deffro'r dyffryn
> A brwd yw coelcerth y bryn
> A welir ail Lywelyn?
>
> (A fervour is stirring in the vales
> And bonfires burn brightly on the hills
> will we see a second Llywelyn?)

It continues in this vein; throughout the land, timid men are straightening their backs. An impotent people is rousing itself, inspired by the unassuming Barry John. Anyone who has known his genius can never grovel to foreign crowns, etc.

If the chords struck in this swelling diapason of praise are in celebration of spines stiffened, pride asserted, a captive, deferential people liberated by King John, the herald of a second Llywelyn (the first was the last independent prince of Wales), such voices fall mute after 1979, the year of the first devolution débâcle and the end of a decade of Welsh rugby dominance. It is the English-language poets of Wales who most bitterly articulate the frustration of dashed nationalist hopes, and turn vengefully on the eighty-minute patriots of the Arms Park. Alun Rees, for instance, is impressed by the fervour of the international crowd but wishes it were applied elsewhere (Rees, 1987: 93):

> To see this, all the same, is to regret
> That sixty thousand with this splendid fire
> Urge fifteen on to drive the English back
> If only they would urge *themselves* like that.

Similarly the 'dark thought' occurs to Raymond Garlick as he passes the Arms Park and hears its ritual chants (Garlick, 1986: 100):

> How outside the stadium
> So many of these are dumb
> For their country – who acclaim
> Its crowning in a mere game.

More rancorous is Nigel Jenkins's splenetic 'Land of Song', a tirade against what he perceives to be the shallow patriotism and boozy, hymns and arias male chauvinism of Welsh rugby culture; sub-headed 'In memoriam 1 September 79', the date of the first devolution referendum and its rejection, its theme is 'shame dressed as pride' (Jenkins, 1981: 43).

A Pontypridd-accented growl of dissent emanates from the short-story writer and playwright Alun Richards, who has never been embarrassed by his love for rugby. As well as being one of the sharpest chroniclers of modern South Wales, no-one has written more perceptively about the Welsh grammar school ethos of the 1930s and '40s and the particular role of rugby within it, with its hierarchy of talent and gradations of teams, its opportunity for esteem and prestige, and its pervasive, hegemonizing influence. In his autobiographical *Days of Absence* we are not allowed to forget that Pontypridd is a breeding ground of sporting excellence, that three world boxing champions have been born within a radius of six miles of it, one of them Freddie Welsh, and that his grandmother's cousin, who lay in bed one night, laid a burglar out with one punch (Richards, 1986: 32).

Pontypridd Grammar School in the 1940s clearly *was* a nursery of quite extraordinary talent, producing, for example, the half-backs Glyn and Wynford Davies who played for Wales from school in the first post-war but unofficial international season. Alun Richards's own inclusion in the First XV gave his last years at school a sense of belonging hitherto missing in his own personal life: 'Suddenly I was physically different and caught up in the most powerful of social forces' (ibid.: 103). He had found the key to one of the few Welsh activities in which excellence was in evidence everywhere around him; and not just excellence but the elusive grace and flair of the truly great players.

The inability to cope with this specialness in later life is the theme of several of his short stories, in the collections *Dai Country* (1973) and *The Former Miss Merthyr Tydfil* (1976) particularly, which beautifully re-create the middle-aged sentimentality of the Welsh ex-grammar school fraternity, its beery bonhomie and, among the highly varied range of social types he portrays, marvellous South Wales women. The stuck-up Esmé in the story 'Fly half' (Richards, 1973: 46–61) is married to that rarest of beings, a much capped stand-off, one of the greatest, 'a man to be put amongst the immortals, Trew, Willie Davies, the two Cliffs, even 'King' John, who did other things better but shirked a physical game and couldn't beat a man off either foot ... It was this beating a man off either foot which was apparently important. In thirty years only two men could do that, one was Bleddyn and the other was her husband.' Esmé was Cardiff, a Tory Lord Mayor's daughter, and had not known him in his heyday but he was something very special then. People who had known him, now in their forties, spoke of him as a divinity:

> He had an eye for an opening and – more important than anything else – absolute confidence, a wicked acceleration over twenty yards, and a wonderful pair of hands. He had once sold a dummy which deceived even the referee who blew up for a forward pass and couldn't then reverse the decision, or so the legend ran ... People who knew went on for hours in this vein ... The game, the past, his continual wallowing in it, aided and abetted by everybody he seemed to meet ...

even on holiday in Portugal, 'added up to a kind of cancer' Esmé wishes she could exorcise, but cannot. In desperation she demands: 'Have you ever thought what it's like to grow up?'

Whether this is evidence of the essential juvenility of sport and its ability to retard maturity and hamper adjustment to a non-starring role in the adult world after retirement from the game, or merely a harmless nostalgia for a vanished youth, either way we have come full circle. Tom Buchanan, 'one of the most powerful ends that ever played football at New Haven' was a national figure, too, in a way, (Fitzgerald, 1990: 11–12)

> one of those men who reach such an acute limited excellence at twenty-one that everything afterwards savours of anti-climax.... Tom would drift on forever seeking, a little wistfully, for the dramatic turbulence of some irrecoverable football game.

Emyr Humphreys elaborates on this theme in his story 'The hero' (Humphreys, 1968: 49), when the young lawyer Gwilym Tist, a prospective parliamentary Labour candidate, takes two older academics to what is for one of them his first rugby international. What impresses Dr Hudson beyond even the size of the crowd, the arena and thirty young gladiators in the peak of fitness ready to do battle, is

> the longing in the stands for a vanished youth ... Rows and rows of gray-haired men with red faces from drinking, smoking and over-eating, reliving an idealised youth, identifying with the young heroes in the arena. To see that collectively, that was interesting.

It was not a matter of righting Wales' ancient wrongs, of pulverising the oppressor, of beating England, all-comers, or anybody. It was not even a matter of winning. It was avoiding losing. Avoiding failure. His companion asks:

> What's the difference? There is a difference. Not losing means avoiding failure ... Analogous to postponing death.

It is that youthful quality that is the primary appeal of sport and the essential virtue of its heroes. As John Updike's Harry Angstrom says (Updike, 1991: 62), being mature is 'the same thing as being dead'. Maturity is death, the death of youth, and therefore to be regretted. The Celts are very good at regretting.

NOTE

1. *cywydd* and *englyn* are tightly metrical forms of poem, strictly governed by rules of length of line and syllable, and written in *cynghanedd*, an ancient and complex system of internal rhyme, assonance and alliteration. See Stephens, M. (ed.), *The New Companion to the Literature of Wales* (Cardiff, 1998) for further elucidation.

6

STADE RENNAIS: STANDARD-BEARER OF BRETON IDENTITY

Michel Raspaud

(translation by David Bailey)

According to various works devoted to sport in the geographical and historical area of the 'Brittany' region, that politico-administrative entity in western France that covers the four départements of Côte-d'Armor, Finistère, Ille-et-Vilaine and Morbihan, Brittany has certain specific features arising from a kind of 'tradition' of producing sportsmen and champions. It is quite easy to understand that boat racing is deeply rooted in the region's economic history and that, due to the development of leisure activities and modern sport, this has led to the rechannelling of skills and energies into a territory and cultural penchants for yachting and offshore racing, producing such figures as Eric Tabarly and Olivier de Kersauzon. However, there seems less apparent reason for the predilection for cycling and football, which official sporting media claim have met with particular success among the local population, in terms of both actual playing and the production of great champions. Thus, the names of Petit-Breton, Jean Robic, Louison Bobet or Bernard Hinault in the case of cycling, or Jean Prouff, Raymond Kéruzoré, Stade Rennais, En Avant Guingamp, and even FC Nantes in the case of football, are often chanted like spells to corroborate this close relation between sport and Brittany.

However, sport has been grafted onto other deeper and more essential features. Indeed, Brittany, like several other regions of France (Corsica, Languedoc, the Basque country, Alsace, etc.), is said to have kept alive a number of particular local characteristics and cultural traditions, such as its language, architecture, costume, certain festivals, etc., which mark it out from the rest of the country. For the last two or three decades, these characteristics and traditions have been taken over by the cultural and political élites, who are promoting them as consubstantial elements of

Breton identity. The origins of organizations, set up by départements and the Brittany Region, such as the Institut Culturel de Bretagne, predate the decentralization of 1982; the first Festival Interceltique de Lorient of 1971 was a militant and more spontaneous experiment, replacing the moribund Festival de Brest.

The increasing success of Lorient's event clearly demonstrates the entrenchment that the festival's promoters wish to stress, setting Breton culture against a wider background than the administrative region, namely that of the Celtic cultures that continue to make their mark on the extreme westerly parts of Europe (Galicia, Brittany, Ireland, Wales, Scotland). A book like *Le Cheval d'orgueil* (1975), by Pierre-Jakez Hélias, in which the author recounts his childhood between the two World Wars in the *pays bigouden*, is no doubt important in restoring legitimacy to a culture that has been crushed on the one hand by the state's desire for uniformity, expressed through compulsory schooling, and on the other hand by industrialization and migration from the countryside towards the large regional cities (Rennes, Nantes) and Paris, as well as by the development of radio and television, and mass culture.

After the growth of the consumer society in France of the 1950s and '60s, the economic situation of the 1970s provided a favourable climate in which to express local idiosyncrasies, which were in fact claims to identity. Via changing social values, the resurgence of regional cultures may be understood as expressing a challenge to the standardization of lifestyles, in the same way as do claims for sexual freedom, feminist movements, attempts to 'get back to the earth' and the resulting formation of rural communities, anti-nuclear protests, etc.

Song, a minor but widely disseminated art form, was a vehicle for popularizing the constituent features of Breton culture (*bagad, fest-noz...*). At the time, singers such as Glenmor, Gilles Servat and especially Alan Stivell met with success well beyond their geo-cultural area of origin. The Breton language, today, is taught officially in a number of primary and secondary schools and is no longer considered a stigma, a sign of social backwardness and consequently of not belonging to the nation.

Nevertheless, leaving aside musical or literary works, there is little or nothing to be seen of the other constituent features of Breton culture and identity. For example, the traditional trials of strength – considered to be typical of Celtic cultures, such as the Scottish Highland Games (Cadiou, 1995) – and Breton wrestling (*gouren*), are found more often in genuinely Breton celebrations such as the *pardons* than in these major festivals. It is true that these physical pursuits are considered to be quaint relics of the past, even though they are still very much alive in certain parts of the region, such as the Trégor area (Péru, 1985). However, the fact that they have survived is an indication that, in spite of transformations in the rural and agricultural living conditions that produced them, the communities in which they originated still find them meaningful.

As in the rest of the country, of course, modern sport – whether of British origin or not – began to appear by the second half of the nineteenth century, gradually replacing traditional physical activities. Nevertheless, beyond the forms surviving in the *pardons*, soule, for example, a violent game that was banned on several occasions in the course of the last 500 years, lasted long enough to be seen in the Morbihan region just before the First World War (Cadiou, 1995). Soule, which is not unlike certain other Celtic games such as hurling or cnapan, and of course modern football and various forms of rugby, is often claimed to be the ancestral form of these games by various sports historians. In this way, Brittany is presented as possessing sporting characteristics that make it firmly rooted in the history of sport, and yet at the same time is assigned particular features that distinguish it from other regions of France.

BRITTANY, REGIONAL IDENTITY AND THE CELT

This logic of assignment goes back to the notion of the various French provinces having specific features, an idea that came into being during the Revolution and Empire periods, at the time when the provinces ceased to be political entities (Bertho, 1980). Each province was recognized as having a history, with its monuments and outstanding figures, its geography, soil, climate and inhabitants, its peasants with their lifestyle and the characteristic traits of their race. By 1830, the categories describing each province were fixed. As far as Brittany is concerned, three major factors can be identified. The Bretons were 'recognized' as true Celts, who were themselves accepted as the ancestors of the Gauls. The West was uniformly seen as *chouan* (those who had taken part in the peasant revolts against the Revolution), and the province as a whole was economically backward. These three factors cast Brittany in an archaic mould, while the urban bourgeoisie – which was becoming curious about the rural world of the provinces – retained only what seemed to be the most visible outward signs of civilized society: Breton folklore (Bertho, 1980). Soule must be considered as falling into this category.

Books dealing with the subject of sport in Brittany, and football in particular, usually insist on the Breton identity of its athletes and teams (Aubour, 1972; Cadiou, 1982; Le Boulanger, 1995; Loire, 1994; Ollivier, 1980, 1981). Via its football teams, it is Brittany that is being represented, challenging the other provinces. A sort of hierarchy has thus been set up, stigmatizing failure and showering praise upon success.

However, while this article seeks to determine the Breton identity of Stade Rennais, it is necessary to bear in mind the fact that 'Breton identity is probably indefinable as it is a movement and not a thing' (Chappé, 1995: 106). It is not a question, therefore, of identifying the characteristic traits of Brittany in Stade Rennais, but of showing how, at a particular period in the history of France and Brittany (1945–75), it became a representative figure of their region for the Bretons.

STADE RENNAIS, A GLORIOUS HISTORY

Stade Rennais was founded on 24 March 1901. Three years later, on 4 May 1904, it amalgamated with FC Armoricain, itself created by the alliance of FC Rennais and Armoricaine (30 January 1902). At the time, it became known as Stade Rennais Université-Club. There was nothing to distinguish it from the other football clubs created in France, which were influenced by both the English – via US Servannaise, the club from Saint-Servan near Saint-Malo – and the secondary school/student world, as witness its name (Loire, 1994; Wahl, 1989). In Brittany more than in the rest of the country, there was strong competition between Catholic and secular sports clubs (Lagrée, 1992; Wahl, 1989) and this may perhaps help to explain the rapid development of football in this region.

Before the advent of professionalism in France (1932), Stade Rennais won the title of Champion of Brittany seven times between 1904 and 1918, and then three times that of Champion of the West. But, more importantly, it was successful at national level. It won the Allies Cup (French Inter-federation championship) in 1916, but it lost the final in 1917. In 1922, it also lost the French Cup final (0–2 against Red Star, the best French team at the period). However, the outstanding feature of Stade Rennais was the fact that, from 1929 to 1932, it refused to play in either the Western League championship, as it did not agree with the rules, or the French Cup. It recruited Czechoslovak and German players and played friendly matches against major teams from abroad. But the club faced sanctions and fines, and could not use players who had not been authorized to leave their federation. This, however, did not prevent the Fédération from selecting Stade's best players for the national team! These problems were solved when it joined the French Professional Championship in 1932. Stade took part in the French Cup Final again in 1935 (when it was beaten 0–3 by Olympique de Marseille), but its poor results led to its being relegated to Division 2 in 1937. It was unable to return to Division 1 in 1939, as the championship was upset by the war, but in 1945 Stade was back in the first division. In spite of good results in 1946 (5th) and 1949 (4th), it was relegated to the second division once more in 1953.

In 1954, Mr Louis Girard was elected president of the club. Young (41 years of age), and a former Stade footballer himself (goalkeeper), he was a public works contractor and quickly surrounded himself with men from the same background, true to a tradition that had characterized the club. During his fifteen years as president (1954–69), Stade returned to Division 1, where it performed consistently well (1958–75), winning its first French Cup (1965). However, faced with the club's financial difficulties, Louis Girard resigned and, after a few months of confusion, Jean Rohou was appointed in 1969. He was also a public works contractor, mayor of Carhaix (a town 95 miles from Rennes), former president of a local club (Dernières Cartouches de Carhaix), and councillor in the département of Finistère. Under his presidency (1969–72), Stade Rennais won its second French Cup in 1971.

Subsequently, with mediocre results, financial difficulties, and the arrival of a president who lacked experience, Stade Rennais found itself back in the second division. Another twenty years of hard work would be needed before it could once again take its place among the elite in 1994.

THE CONSTRUCTION OF STADE RENNAIS' BRETON IDENTITY

It was during the decade from 1965 to 1975 that Stade Rennais, perhaps more than before, became the real standard-bearer of Breton identity. The two French Cup victories, then its financial difficulties, and finally the sad recognition in March 1975 that 'there is no longer any style at Rennes, which is completely dead' (Moreau, 1995: 26), all underline the fact that its supporters, and Brittany as a whole, were deeply attached to Stade. From this point of view, the changes that occurred between the two French Cup victories were significant.

In 1965, 30 years after it had lost the final for the second time and under the leadership of its trainer Jean Prouff, Stade Rennais managed with some difficulty to beat Sedan. The same year, FC Nantes won the French championship and the local press (the daily *Ouest France*) described these triumphs as 'an admirable Breton double', stressing that 'it is Brittany that should be fixed to the masthead'. Before the first cup final, Stade received telegrams of encouragement from Bretons all over the world (Madagascar, the Meteorological Studies Centre in the Kerguelen Islands, the French Polar Mission in Terre Adélie, and officers and sailors on board the *Commandant-Bory* off the coast of Gabon). The mayor of Rennes (Mr

Henri Fréville) and the region's préfet of course attended the match. However, it was the city of Rennes and the West that received most of the attention, rather than Brittany itself.

Rennes and Stade were linked up with a glorious past, and with the two lost finals of 1922 and 1935. On 21 May, *Ouest France* ran an article on Maurice Gastiger, who, although born in the east of France, played with his brother Pierre in the 1922 final. It was also stressed that Jean Prouff himself played with the junior Stade team against Red Star on the eve of the 1935 final. Two former Rennes footballers, Robert Colin and Maurice Guénard (the latter having played with professionals from Stade) cycled to Paris to attend the final. The selection of the two teams taking part in the final highlighted Stade's recruitment policy, since only four of the eleven players began their careers with the team. And while, on 22 May, the eve of the 1965 final, old members of Stade were playing against the Union Sportive des Bretons de Paris – recalling the large numbers that had left the region's rural areas – the reference to Brittany was largely anecdotal, with the supporters' decision to adopt a baby piglet called Rodrigue as their official mascot, in response to the little wild boar of the team from the Ardennes (18 May).

The only real reference to Brittany was on the front page of *Ouest France*, which noted, after the victory, that 'the team from Rennes has given Brittany its first Cup' (28 May). This – positive – title is in stark contrast to 'The West disappointed' that had appeared after the first final (24 May). Otherwise, the comments pages make no explicit reference to the idea of Brittany. There is just a passing reference to the fact that, after the last championship match in Strasbourg 'on Sunday night, Breton supporters will acclaim Stade Rennais players who have just won the French Cup' (29, 30 May). 'Rennes welcomes its team in triumph' reported the newspaper when 50–60,000 people filled the city streets, mayor Henri Fréville remarking that 'the crowd reminded him of the atmosphere on Liberation Day' (31 May).

The 1971 final took place in a completely different context. First of all, Stade had already won the Cup. Secondly, French football was undergoing a thorough change after the disastrous late 1960s. Lastly, the major political and sociological upheavals connected with the events of May '68 had brought about serious changes in society. In particular, regionalist claims, some of which were accompanied by radical, violent nationalist movements, were actively pushing for the creation of a cultural identity with a positive image. Sporting events, like cultural festivals, became favourite ways of demonstrating this identity. In 1971, *Ouest France* spoke quite differently of Stade Rennais. During the second leg of the semi-final against Olympique de Marseille (who were to become French champions), the headline was devoted to their exploit in qualifying after the penalties (2 June). The Lorient Road ground became part of the history of football and world sport via references to the 'Rennes players' "Brazilian night"' (3 June), while the crowd was compared to those at Wembley or Cardiff Arms Park. Before the Final (20 June), telegrams of encouragement arrived from 'exiled' Bretons everywhere (9 June). 12, 000 postcards were sent to one of the city's department stores and the supporters found a worthy successor to 1965's piglet Rodrigue, but this time gave it a Breton name, *Trech't*, which means 'victory'. Certain people complained about this choice of 'an animal that has never been used as the emblem of Brittany', while others replied that it was never intended to be a regional symbol, just a good luck charm (*Ouest France*, 15 June).

The main point, however, was that the Bretons' joy was completely out of keeping with what happened in 1965. That year, the press had announced only five days before the final that there were still places available (the number of supporters from the West was estimated at 6000), there was only one special train travelling to Paris (1600 people) and coaches would leave only from *the four corners of the city*. Six years later, 10, 000 tickets were sold in Rennes on the first day alone and 4000 more had to be ordered from the Fédération. Three special trains, each carrying 1000 people, left Rennes, with another from Quimper and another from Brest. 'All over Brittany, transport companies are stretched to the limit by reservations' (10 June) and 100–150 coaches were to leave for Paris. There was even a special charter flight. There were not enough club hats and shirts to meet demand ... René Cédolin, the only survivor of the first final along with Louis Cardiet, commented that 'the atmosphere is more impassioned than in 1965, when we were left in peace' (*Ouest France*, 17 June).

References to the past this time were more cultural and no longer simply sporting. The journalist Alain Cabon (*Ouest France*, 21 June) wrote that '[he had] relearned [his] songs on the road to Colombes, because yesterday Colombes was both Sainte-Anne-d'Auvray, Lisieux and Le Folgoët together, including the faith and popular fervour'. There was much discussion about the places of origin of the supporters, and comments made on car registration numbers: 22, 29, 35, 56, the four Breton départements (44, Loire-Atlantique, did not get a mention). André Maussion, on the front page of *Ouest France* (19–20 June), mused about this 'astonishing migration [which] is an event that goes beyond the boundaries of sport alone'.

Michel Castaing (*Le Monde*, 22 June) noted the size of the 'Breton tide' that was estimated to be more than half of the 46,800 spectators, and underlined the fact that 'increasingly, an entire region is supporting its "regional" team. This cup final was a more or less conscious, avowed opportunity for the Rennes supporters to give an idea of Breton unity – let us not speak of independence, as the shadow of the Breton Liberation Front does not seem to have fallen over Colombes – and for the Lyon supporters to affirm the administrative supremacy of their regional capital and also its sporting supremacy that might be challenged by Saint-Etienne.'

The victors' return (Stade won 1–0) bore no resemblance to what had happened six years before. From the station (where trains had to be stopped for more than half an hour) all the way to the square in front of the Town Hall, 'tens of thousands of Bretons' – 100, 000 according to some – 'from all over the West' gave an immense ovation to the players (*Ouest France*, 22 June). Marcel Aubour, the goalkeeper and hero of the semi-final against Olympique de Marseille (in which he stopped several penalties) who had been photographed using artichokes to play bowls during the match, began singing the Breton folk song 'Ma Bretagne' from the balcony of the Town Hall. 'I just felt the impulse to start singing the Breton regional song (...) the Bretons were surprised at first, probably astonished, and then they all clapped, giving me the most fantastic, sincere and moving ovation ever' (Aubour, 1972: 161). A year later, hurt by the unjust criticism of a Paris journalist, he decided to abandon football. A supporter wrote to him saying that 'no Breton can forget that you sang "Ma Bretagne" from the Town Hall balcony' (Aubour, 1972: 128).

However, while non-Bretons playing for the team were gradually 'naturalized', the press and public focused more on the young and talented local hope, Raymond Kéruzoré. Only 22 years of age, he delighted supporters and critics alike by his creative, elegant playing, and he seemed destined for a remarkable career. His trainer, Prouff, understood this well and left him complete leeway in the field. The press emphasized his Breton origins by nicknaming him Korrigan de Châteauneuf-du-Faou (his birthplace, a few miles from Quimper). Raymond Kéruzoré is *the* emblematic player of Brittany, a real 'legend'. A long-haired intellectual, a Breton bard without the beard, he unfortunately never managed to express himself fully outside the Breton context. He left Stade Quimperois for Rennes in 1968 and then joined Marseilles in 1973, but never settled in. In 1974 he returned to Rennes, where a dispute with the trainer, Antoine Cuissard, led to his leaving the club (now back in the second division) for Stade Lavallois in 1975. With them, he immediately returned to the first division. After that, he joined Brest (1979–81), then Guingamp, firstly as trainer-player (1981–4) and then as trainer (1984–6). He then returned to Brest (1986–7) before coming back to Stade Rennais (1987–91), which he brought back again into the first division (1990). However, the final years were difficult ones, with relationship problems seriously affecting Kéruzoré's talent. He then left Rennes for FC Tours (1991–3) before returning to his original point of departure (Quimper). Thus, with the exception of the Marseilles episode, Kéruzoré only played for and coached Breton or Western clubs.

This is in stark contrast to the other major figure of Breton football, Jean Prouff, the club's trainer during its heyday (1964–73). Prouff was at home wherever he went, between stretches with Stade Rennais in the North, at Rheims, during which period they won the French championship (1949), or with Rouen. He then became a trainer–player (Caen, Aix-en-Provence, Philippeville (Algeria), Guingamp) and subsequently trainer (Boulogne, Red Star). On information from Gabriel Hanot, he took charge of the Polish national team, which won sixth place at the Rome Olympic Games (1960). He then trained Standard de Liège, taking them to the European Cup semi-final in 1962 (where they were eliminated by Real Madrid). A sports teacher at Lille (indeed he never completely abandoned his profession), he was called upon by Stade as their trainer, Antoine Cuissard, had problems with the players. François Pleyer went up to Lille, and told him simply 'I have just come to fetch you' (Prouff, 1997).

Prouff and Kéruzoré always maintained close professional relations, as when the latter became a trainer, Prouff followed him to Guingamp, then to Brest and Rennes, either to 'cover' him (Kéruzoré still had no diploma) or to look after technical matters. This friendship, which went hand-in-hand with Kéruzoré's deep respect for his elder – he always addressed him formally – is an expression of the historical continuity of football at Rennes. However, a remarkable aspect of the Breton identity of Stade concerns its choice of trainers. Right from the time it became professional (1932), with the exception of the very first years, it was always managed by former club players, even if they were foreigners (the Austrian Peter Schneider, or the Spaniard Salvador Artigas). In the early 1980s, this phenomenon became less systematic, as certain trainers had no links with Rennes or Brittany, such as Jean Vincent or Pierre Mosca. But it became a feature once again with the arrival of Kéruzoré (1987), and then Didier Notheaux (1991). And while Michel Le Milinaire (1993) and Yves Colleu (1995) never played with Stade, they are both nevertheless Bretons.

FOOTBALL, ECONOMICS, POLITICS

The history of Stade Rennais cannot, however, be separated from the economic and political context. Firstly, its setting was the 'glorious thirty' years of economic development in France, from the Liberation to the middle of the 1970s. Brittany was not exempt from this: the modernization of agriculture, the development of agroindustries, and the creation of jobs in industry were of particular benefit to the département of Ille-et-Vilaine, while the population of Rennes, the regional capital, grew through the influx of new workers. All of this went hand-in-hand with the new awareness that Brittany vitally needed to develop, and led to the creation in 1950 of the Comité d'Etudes et de Liaison des Intérêts Bretons (CELIB), which was to spur development. At the same time, the regionalist movements were being transformed, becoming more radical or legalistic, in tune with changes in the political arena. Then the cultural movements took over in promoting Breton identity. The administrators who managed Stade throughout this period took advantage of this development, and introduced their know-how into the club's management and modernization. Most of them were drawn from the construction and public works sector (Odorico in the 1930s, Girard, Rohou and Lemoux later), but they gave way to industrialists during the building crisis in the 1970s.

Throughout its history, Stade Rennais has also received support, both concrete and symbolic, from local politicians. Thus, even before World War I, M. Janvier, the city's mayor, was the club's honorary president, and it was he who placed the ball in the middle of the field for the match inaugurating the new ground in 1912 (Loire, 1994: 45). Subsequently, in the 1930s, the city helped the club with subsidies to wipe out its deficits, arranged for municipal councillors to sit on the board of management during crisis periods, and enlarged and modernized the ground, which had become its property.

During the serious crisis of autumn 1969, the club's new president, M. Rohou (mayor of a town in Finistère and member of the regional council) declared that he intended 'to save the club with the help of [his] team, the municipal council and the supporters'. He went on to stress that 'Stade Rennais is a matter of concern for the whole of Brittany (...) I will manage it like a company, and consider the players as executives taking part in the life of the club' (Moreau, 1995: 40). The supporters themselves organized a 'rescue operation' throughout Brittany. Four years later, when new budget problems arose, Mr Lemoux, aware that Stade had to be the club for a whole region, launched an appeal to Breton companies and had 20, 000 stickers printed with the words 'I am Breton. Come on Rennes' (Loire,

1994: 364). This demonstration of identity must also be seen against its background, that of Brittany at the start of the 1970s, disturbed by many different social upheavals: radicalization of the regional question, and trials of various separatists accused of bombings, the manifesto by Breton artists against show business, the strike by workers at the Joint Français, claiming equal pay with those in the Paris region, the 'milk war', challenges to the development of hypermarkets, etc. Throughout the region, support groups and demonstrations were organized, mixing red flags and Breton flags. The latter appeared for the first time in public during the mad evening in 1971 when the whole of Rennes welcomed back the triumphant Cup winners team (Caro, 1997).

This feeling that Stade Rennais represents Brittany and forms part of its cultural heritage is illustrated by a symbolic fact. When it was again faced with financial difficulties in 1987, the club was transformed into a semi-public company, in which the city council (left-wing) owned 47 per cent of the shares. To chair the company's board of supervision, an invitation was issued to one of the most famous Bretons, Hervé Bourges, former Chairman of the public TV channel TF1 (Bouchet, 1988). But these deliberately Breton leanings have always existed with regard to the public at the Lorient Road ground and the recruitment of regional players, in spite of the emergence since the 1970s of other first division challengers at Laval (1976), Brest (1979), and Guingamp (1995), and second division too (Lorient, Quimper, Saint-Brieuc).

CONCLUSION

The supporters of Stade Rennais chose a little piglet as their mascot for the Cup finals. However, this good-natured fans' emblem underwent a major transformation, as the French name it was given in 1965 was changed to a Breton one in 1971. This symbolism became more radical at the same time, with the Breton flag beginning to appear among the public. Thus within a few years, Stade acquired a definitely *Breton identity* in the eyes of both Brittany and France as a whole. In spite of the club's irregular performance both on the field and economically, the (brief) emergence of a competitor at Brest and then at Guingamp, Stade has always been the principal standard-bearer of Brittany. Today, however, it represents urban Brittany and is opposed to Guingamp, which enshrines the values of deep, rural Brittany.

At the same time, the homogeneous universe of the Rennes supporters has fragmented into three separate entities: Allez Rennes, the oldest group (created in 1961, with 500 members) split to give birth to the Socios (950 members). Simultaneously, a third group, Roazhon Celtic Kop, was created. Unofficially formed in 1987 and transformed into an association in 1991, this little group (150 members) is younger and rowdier than the other two (Caro, 1996). Mostly, however, they have exacerbated the Breton identity by their behaviour, slogans and symbols, which pleases neither the other supporters nor the club, which is trying to build itself a smooth image. These supporters stigmatize the existence of the regional competitor (Guingamp) by stating that 'we do not like any other team, be it Breton or French; the only thing that counts is the red and black shirt with the two ermines (i.e. the true one and not the copy worn by a minor Breton town currently in the first division)' (Caro, 1996: 42). They proffer slogans in which they declare that 'a good Laval player is a dead one' or have 'death rather than defilement' printed on their scarves (Boizard, 1997). Of course one must understand that affirming group identity means denying the existence of others (Bromberger, 1995).

But much more interesting for the question of regional identity is the fact that they have introduced the Breton form of Rennes into the name of their association, placing it alongside a Celtic reference, thus falling in line with the cultural trends that have been developing since the 1970s. The identity of Rennes is no longer confined simply to Brittany, but has been opened up to the entire Celtic world, which is perhaps just another way of rooting oneself in Europe. However, the most significant feat of these supporters is to have made the largest *gwenn ha du* (Breton flag) of all time, measuring 270m^2, and to have unfurled it in the Mordelles stands during the 1994–5 season. This photograph of the Breton flag was then used to illustrate the official Stade Rennais calendars.

7

SHINTY AND THE CELTIC CELEBRATION OF NEW YEAR

Hugh Dan MacLennan

The game of camanachd is peculiar to the Celts of Scotland and Ireland – peculiar that is to say, to the old Scottish (not Scottic) or Gaelic-speaking people. Its antiquity therefore goes beyond the time when the Scots first came from Ireland into Scotland, or, as it was then called, Caledonia. The Scots brought shinty with them from old Scotia or Ireland in the early centuries of the Christian era. The antiquity of the game among Scots is indisputable.

(*Littlejohn Album*, Aberdeen University)[1]

The Celtic peoples were one of the great founding civilizations of Europe, an exciting, innovative race whose cultural impact has long since been underestimated. This chapter will detail two specific aspects of that enduring cultural legacy: their linguistic and sporting traditions as manifested in the celebrations and consciousness of the modern Gael. What follows will go some way to explaining some of the formative influences which have shaped one of the main elements of Celtic cultural celebrations, the New Year festival and its sporting appendages.

FORTISSIMUS HEROS SCOTORUM

Shinty – in Scottish Gaelic *camanachd* or *iomain* – is a game of great antiquity. The evidence we have of the place sport played in the ancient Celts' training for war fully justifies Father Ninian MacDonald's assessment that the modern form of the stick and ball game known as shinty has been 'consistently practised from the remotest periods of our racial history' (J. N. MacDonald, 1932: 30). Nor is there any doubt but that some early form of the stick and ball game we now know as shinty was played in pagan times. Whether it was, as has been suggested, 'a recognizable relic of a very ancient, pagan, magical fertility rite', I doubt

(*West Highland Free Press*, 13 January 1989). The folklore collector Robert C. MacLagan (1910: 3–42) also postulated some phallic significance in relation to the shinty stick, although he was prone to finding phallic significance more or less wherever he looked.

The game we now know as shinty, and its attendant baggage – the Gaelic language and culture – was introduced to Scotland nearly two thousand years ago by Irish missionaries. Indeed, 1400 years after St Columba's death, it is worth noting that the venerable saint is said to have arrived on these shores as a result of a little local difficulty at an Irish hurling match. What started as the world's first debate about copyright (as popular lore would have it, anyway) – 'to every cow its calf and every book its copy' (Marsden, 1991: 36ff) – eventually ended up with a bloody resolution on the battlefield. The upshot, whichever version of the historical tale we accept, was that Columba arrived on these shores.

The venerable saint may currently have the highest profile of anyone who came to Scotland from Ireland, but he was by no means the only man with outstanding credentials. Amongst the heroes of the Heroic or Red Branch Cycle – the great heroic cycle of Irish mythology – the most remarkable and renowned is without doubt Cù Chulainn – *Fortissimus heros Scotorum*. The greatest of all the Irish heroes was originally known as Sètanta. He won his name by driving a ball through the foaming mouth of a dog, forcing the brute's entrails through the other end. This prodigious feat, we are told in *Táin Bó Cuailgne* (The Cattle Raid of Cooley), ensured that the women of Ulster went forth to meet him 'stark naked', baring their breasts, at which, our hero was 'placed in three vats of water to quench the ardour of his wrath' (O'Rahilly, 1984: 162, 170–71).

As Anne Ross (1986: 95–7) informs us in her *The Pagan Celts*, board games were very popular among the ancient Celts, and no doubt helped to pass the long evenings. Field games were also encouraged. The hero Cù Chulainn excelled at such games:

> He took his little javelin for casting and his toy spear with its end sharpened by fire; and he began to shorten the journey by playing with them. He would strike his ball with the stick, and drive it a long way from him. Then with a second stroke he would throw his stick so that he might drive it a distance no less than the first. He would throw up his javelin and would cast his spear, and would make a playful rush after them. Then he would catch his hurley stick and his ball and his javelin; and before the end of his spear had reached the ground he would catch its tip aloft in the air.

'Seven years was his age', it is said, 'when he took arms, seventeen when he was in pursuit of the Táin Bó Chúailgne, twenty-seven when he died.' It is not surprising to find that such a warrior excelled in the wielding of the caman. The training for warfare which the club-ball *(ag immain liathroidi)* represented, was central to life. We are told that King Conchobar divided his day into three parts (J. N. MacDonald, 1932: 36):

> the first being devoted to watching the boycorps at their sports, especially that of Caman; the second to playing of chess and of draughts; the third to pleasurable absorption of meat and drink until drowsiness set in, which was then promoted by the exertions of minstrels and musicians to induce favourable placidity of mind and disposition.

It is a measure of sport's importance in Celtic life that the Brehon Laws, the codification laid down in ancient Ireland by the *brehons* or judges dating from the seventh or eighth centuries AD, impinges on virtually every aspect of life, including the ancestor of modern shinty and hurling (O Caithnia, 1986: 30).

Ancient Irish law is characterized by an extreme, and at times ludicrous schematism. While the contents may be regarded as a largely theoretical construction (built, without doubt on a realistic foundation), they bear a very limited relation to life in ancient Ireland. The laws regarding hurling are no exception. Only officially sanctioned contests were validated with the detailed penalties carrying the full force of law, for reasons which are elaborately explained. The basic essentials of a game as detailed in the laws were: a hurley, a ball, a goal, and a field.

According to O Caithnia (1986: 30), early lawyers made a distinction between three aspects of the sport: a match *(fianchluiche),* a bout of 'pucking around' or 'slogging' *(ruidilse cluiche)* and specifically dangerous fouls *(colchluiche).* The fourth foul was *taithe tuilche,* which probably meant lying on the ball. Apparently the law dealt differently with injuries arising out of all four forms of play. It is this elaboration which is brilliantly satirized by Flann O'Brien (1960: 9) in his classic *Snàmh-dà-eun* (At Swim Two Birds):

> Finn MacCool was a legendary hero of Ireland. Though not mentally robust, he was a man of superb physique and development. Each of his thighs was as thick as a horse's belly, narrowing to a calf as thick as the belly of a foal. Three fifties of fosterlings could engage with handball against the wideness of his backside, which was large enough to halt the march of men through a mountain-pass.

Hurling, shinty's sporting and cultural cousin, has such a distant ancestry that it is impossible to pin down its origins. According to the evidence of Irish myth and legend, the game had its devoted followers more than a thousand years before Christ. The first recorded mention dates it to the battle fought at Moytura, near Cong, County Mayo, in 1272 BC between the native Fir Bolg and the invading Tuatha De Danann, who were demanding half the country. A battle was inevitable. While the sides were preparing for the fray it was agreed to have a hurling contest between twenty-seven of the best players from each side and it went on 'till their bones were broken and bruised and they fell outstretched on the turf and the match ended.' The Fir Bolg won and then fell upon their opponents and slew them (King, 1996: 1).

The Tailtean Games, organized originally in honour of Prince Lugh Làmhfhada's foster-mother Tailtiu, were held in Ireland as far back as approximately 1800 BC, and they continued until approximately 1180 AD. They are apparently the oldest recorded organized sports in the world. Stick and ball games would have been central to their performance.

It has been estimated (Terry, 1997) that in Celtic Ireland there were three team games and more than twenty individual sports, many of which can be identified with, or connected to, warfare. Boys and girls trained regularly at summer training camps and there were sports at annual fairs and feasts. Perhaps the most famous warrior camp was the one run by Sgàthach, the warrior queen who taught advanced battle techniques to Irish heroes in the south end of the Isle of Skye. Cù Chulainn, in order to complete his training in arms, was sent by his uncle to be instructed there. The celebrated institution was surrounded by a circle of water and could only be reached by a bridge, which when stepped upon, tilted the person into the water (Gregory, 1970: 44).

When Cù Chulainn arrived, he found a number of Sgàthach's pupils and other warriors engaged in a game of camanachd outside the gates of the fortress (MacNeacail, 1993: 15):

'We'll have a game of shinty,' was the first thing she said, next time I saw her, then she picked up a caman, with its bent end of hard flat edges, that she had hooked in to her belt, and a hard wooden ball from a pocket in the front of her dress. I thought, this is a waste of time. I'm supposed to be here to learn the arts of war, and she's going to play a game. But I didn't say anything to her – after all we didn't have teams, so how could we play a game like shinty? Then she gave a shriek of a whistle that nearly tore the inside of my ear out! And suddenly we were surrounded by sturdy men with camans in their hands. 'Choose your team,' she said, 'I'll be watching how you play. A good player will make a good warrior.'

CULTURAL ICONS

So much for some of the myth. What of the fact and historical evidence? The earliest we have is in an Irish document dating to the twelfth century – a version of the deeds of the ubiquitous Cù Chulainn, where the word *caman* is clearly seen (Ó Maolfabhail, 1973: 130). Sometimes it is hard to tell fact from fiction. The Club of True Highlanders (founded in 1815) in their book, published in 1881 (*Book of True Highlanders*, 1881: 50), detailed shinty as being:

> undoubtedly the oldest known Keltic sport or pastime. The game is also called Cluich bhall, shinnie, shinty, bandy, hurling, hockey, and at one time was a universal and favourite game of the whole of Keltland.... The origin of this game is lost in the midst of ages ... indeed, it is said, and, no doubt, with great truth, that the game of Camanachd, or club playing, was introduced into the Green Isle by the immediate descendants of Noah. On such authority we may rationally conclude that it was played by Noah himself; and if by Noah, in all probability by Adam and his sons.

Fifteen years later, in a magazine article entitled 'New Year's Day Shinty Match – a Time-honoured Custom', it was stated that there was 'no event of greater importance in connection with the celebration of the advent of the New Year in the Highlands than the New Year's Day Shinty Match – "a very ancient custom"' (*Celtic Monthly*, V, 1896: 64):

> The game usually takes place on an extensive stretch of sand at the sea shore, where that is available, or in inland places on the largest field procurable, and to it flock young and old from the adjoining parishes. Usually there is no limit to the number of contestants, and the young men enter into the fray with a dash and energy that threatens danger to head and limb.

It was usual in the Highlands, to have the principal games of shinty at New Year or Old New Year – 1 January or 12/13 January. In these contests, often between two districts or parishes, there was no limit to the numbers taking part. Players arrived and departed at will, and often play continued from the forenoon until darkness fell. The extent to which shinty was central to the celebration of the New Year festival is confirmed by nineteenth-century folklorists and collectors from R. C. MacLagan, Alice Bertha Gomme and John Francis Campbell onwards, through to Mrs M. MacLeod Banks in the first half of this century. Jamieson's classic *Dictionary of the Scottish Language* also acknowledges the place shinty had in the celebration of New Year.

From 1560 onwards, the Reformers had been doing their best to abolish Christmas and many religious customs probably attached themselves to the New Year instead. When the calendar was changed in 1752, the customs of Christmas and New Year became further entangled. Christmas (New Style) on the new 25 December attracted any new or revived Christmas practices. This was followed by New Year (New Style) on 1 January, with a reversion to any surviving Christmas customs for Old Christmas on 5 (later 6) January, with a return finally to New Year customs for Old New Year on 12 (later 13) January.

The celebration of Epiphany on January 6 was obviously an occasion of great importance in Catholic communities, 'a day of great solemnity and rejoicing', and shinty often featured (*Highlander*, 19 January 1881):

> After the celebration of Mass, in their neat and well built church of 'St Mary and St Bean' at Marydale, the congregation, men, women, and children, headed by the local piper, marched to Cannich Bridge, where many more had assembled from the surrounding glens, in expectation of the match appointed to be played on that day, by the Strathglass Shinty Club.

In an area such as Strathglass, play was held on St Stephen's Day, 26 December; St John's Day, 27 December; New Year's Day, 1 January; and Epiphany, 6 January. As soon as mass was over, people and priest set out for the fields of Balnahaun and Baile na bruach. The Brae and Glen Cannich united against those from the whole Strath, each man considering that the honour of his district rested on him (*Highlander*, 5 March 1880).

Ronald Black's assessment of the situation regarding the date of New Year as a 'hopeless mess' is fair, as is his conclusion that this period was effectively a 'dead' time of year agriculturally, resulting in what amounted to an annual three-week winter close-down (*West Highland Free Press*, 22 December 1995). The terms Nollaig and Callainn (or Calluinn) were freely interchangeable, used to signify precisely the same occasions and festivities. Nollaig could describe both Christmas and the New Year, and when a distinction was required, the former could be called Nollaig Mhòr (Big Christmas) and the latter Nollaig Bheag (Little Christmas).

Whether Nollaig Mhòr or Nollaig Bheag, it is clear that New Year, and particularly Hogmanay, was a time of great celebration and one of great significance in people's lives – *Oidhche nan luireach 's nan caman* (the night of the cloaks and the camain) marked in *Rannan/Duain Calluinn* – Hogmanay verses (*Oban Times*, 8 January 1870).

Even when shinty was at its lowest ebb in the mid-nineteenth century, play at New Year was a crucial element of its survival and continuation.

Mrs M. MacLeod Banks (1939: 111), in *British Calendar Customs* introduces shinty as follows:

> The chief game in Scotland at New Year was Shinty, or Shinny, the second probably the oldest form of the name. Played with a bent or curved stick, the caman, its Gaelic name was Camanachd, shortened to Cammock; it was also known as Iomain, driving, though this name applied as well to football, or any game in which a ball was driven forward. It is honourable as a game for heroes in early Irish as well as Gaelic legend.

Eighty-eight years ago, the Argyllshire collector R. C. MacLagan wrote a paper on 'Calluinn – Hogmanay', a 39-page discourse on the beliefs and customs associated with New Year (MacLagan, 1910); '(in) an attempt to explain the origin of certain local customs connected with the observance of the New Year, and show their probable connection with the ancient civilisation existing among the rulers of Great Britain in the early years of our era'.

Shinty is dealt with in passing, among customs Latin and Greek, Welsh and Breton, as MacLagan describes the 'wild and lascivious' nature of Hogmanay and New Year celebrations. This is mixed with a convoluted discourse on the precise date on which celebrations did or should have taken place.

MacLagan's account of the shinty and Oidhche Challuinn is very similar to that detailed by several contemporaries. There is no reason to suspect that he was anything but familiar with the traditions of the *caisean-uchd* (the skin covering the breastbone) which was attached to the 'business end' of a shinty stick.

It is clear that from the middle of the nineteenth century, and before, there was general acknowledgement that the maintenance of traditional customs, including shinty play, was in decline. Ministers who drew up the *New Statistical Account* in the decades before 1850 recorded the passing of the time-honoured customs. The 'taste for amusements' had gone. Christmas and New Year's shinty matches 'are now abandoned, and exchanged, it is to be feared, in many instances, for pastimes of a less equivocal character'.

In the parish of Moy and Dalarossie (*New Statistical Account*, vol. XIV: 107):

> few or none wear the kilt and belted plaid; and the ancient superstitions, with the ceremonies connected with them, are vanishing away. The game chiefly played is the club and ball, which forms the winter amusement; and the collecting of the people for a trial of skill at this game is the only remnant of the old mode of celebrating Christmas and new year holy days.

Part of the reason for such a decline in traditional pastimes was simply the absence of people – emigration was taking its toll. Across the Highlands and Islands, the story was the same (*New Statistical Account*, vol. XIV: 107):

> The club or shinty used formerly to be much played on Christmas and New Year's Day O. S.; but this pastime is now almost abandoned to the boys ... the practice has now almost totally died away.

It is also clear that many people held the clergy themselves responsible. In an address to the Gaelic Society of Glasgow in 1890 on 'Social Life in the Highlands', John G. MacKay, Gaelic activist and land politician, railed against the ministers who were, he alleged, preventing the youth of the country from enjoying themselves (at shinty and caber-tossing and the like) and engaging in 'manly exercises in a rational manner' (*Transactions of the Gaelic Society of Glasgow*, vol. 1: 187–91).

Alexander Macdonald in his famous paper on historical and traditional aspects of shinty, presented to the Gaelic Society of Inverness, also pointed the finger at the clergy. He said, quoting the famous Gaelic scholar Dr Alexander MacBain (*Transactions of the Gaelic Society of Inverness*: vol. XXX: 47):

> The great shinty matches took place on winter holidays, and the greatest day for it was New Year's day. Till late in the 18th century it used to be played to and from the Church, but the wave of Puritan piety that rolled over the Highlands about 1750 put an end to Sunday shinty, and, indeed, did much to destroy not only shinty but all manner of Highland sports, both outdoor and indoor. Still, shinty held on.

In many districts, the game had virtually died out however towards the middle of last century, but tended to continue in places such as Badenoch, Lochaber and Strathglass. There was perhaps no better example of the extensive system of patronage operated by the landed gentry than in Badenoch where Cluny MacPherson and the Grants of Rothiemurchus frequently entertained their tenants at the annual *cluidh-ball* (ball play). Elizabeth Grant (1898: 267–8), for example, described the ba' – 'our Scotch substitute for cricket, the hockey of the Low country' – which was obviously shinty, thus:

> The Highlanders are extremely fond of this exciting sport, and continue it for hours on a holiday, exhibiting during the progress of it many feats of agility. There are always spectators in the crowds applauding the fine strokes, many of the women taking a pride in the success of their particular

friends at the Ba' playing. Our people kept up the game till dark, when all the men, above a hundred, went to dinner in the barn, a beef and several sheep having been killed for them.

In R. C. MacLagan's important *The Games and Diversions of Argyleshire* (1901) we find as part of a fifteen-page section on the history of camanachd – *cluich air a chaman* – one of the earliest written 'definitions' or descriptions of what shinty was perceived to be. Shinty's significance in the overall celebration of New Year may be gauged from this, part of the preamble to a detailed description of the preparation for play on the island of Islay (MacLagan, 1901: 27–8):

> It is still in the recollection of some when there were here gathered on New Year's morning crowds of players, cheered by the presence of six or seven pipers, play being carried on during the whole day, with the late Lairds of Islay and of Balinaby superintending, of course, both in the kilt, as was the fashion with Campbell of Islay. One reciter has lively recollections of two men, MacNiven and MacLauchlan, both old and grey-haired at the time, but recognized as distinguished players, taking a prominent part. They divested themselves of nearly every article of clothing; their feet were bare, with a handkerchief tied round their heads, yet wet with perspiration.

One other vivid account of shinty's role in the celebration and tradition of New Year appears in Volume 3 of F. Marian McNeill's, *The Silver Bough* – a lengthy description of the ritual of Hogmanay guisers which McNeill (1961) claims as 'one of the most ancient and curious pagan survivals in Scotland'.

> Hogmanay of the Sack,
> Hogmanay of the Sack,
> Strike the hide,
> Strike the hide.
> Hogmanay of the Sack,
> Hogmanay of the Sack,
> Beat the skin,
> Beat the skin.

McNeill (1961: 93) goes on to detail how no less a personage than Dr Samuel Johnson also came across shinty at New Year. In his *Journey to the Western Isles* (1776) he mentions this 'old game', which he was told was played on New Year's Eve at the hall or castle of the Laird. It is described by his companion, James Boswell, who perceived shinty as a 'curious custom' rather than an intrinsically sporting occasion.

The *Oban Times* of 8 January 1870 devoted no less than eighteen column inches to an interesting article on 'New Year Customs in the West Highlands'. As many as forty people with sticks would do the Calluinn (Hogmanay) round of the houses in the locality. The grand finale is the shinty match, involving as many as 2000 people, 'usually about 10 a.m. on New Year's morning'.

> Usually the stakes were simply the honour of either half of the district, but occasionally a hogs-head of whiskey was given to the winners by the proprietor. This liberality led to such scenes of drinking, and sometimes of fighting, that in recent years he wisely refrained from a present in the train of which were consequences so disagreeable.

It is clear that across the Highlands at this point, New Year was being celebrated in a time-honoured fashion. The low point of mid-century was eventually overtaken by a fervent rush of Celtic awareness and the desire for the upper or middle classes once again to exert their traditional rights. Order and organization became the order of the day and the spontaneity of previous celebrations was set aside. R. C. MacLagan declares that in Argyllshire, which was not noted as an evangelical area, shinty was played (1901: 27):

> to a considerable extent all December and January. But on New Year's Day great crowds turned out to the various shinty fields, all ages, boys, young men, and even men of sixty and upwards.

One of the earliest newspaper references to a New Year celebration involving shinty is to be found in the *Edinburgh Evening Courant*, which reported in January 1821 that:

> On Tuesday last, one of the most spirited camack matches witnessed for many years in this country (Badenoch), where that manly sport of our forefathers has been regularly kept up during the Christmas festivities, took place in the extensive meadows below the inn of Pitmain. On Christmas and New Year's Day matches were played in the policy before the house of Drakies, at the camack and football, which were contested with great spirit.

In the *Inverness Courier* of 18 January 1826, it is reported that a 'camanach' match had taken place in Strathglass:

> Upwards of 150 Chisholms and other natives of Strathglass had their usual match at Shinty. The match was betwixt the Braes and the Strath. The Braes men supported the character for superior activity and expertness, which they are said to possess, and though less numerous carried the day.

The whole collapse of Highland society in the nineteenth century due to the most hostile of circumstances was reflected in the parallel decline of the game. A dispirited, downtrodden and fever-ridden population had little reason to celebrate and less energy for shinty. Notwithstanding the poverty and distress of the bulk of the population, however, what was obviously the annual New Year play was still maintained in some areas. New Year camanachd was clearly very much part of the tradition in the Western Isles. A significant corpus of material survives in the oral tradition, most notably the Uist story of the 'Spectre Arbiter' (*Celtic Monthly*, January 1893). At the end of January 1895 'a friendly game' was played on the Sollas machair in North Uist (*Oban Times*, 26 January 1895):

> After likely play for two hours, the match concluded in a draw – two goals to each team. Players and spectators were then supplied with refreshments through the liberality of Mr Orde. A dance followed (before leaving the playground) to the stirring music of the bagpipes, played by Mr Angus MacDonald, Middlequarter. Mr Orde proposed to try a friendly game on an early date with a team from the west side of the island, which was agreed to with applause. To show him how his interest to keep up one of the oldest Highland games was appreciated, Mr Orde was carried off the field shoulder high.

It is remarkable that shinty survived at all, far less exploded on a more or less unsuspecting public towards the end of the century. It is quite clear from contemporaneous accounts that shinty was of much wider interest and importance than just being the expression of some local conflict, or a landlord's patronage. The view from outside, one of the fullest in the nineteenth century, was as follows in the *Penny Magazine* of 31 January 1835. Produced by the Society for the Diffusion of Useful Knowledge, its cover provides us with an early visual representation of the game, remarking that shinty has a 'considerable resemblance to that which is denominated "hurling" in England'.

> The writer witnessed a match, in which one of the players, having gained possession of the ball, contrived to run a mile with it in his hand, pursued by both his own and the adverse party until he reached the appointed limit, when his victory was admitted. Many of the Highland farmers join in with eagerness in the sport, and the laird frequently encourages by his presence this amusement of his labourers and tenants.

Compare, however, this 'outsider's' view of a New Year match between a number of parishes in Sutherland, also dated 1835 (*Shinty Yearbook*, 1975–6: 25–7):

By order of the Countess of Sutherland, they were served on the field when done with plenty bread and whisky. The proceedings did not all terminate here, for beside the burn at Golspie Inn there were two whole stalled oxen roasted with horns and hoofs on – of course the hide and entrails were cleared away, that was all. Whisky was served and drunk out of bowls, the ox was cut up and a slice of bread given to any that would take it.

These accounts detailed above show that the patronage offered by the lairds and gentry was well established across the Highlands, and indeed Scotland, in the nineteenth century and particularly at New Year. Sir Aeneas MacKintosh describes the camack or shinty matches as follows, in 'Notes Descriptive and Historical, Principally relating to the Parish of Moy in Strathdearn', written in 1892 (Grant, 1960: 90):

Playing at Shiney is thus performed – an equal number of men drawn up on opposite sides, having clubs in their hands, each party has a goal, and which party drives a wooden ball to their adversaries goal, wins the game, which is rewarded by a share of a cask of whiskey, on which both partys get drunk. This game is often played upon the ice, by one parish against another, when they come to blows if intoxicated, the players legs being frequently broke, may give it the name of Shiney.

In 1873, the *Oban Times* was reporting that on New Year's Day, despite some atrocious weather, games were played in Ardgour, Tobermory, Ballachulish, Acharacle and Kilninver. The fact that these matches were reported in such a way, may suggest that the events were the exception rather than the rule. Meanwhile, a year later, no less than forty to fifty men contested a New Year's Day match at Ballachulish for two and a half hours (see also, for example, the *Oban Times*, 11 January 1873; 17 and 24 January 1874), while on Skye 'scores of shinty players were at once on the fields, and not till dusk did they finally cease'.

The same paper reported just a few months later, without making any connection between the distress and the celebrations, that 'the island is gradually becoming an intolerable place for human beings to live in', as they departed in droves for New Zealand. Meanwhile, *The Times* of London and the *Glasgow Daily Herald* carried a report of a match at Inveraray, refereed by John Francis Campbell, detailing how 'genuine Fenians of the old breed occupy their leisure in their native land'. There were thirty-nine men on each team for what was to be 'a peaceful battle between dwellers on opposite sides of the beautiful loch'.

For hundreds of years a shinty match has been played beside the old pillar at the New Year; but this was something more important than usual, and the excitement was in proportion. Lords and labourers, volunteers and their officers, farmers and burgesses, fishermen, shepherds, tradesmen, all armed with shinties, clustered about the old stone, and stripped to their work, while spectators clustered under the trees, and hung in clumps on the turf slopes, wherever a view of the coming battle could be best obtained (*Oban Times*, 6 January 1868).

Chaotic scenes obviously developed at some matches at New Year, strong drink was nearly always taken, and there were few rules, if any. It was only when the Camanachd Association was formed in 1893 that matches were regularized. It was perfectly possible to celebrate the New Year in the customary fashion, and it should not be assumed that all New Year matches ended up as orgies of violence and destruction: aqua vitae, does, however, appear to have been the common catalyst. On the Machair in Colonsay, on Cnoc nan Gall ('The Hill of the Strangers'), where the golf course was eventually situated (Grieve, 1923: 298),

> on each New Year's Day, the game of eomain (sic), or shinty, was played. It was a time of festivity and rejoicing, and on these occasions it was considered necessary to have whisky for the refreshment of the players and their friends. The keg containing the aqua was set up on the top of Cnoc nan Gall.

It was also possible to conduct New Year shinty matches in perfectly good order in the urban setting, for example, in the city of Glasgow. One of the most vivid accounts of matches played towards the end of the nineteenth century survives in a collection of songs composed by *Màiri Mhòr nan Oran,* Mary MacPherson of Skye. On Old New Year's Day, 1876, the Gaels of Greenock challenged their compatriots of Glasgow to a shinty match, which was repeated the following year, at sixty-a-side.

In a letter to John MacLean, Bernisdale, Màiri Mhòr tells how she was 'blinded with perspiration' as she baked bannocks for the occasion.

Chan fhacas a riamh,
A leithid de thriall,
Air sràidean Ghrianaig cò-lamh ann.

There has never been seen
A throng of its kind
Conjoined on the streets of Greenock.

We go tomorrow to Queen's Park – three score strong Highland lads; thirty in the kilt, and thirty in knickerbockers, with their sticks on their shoulders, pipers before and after them. And I with a horse and cart full of creels of bannocks, kebbocks of cheese as big as the moon, and a drop of Ferintosh to put spirit in the lads. (*Dàin agus Orain Ghàidhlig le Màiri Nic-a-phearsain,* 1891: 183.)

There was also a very active urban shinty scene beyond Hadrian's Wall in the nineteenth century. This was at its most vibrant during the festive season, particularly in the 1870s and the two decades thereafter (*Shinty Yearbook*, 1890: 53, and *Highlander*, 6 January 1877). The Manchester Camanachd Club, for example, held interclub matches on Christmas and New Year's Days, and they also played a 30-a-side game against a local Scottish organization, the Manchester and Salford Caledonian Club on Christmas Day, 1877 (*Highlander*, 5 January 1878).

Two years later, the Lowlanders in Birmingham challenged the Highlanders there to play at Aston Park on Christmas Day, with even numbers on each side. The Highlanders won 6–0. There was also a match in connection with Birmingham Celtic Society on the 27th at Sutton Park, which resulted in a draw. 'A good number' were present 'on a very wild day'.

Shinty in its organized form has come a long way since it fought to survive in the glens of the Highlands and much further afield, in public parks as far from its main heartland as Wimbledon, Manchester, and even in Aberdeen, where the North of Spey Club met on the links on 1 January 1849 'for conducting the long established Celtic game' (*Inverness Courier*, 11 January 1849). But it is clear that in fact shinty play at New Year had a world-wide dimension, impinging on a foreign consciousness even at the end of last century (*Celtic Monthly*, vol. V, 1896: 64): 'in the "land of brown heath and shaggy wood," the southern cities, or in distant lands across the sea.'

When the settlers from Wester Ross arrived in Pictou, Nova Scotia in 1773, aboard the *Hector*, there was a piper in the company (MacKay, 1980). I doubt, however, if the assembled masses had had the opportunity, the time, or the inclination, to pack shinty sticks amongst their meagre possessions. But once they got to Canada and Australia they took up where they left off at home in many respects. Clearly there was no shortage of trees to inhibit the settlers in Canada. Their sports and pastimes were, after all, just about all they had in the face of extreme adversity. And we know this from the store of songs which have survived. Thus it is confirmed that it wasn't just in the Highlands of Scotland that New Year or the *Calluinn* was celebrated.

In the summer of 1995 in Mabou, Cape Breton Island, Effie Rankine of North Uist recited for me a version of '*Tiugainn a dh'iomain*' her mother had learned in North Uist.[2] She also gave me this short verse from Mabou, which shows how the tradition survived on the other side of the Atlantic:[3]

> Oidhche Chullainn, Challainn, chruaidh
> Thàinig mi le'm dhuan gu tigh
> Mis' Alasdair Mac Iain Mhòir
> Gabhaidh mi mòran leis a mhòran
> Gabhaidh mi an t-ìm leis an aran
> Agus gabhaidh mi an t-aran leis fhèin
> A'chailleach chòsagach, chòsagach
> Na geàrr d' òrdag
> leig a staigh mi.

The despair of the Gaels in Canada given their situation, the maintenance of tradition in the face of complete adversity and the natural longing for home through their songs, is also reflected in what survives of the Highland and Gaelic tradition in Australia. Many Gaelic/ Highland/ Scotch/ Scottish/ Caledonian Societies flourished and were the conduit for the cultural anchors the emigrants put down – figuratively, if not in fact.

It is clear, despite the claim that in Australia, 'shinty itself is unknown' (Prentis, 1987: 119) that shinty was, in fact, one of the cultural anchors which sustained life there. The game survived, in some shape or form, well into this century. Malcolm Prentis's view of shinty may be somewhat dismissive, but he may be forgiven to some extent for making the assumption that the 'broiling heat' of an Australian New Year was not conducive to the celebration of the *Calluinn* with *caman* in hand. Early settlers such as Niel Black from Argyll evidently thought it so, as he tells us in his diary entry for 1 January 1840 (La Trobe Library, Melbourne):

> The mode in which the New Year was welcomed out here was to keep up a constant firing ... but was not troubled with first footing. We had a quiet New Year, different indeed from any I had ever seen before. It would have been hard work here to play the Shinty or dance in the heat we have had at present but I thought it might be done.

From the earliest years of their settlement in Australia, Scots were conscious of their distinctiveness and were quite deliberate in maintaining this. New Year provided the settlers with the perfect vehicle to express their 'Scottishness' right through to, and beyond, the turn of this century. Geelong in Victoria had its own society which was established by Highlanders to maintain the culture and traditions of their people: Comunn na Feinne (Fingalian Society) which lasted from 1850 to the 1940s.[4] The Comunn na Feinne Highland Gathering on New Year's Day

soon became the premier festival event for the Geelong district. The first
Gathering in 1857 commenced at 12 o'clock noon precisely and was
advertised thus (*Geelong Advertiser*, 22 December 1856):

> Sports at Inverleigh, on New Year's day – Races! Shinty!! Highland Games!!
> A splendid hog's skin saddle and bridle, and jockeys whip and spurs &c to be
> run for. Open to all horses. After which, great Shinty Match and other sports.

CÙ CHULAINN, THE CAMAN AND THE CALLUINN

From the middle of last century, shinty play during the festive period was
very much part of the Highland social scene, even if the 'sons of the Gael',
scrambling to survive against the depredations of landlords and the
catastrophic effects of the great famine in the Highlands, might not have
recognized much of the ancient and noble game. Conchobar or Cù
Chulainn might not either, or would they?

It was in the rural areas of the Highlands that the tradition of playing
shinty at New Year survived best, particularly and towards the end of the
century, following a period of almost terminal decline. The accounts of
shinty play at New Year preserved in the *Celtic Monthly,* the *Celtic
Magazine,* the columns of the press (particularly the *Highlander, Oban
Times, Northern Chronicle* and *Inverness Courier)* and elsewhere have all
contributed to the survival of shinty as a meaningful part of Celtic, Gaelic
and Highland culture.

New Year matches are still a regular feature of festive celebrations. The
most enduring example of the tradition is probably the Lovat Cup match,
played first of all between Lovat and Beauly in 1904. Presented for play
between the two clubs by Lord Lovat, (the first President of the
Camanachd Association) the challenge match was originally played on
Christmas Day but eventually became a New Year fixture, with games
recorded at Beaufort Castle, home of Lord Lovat, as early as 1850.

The playing of New Year matches has, in recent years, undergone
something of a revival. Games have been played in Lewis, Skye,
Glenorchy, Oban and Fort William (between Masonic lodges), sometimes
in curious if not bizarre circumstances. In Kyleakin, for example, in the
immediate post-war period, the married and single men met in a challenge.
Unique to the Kyles of Bute, however, was the meeting on New Year's
Day of the 'Sleeve Waiscoats' and the 'Powder Monkeys', the former local
boys who worked on the yachts during the sailing season, the latter
workers at the Powderworks at Millhouse; and in Fort William the
'Teetotallers' played the 'non-Teetotallers'.

The shinty players still participating in New Year festivities are indulging in a 'time-honoured tradition'. Few would recognize the historical pedigree of the events they celebrate, usually as 'a most effective way of clearing people's brains after their libations'.

Wherever the celebrations, in Ireland in the sentiments expressed in the song 'Airdi Cuan' or elsewhere, the celebration of the Calluinn with the caman was a universal cultural experience shared by Celts.

> Is iomai Nollaig 'bhi me fèin
> I mbun abhann Doinne is me gun chèill
> ag iomain air an trà bhàn
> is mo chaman bàn I mo dhorn liom.[5]

There's no game ever I saw I could compare to shinty. Talk about cricket, that's nothing to it. Shinty was suited to a New Year's day; it kept the spirits up and the body warm. (*Celtic Magazine*, **1** (1896)

NOTES AND ACKNOWLEDGEMENTS

1. Littlejohn Album, Aberdeen University, Special Collections Section. My thanks to Brendan Harvey, Belfast, for his assistance in the preparation of this chapter.
2. See also John L. Campbell, *Songs Remembered in Exile* (1990: 80–1), for a Cape Breton version of the song, dating from 1937. A similar version is to be found in *Tales until Dawn* by John Shaw (p. 390). A Mull version is held in the archives of the School of Scottish Studies (SA 1953/70/A4); see also MacLagan (1901), pp. 32–4, for further variations.
3. Translation of verse: 'I have come here to the house with my verse/I am Alasdair son of big John/I will take anything you offer/I will take butter with the bread/or I will take bread with nothing on it/O long-coated old woman/don't cut your finger/let me in.'
4. My thanks to Dr Cliff Cumming, Deakin University, Geelong, for his assistance here.
5. Thanks to Brendan Harvey for bringing this verse to my notice; also the article 'New Year Old Style in the Highlands', from which the following quotation was extracted.

8

THE GAELIC ATHLETIC ASSOCIATION AND ORGANIZED SPORT IN IRELAND

Marcus de Búrca

MICHAEL CUSACK, THE GAA AND THE CELTIC DIASPORA

In the opening chapter of *Scottish Sport in the Making of a Nation*, Jarvie and Walker (1994: 7) advanced a set of six interconnected propositions. In summary form, the principal arguments advanced there were that sport can be an instrument of national unity, can help to consolidate cultural nationalism and national consciousness, and can contribute to the search for cultural identity. In this chapter I hope to show how these arguments taken together were exemplified in Ireland in the second half of the nineteenth century through the foundation in 1884 of the Gaelic Athletic Association (GAA), which for almost all of the twentieth century has been the biggest and most influential of Irish sports bodies. In particular, this chapter will demonstrate how these ideas dominated the thought and actions of the founder of the GAA, Michael Cusack, whose influence on the subsequent foundation and development of the modern Irish nation state has in my opinion been understated. Instead of being, as he is widely portrayed, merely an early advocate of Irish field games – and, incidentally, the prototype of The Citizen in a memorable episode of James Joyce's *Ulysses* – he had, I will argue, a much broader agenda which at a vital stage of his life and intermittently thereafter embraced the whole Celtic diaspora. That he failed to realize this dream was due in large part to his own chequered career in the GAA and to the eclipse of the GAA in the 1890s, but also to a lesser degree to an apparent lack of commitment to Cusack's Celtic cultural agenda by the Scottish community in Dublin just over a century ago.

To appreciate the magnitude and scale of Cusack's achievement in the last two decades of the nineteenth century, and his lasting impact on Irish cultural development to this day, one has merely to look back at the state of sport in Ireland in the first half of that century. As late as 1850 none of the three major football codes now so widely played and followed in Ireland was played there on an organized basis. Soccer reached Ireland via Belfast in the late 1870s. Rugby, though played in Ireland from the 1850s, was not properly organized until the foundation in 1879 of the Irish Rugby Football Union. What became Gaelic football only took off on an organized basis after the foundation in 1884 of the GAA.

As for the national (or more correctly Celtic) game of hurling (which is similar to shinty and was also played in the Isle of Man, see Chapter 11), it suffered a disastrous decline in the decades following Irish famines of the late 1840s. Back in the late 1700s it had enjoyed a boom period when it was sponsored on a semi-professional basis by some Anglo-Irish landlords, a class just then going through its own cultural identity crisis (O Caithnia, 1980). However, a deterioration in landlord–tenant relations in the early 1800s ended this boom. Consequently by the 1870s, shortly before Cusack's intervention, this Celtic version of the ancient ball game played with sticks was well-nigh extinct except in widely scattered pockets of remote parts of Ireland (de Búrca, 1980: 3–6). Two other factors had hastened the near-demise of hurling: the impact of the famines on rural areas and the consequent mass migration (mostly to the United States) from the Irish countryside.

As for athletics, a similar decline had occurred in the first half of the 1800s. Such sparse evidence as has survived suggests that unorganized rural sports, with traditional events like weight-throwing, often actively encouraged by well-disposed rural landlords, were common until the 1840s. But then famine, migration and increased agrarian tensions also killed them off. Writing his memoirs in the 1870s, the Home Rule MP and journalist, A. M. Sullivan, recalling the effects of the famine on ordinary folk, commented: 'Their ancient sports and pastimes disappeared and in many parts . . . have never returned. The outdoor games, the hurling match . . . are seen no more' (Sullivan, 1877: p. 68). Inside a decade, however, Michael Cusack changed all this.

From the 1850s a change came, and athletics (both on the track and across country) led the way in the growth of modern sports in Ireland. Even more surprisingly, the revival came in large part from the Protestant community (overwhelmingly non-nationalist in outlook) in the larger towns and cities, as well as from the rising white-collar classes, also mainly of unionist persuasion. Trinity College Dublin, founded in the Elizabethan era to propagate the new state brand of Christianity, had its Dublin University Athletic Club from 1857 (de Búrca, 1989: 44–5). It was, however another ten years before a second club appeared in the capital in the shape of the Civil Service Athletic Club, whose members were as loyal to the political establishment as their rivals in the nearby university (ibid.). But rural Ireland, where traditional amateur athletic contests had been common until the late 1840s, appears to have joined this revival too. It is true that the Irish provincial press rarely carried reports of sports meetings before the 1870s. But the case of Michael Cusack himself, who participated in running, jumping and weight-throwing from at least his period as a teacher in Co. Galway from 1867 to 1871, shows that – assuming they had ever become wholly extinct – rural athletics in Ireland were at last on the way back.

However, it was Dublin which led the revival. There in 1871 and 1872 respectively were founded the Irish Champion Athletic Club (ICAC) and the Dublin Amateur Athletic Club, the former significantly having started life as the Royal Irish Athletic Club. The ICAC was different from the others in that it assumed the role of a governing body for athletics, awarding prestigious medals at its annual championship meeting, held from 1873 at the sports ground in Lansdowne Road which for over a century now has been the headquarters of the IRFU, and more recently the venue for all international soccer games played in Dublin (de Búrca, 1989: 44–5). In addition, unlike the others, the ICAC drew members from a wider pool which included students from the four Queen's Universities (in Dublin, Cork, Belfast and Galway) and also from some of the exclusive (Protestant) High Schools in the Greater Dublin area.

CLASS, IRISH ATHLETICS AND MICHAEL CUSACK

It was into this exciting scene – exciting, that is, for one who had been an enthusiastic field and track athlete from his teens – that the 27-year-old schoolteacher from the remote Burren area of Clare, Michael Cusack, arrived in 1874. Having taught in various Irish provincial locations (including Galway, Down, Kilkenny and Kildare), he had just secured a post in the new French College at Blackrock near Dublin (so called because it had been founded by a French Catholic religious order), which from that moment was destined to become the cradle of Irish rugby (de Búrca, 1989: 29–31). Although he is known to have competed at athletics meetings in Dublin in 1875, soon after his arrival in the capital city he became involved in the management (and hence the politics) of Irish athletics. From the start he was critical of what he saw; not yet obvious to those he criticized was the fact (or at least the probability) that Cusack had another agenda, of a distinctly political as well as cultural nature.

In truth, there was much to be critical of in the world of amateur athletics in Dublin of the mid-1870s. For one thing, it had a distinct anglophile atmosphere – something about which, though it must have jarred on his nationalist upbringing, Cusack did not initially complain. What did irk him, however, was the exclusive elitist set-up – something intolerable to an athlete who had for a decade or more been accustomed to a mixture of the classes and a distinctly non-political atmosphere at rural athletics meetings he had participated in all over Ireland. There landlord and tenant, white-collar youth and farm labourer, nationalist and unionist athlete, all put aside for one day each week the cultural, political and religious differences that separated them on the other six days. This was what Michael Cusack had become used to since 1867, whether it was in the local school (built by one of the titled gentry but managed by a Catholic priest) in Galway, the Catholic seminary in Newry, the exclusive Protestant Kilkenny College or the equally exclusive Catholic boys school (later to welcome James Joyce) in Kildare – at all of which he had taught before he settled in Dublin in 1874.

But there was even more to the Dublin athletic scene that Cusack disliked (de Búrca, 1989: 49–50). He found practices being tolerated at meetings there that went close to making a mockery of amateur sport. Betting was going on openly; handicaps were fixed so as to favour friends of organizers or officials; money prizes were commonly awarded; results were often rigged in advance. At one 'fashionable' meeting in Trinity College's College Park rioting broke out which forced the authorities to ban the next fixture. Little wonder that Cusack began to protest, first semi-privately and discreetly as befitted a newcomer to the city, but gradually in blunter more critical language and eventually in the columns of the sporting press. No wonder, too, that he began to associate what passed for amateur athletics with the political outlook of those in charge.

For the moment, however, business in the shape of his chosen profession of teaching came first with Cusack. In the autumn of 1877 he opened his own 'grinding' school in Dublin – Cusack's Academy, as it soon became known. To it came young men anxious to pass the entry examinations for the Irish, British and Indian civil services (including Dublin, London and Edinburgh court offices), the police force, the commissioned ranks of the army and the teaching and medical professions. Soon he became known as the city's best 'grinder', employing other grinders and moving to larger premises as his roll-book grew and earning an astonishingly high income by the standards of the time. Significantly it was from Trinity College – the cradle of modern Irish athletics – that Cusack drew many of his pupils, so that one may surmise that getting involved in athletics paid off (de Búrca, 1989: 39). Similarly one may question if the motive for affiliating his academy rugby team to the IRFU from 1880 to 1883 (ibid.: 43) was solely to benefit the health of his students!

During his first five years in Dublin one finds Cusack being in several athletic clubs, including French College Club – for a few years he was an avid cricket fan – and Trinity College Rowing Club. Then in 1879, after an absence from athletics for a couple of years, he returned to accept an offer of a seat on the council of the prestigious IAAC, the first body to try to introduce an orderly management system into Irish athletics. A year later he was a prominent member of another new club, the Cross Country Association of Ireland, and later still a member of the City and Suburban Harriers. By then the IAAC, as a result of some internal dispute (in which Cusack was involved) had been wound up. Then in 1882 Cusack was a founder of yet another club, the Dublin Athletic Club, intended to replace the IAAC, the DAAC and the CSAC, all of which had now come to grief (de Búrca, 1989: 55).

In all of these clubs Cusack tried to clean up Irish athletics, to restore to it the genuine amateur status it had enjoyed for perhaps a decade or more after its revival in the mid-1850s. One of his commonest pleas was for the restoration to programmes of traditional events like weight throwing and high jumping. That he had to move from one club to another suggests that he met with opposition – whether from those running athletics in Dublin who were unwilling to loosen their grip, or whether because of Cusack's blunt aggressive manner (often accompanied by spontaneous nationalist outbursts) is difficult to state. Personal attacks on fellow athletics officials at meetings or in the press can hardly have endeared him even to the substantial number of such officials who were in agreement with his ideas for reform. Nor can his persistent calls to open amateur athletics to what the Victorians would have called artisans have gained him unqualified sympathy from athletics officials mostly drawn from the professional and white-collar classes.

A series of three articles which Cusack contributed in 1881 to the Dublin unionist weekly, *Irish Sportsman*, gives a fair idea of his views, at least up to 1882 (*Irish Sportsman*, 9 April 1881; 2 July 1881; 1 October 1881; for authorship see *Irish Sportsman* 10 June 1881 and *Irish Weekly Independent* 1902, Christmas Supplement: 29). Starting on a low key, he deplored the recent decline in athletics, which he forecast would lead to a decline in public morality, a view he held all his life. Once again he advocated the restoration of traditional events in jumping and weight throwing. Then, concealing his nationalist outlook beneath a veneer of liberalism, he argued that sport should be a unifying factor in a country like Ireland where political differences were fundamental; 'the platform of sport', he said, should be kept 'clear of the party spirit'. Implicit in this series (as in all his thinking since his arrival in Dublin in 1874) was the desire to see nationalist youth being given a place in athletics – just as he had seen conceded all over the provinces before he moved to Dublin.

As the 1870s gave way to a new decade Cusack, now campaigning for reform of athletics for six years and becoming gradually more frustrated by continued opposition to his ideas, suddenly changed course. The year 1882 in particular was significant for him in another sphere of activity – the promotion of the Irish language, a cause dear to his heart, as one brought up as a monoglot in his native Clare. When in 1879 the moderate Society for the Preservation of the Irish Language split, with the more active of its members founding the Gaelic Union for the Preservation and Cultivation of the Irish Language, Cusack sided with the new GU and played a leading role in November 1882 in the launch of the *Gaelic Journal*, a weekly publication regarded ever since as the start of the modern Irish language revival movement, which by the end of the century had acquired political undertones (de Búrca, 1989: 62).

The effect of this success was to convince Cusack that it was time for him to break with the ruling Dublin athletics clique (as he saw it) and to campaign for a new athletics body to take control of track and field sport for nationalists. As it happened, this decision coincided with – perhaps was influenced by – a revival in Dublin of the game of hurling (for a discussion of the game of hurling in the Old and New World, see Chapter 11), called hurley by its supporters (de Búrca, 1989: 64). Suddenly, it seems, Cusack decided to combine his efforts in athletics with a move to revive hurling. Thus in due course, after several false starts, was born in 1884 the Gaelic Athletic Association for the Preservation and Cultivation of National Pastimes, shortly afterwards abbreviated to the GAA.

Just how formidable was the opposition Cusack had encountered in Dublin athletics in the 1870s may be seen in the subsequent history of Irish athletics. Early in 1885, within months of the start of the GAA, the Irish Amateur Athletic Association was established in Dublin in direct opposition to the GAA, its principal officers those who had been Cusack's main opponents in the 1870s (de Búrca, 1989: 115). Catering mostly for non-nationalist youth and confined largely to provincial towns containing white-collar athletes mostly of unionist background, the IAAA lasted for almost 40 years, until the establishment in 1922 (following the setting up of the Irish Free State) of the National Athletics and Cycling Association (de Búrca, 1989: 71). This latter, expressly formed to permit the new Irish State to compete in the Olympics, replaced the IAAA and the Athletics Council of the GAA, both of which handed over control of amateur athletics in

Ireland to the new NACA, which was then recognized by the Irish Olympic Council.

A NEW DEPARTURE, NATIONALIST POLITICS AND THE CELTIC DIASPORA

Some time in late 1882 Cusack abandoned hope of reforming Irish athletics from within and decided to try from without. It is indeed arguable that had he not made this decision, there would never have been any GAA. Instead, at most a new Irish athletics body, in which unionists and nationalists would have shared control, would have been formed. Instead, too, hurling, to which Cusack now turned his attention, would have become the preserve of those (including a Trinity College law student named Edward Carson) then promoting the (to Cusack) genteel game of hurley. And since the promotion – some would argue the invention – of what became Gaelic football also became part of Cusack's plans, it is also arguable that this brand of football (now by far the most popular in Ireland) might never have been revived and codified.

Although he always insisted that what had forced him to change course in 1882 was his failure to overcome resistance to his reform plan from 1874, it is clear that this was not the whole truth. For one thing, Cusack's own abrasive or confrontational personality was not calculated to win converts to his ideas. Even if one accepts that there is some element of caricature in Joyce's portrayal of the Citizen in *Ulysses*, it is hard to see how such a character could have been endured for long by those in charge of athletics in Dublin in the 1870s. More importantly, even had Cusack been a more charismatic or accommodating figure, there remained the wide political gulf between him and those he had to win over to his ideas for reform of athletics. The time had simply not yet come for nationalists to have a voice – much less a dominant one – in the management of athletics, so that there was something of the inevitable about the parting of the ways which happened in 1882.

Once he made this break, Cusack's ideas began to assume a more political (for which read 'nationalist') tone. It is, of course, probable that all along he had this nationalist cultural agenda, but felt it prudent not to advocate it openly on the various sports committees he sat on in Dublin in the 1870s. Then in the early 1880s several factors came to the fore, one or more of which probably influenced him in coming out openly as a cultural nationalist. Amongst these, as already suggested, was his success in the launch of the *Gaelic Journal*. But there were others too, although it is not easy to state with certainty which were more important to Cusack.

The influence on him from 1879 of P. W. Nally, a Fenian activist and athlete from Mayo with a distinctly political agenda, cannot be exaggerated (de Búrca, 1989: 49). In the West of Ireland Nally had in 1880 successfully organized a sports meeting run by nationalists and open to all classes, precisely what Cusack tried without success to do in Dublin. Back in 1877 Nally had also publicly supported a project (which never got off the ground) to launch a new Irish athletics body. This scheme had been supported too by Maurice Davin, the internationally acclaimed Tipperary athlete destined to join Cusack in 1884 in founding the GAA. Another factor in Cusack's increasingly political outlook was his employment from mid-1882 as an educational correspondent in the weekly nationalist *Shamrock* magazine. In the widely read columns of this publication he began to expound his ideas on a wide variety of subjects of only marginal relevance to education, and continued to do so for the next 30 years, almost to his early death at the age of 59 in 1906.

Over and above these factors, however, was another which must have had even greater influence on Cusack. By the early 1880s Irish Home Rule was seriously on the agenda. With the success of the Land League as a powerful agrarian force in the West of Ireland since 1879, and the election of Parnell as chairman of the Irish Parliamentary Party at Westminster in 1880, there was an atmosphere of anticipation among Irish nationalists that some form of political devolution was just round the corner. It is against this background that Cusack's advocacy of cultural nationalism has to be seen. By a coincidence, in the very month when Cusack was deciding on the place and time of the foundation meeting of the GAA (Thurles on 1 November 1884) an event occurred to which, according to the eminent Irish-American historian Emmet Larkin, the modern Irish nation state owes its origin. In October 1884 an informal agreement was made between the Irish Catholic hierarchy and Parnell, whereby the former gave their support to the de facto Irish State set up by Parnell in 1886, in return for his acquiescence in education being permanently under clerical control (Larkin, 1976). Another 37 years were, of course, to pass before the formal establishment of an Irish State under the Anglo-Irish Treaty of 1921.

Cusack's thesis on (or perhaps programme of) cultural nationalism anticipated Arthur Griffith and Sinn Fein by twenty years. The continued British presence in Ireland had, Cusack argued, almost killed the separate Irish cultural identity. So, if (or when) some degree of legislative independence was restored to Ireland, it was in his view essential that Irish cultural identity be revived, cultivated and preserved so as to provide a kind of moral bedrock for the political freedom which Home Rule would provide. For this reason he wanted Irish athletics to be in nationalist hands, the Irish language to be fostered, Irish games to be supported and other aspects of Irish culture like music and dancing to be encouraged.

A largely forgotten feature of Cusack's ideal of a separate Irish nation was that it included the wider Celtic diaspora, particularly the Scots nation, which he claimed had close affinities with its Irish counterpart. In the course of his career in the 1870s as an athletics administrator in Dublin he had come into contact with the small but vibrant Scots community in Dublin. He struck a lasting friendship with A. Morrison Miller, founder of the Irish Caledonian Society and secretary of the Caledonian Games Association of Ireland. When in 1887, with the active assistance of Miller, Cusack launched his own new newspaper, he called it the *Celtic Times* and stated as one of its aims the preservation of the culture of 'the Celtic Race' (de Búrca, 1989: 149–64). By then the Caledonian Society in Dublin had held at least three Caledonian Games in the city – in 1884, 1885 and 1886 – at all three of which Cusack had officiated. In 1887 Cusack donated the *Celtic Times* Challenge Cup for an annual hurling versus shinty game; this took place intermittently in Dublin at least up to 1919.

Any doubt about the breadth of Cusack's vision of an independent Irish State ought to be dispelled by the extent of his interests as revealed in his weekly *Celtic Times*. This unique venture in Irish sporting journalism ran for the whole of the year 1887 and was the brainchild of both Cusack (who gave up his teaching career) and Miller. By 1887 Cusack had lost his post as Secretary (chief executive) of the GAA, having been ousted at a meeting of the GAA's executive in July 1886, which (curiously) was not attended by its first president Maurice Davin, soon also to part company for good (or ill) with the now faction-ridden Association. Even a cursory glance at the *Celtic Times* shows that its main purpose was to oppose the administration of the GAA and to restore to office both Cusack himself and his co-founder Davin.

Tabloid-size, Cusack's paper ran to eight pages per issue. Since its editor was then at odds with the GAA executive, Cusack could make no claim for his paper as an organ of the GAA in any sense; indeed, such a publication, *The Gael*, began to appear in opposition to the *Celtic Times* near the end of its short life. Thus deprived of authoritative reporting of what was going on in GAA councils or even on its playing-fields, Cusack was forced from the start to widen the scope of his paper by including much news material that had nothing to do with Gaelic games. Most of the weekly editorial columns and other commentary clearly came from his pen; not even his co-founder Davin, also then out of tune with the GAA leadership, contributed a single line to Cusack's paper.

Amongst the non-sporting topics covered by Cusack were socialism (albeit a mild version), feminism (also barely recognizable as such today), trade unionism both in Ireland and the United States, and many analyses of Irish industries, coupled with exhortations to readers to support their products. The formation of a federation of trade councils, which could affiliate internationally, was advocated. The establishment of parish libraries by teachers and clergy in rural areas was suggested, as was the revival of extinct Irish industries like lace-making, sea fisheries, bottle-making, tobacco-growing and brush-making. A visit to Belfast was reported on, with the editor's impressions of the inhabitants' Celtic traits and hard-working, even thrifty, characteristics. An analysis of the maverick American economist, Henry George, who had recently been to Ireland, was spread over two issues. An anonymous article by 'A Scottish Socialist' (possibly from the pen of Miller) with a religious bias was followed in a later issue by the full constitution and rules of the Shinty Association.

That the modern Irish nation state was created in 1922 out of the political and military struggle waged by Sinn Fein against the British administration from 1918 is a truism. Equally manifest is the fact that Sinn Fein itself was controlled from the early years of this century by a group of young or middle-aged intellectuals, who had themselves served their apprenticeship in the various cultural bodies at the end of the old century – the Gaelic League, a rejuvenated Fenian body (the IRB), the literary movement and also, of course, the earliest in time of them all, the GAA that Cusack had founded in 1884 and survived to revive again just after 1900.

To find the real origins of these bodies, one has to go as far back as the middle of the last century to the Irish language bodies he supported and then joined. However, these early 'Home Rule' bodies were not political in any sense, their leading members being ultra-conservative in both outlook and ideology and often belonging to the exclusively unionist community. Moreover, while some of Parnell's MPs could probably speak Irish, hardly any of them took part in these bodies. When in the late 1870s and early 1880s Irish nationalists became a disciplined party at Westminster, they ignored all other forms of nationalist expression or activity. Indeed, Cusack was at times concerned at, and critical of the anglified approach to affairs of Parnell's party.

It is to Cusack's credit that around this time, as he observed the rise of Parnell and his party and its impact on the administration in Dublin Castle, he appreciated the need to strengthen the political movement by providing it with a cultural backbone. Douglas Hyde, the founder of the Gaelic League in 1893, is frequently given credit for an historic statement of policy in the early 1890s on the need for 'the de-anglicisation of Ireland' (Moody and Byrne, 1982: 368). Widely overlooked, however, is the fact that through his sporting revolution and his broadly based cultural campaign that embraced not only field games but also athletics, the Irish language and industry, Cusack had been practising from 1882 what Hyde preached ten years later.

That he appreciated that his forte was in the broad cultural sphere is evident from Cusack's attitude to both wings of nationalism for the brief period when he was in a dominant position in the GAA. His selection as GAA patrons of Archbishop Croke, Parnell and Davitt (founder of the Land League) showed his recognition of the need for broad support from the nationalist leadership. Moreover, although knowing full well that his Association was being infiltrated from the start by IRB men, he took no stand against them until in 1887 when he saw them make a bid for power. Similarly, while accepting the active participation of the clergy in the GAA (many of them then actively engaged in politics) he came out vehemently against an attempted clerical take-over in 1887.

Cusack's new departure in 1882, when he abandoned co-existence with the existing athletic regime and decided to aim at a totally new athletics body controlled by nationalists, represented his considered response to the erosion, especially in the nineteenth century after the enactment of the Act of Union with Ireland Act of 1801, of the cultural identity of the nationalist majority on the island as a whole. It is at least arguable that without Cusack's pioneering efforts in building up the cultural side of nationalism in conjunction with the growth of political nationalism, there would have been no solid foundation on which either the Gaelic League of the 1890s and later the new GAA of the early 1900s (which latter rose out of the re-unification in 1900 of the parliamentary party), were able to build.

That the GAA has had a long-term impact on the character and nature of Irish cultural and political life is widely accepted. It helped to regenerate Irish rural life and gave rural Ireland a separate, defiant, self-reliant and democratic culture with a strong nationalist bias. The Association's use of the British county (shire) unit as the basis of its competitions led to the intense county loyalty which has been a feature of GAA games for a century now. To some extent Cusack's achievement has been obscured by two factors – his own eclipse by colleagues who found him difficult to work with, and later the near extinction of the GAA itself after the disastrous Parnellite split of the 1890s. However, from 1898 onwards signs of a resurgence of the nationalist spirit led both to the end (in 1900) of the split in the parliamentary party and the revival (in 1901) of the GAA itself.

Indeed, as late as that same year, only five years before his death in poverty and ill-health, Cusack failed to regain the post of chief executive of the GAA after 15 years in the wilderness by only two votes at what is regarded the 'revival' annual congress of the Association (de Búrca, 1989: 169).

Finally, it is impossible to appreciate fully the impact of Cusack's ideas both on cultural nationalism and on the importance of the nation's cultural identity without a brief look forward to what happened in Ireland only fifteen years after his death. That the new Irish State of 1922 owed much to his ideals is clear from its official policy of compulsory instruction in primary schools in the Irish language, and from the attitude of the first administration of the Irish Free State in viewing sport 'as an extension of the educational process and as a means of building character and national identity' (Keogh, 1994: 33). Nor was it any accident that (to quote from the same authority), 'The GAA emerged [in 1922] as the strongest sporting and cultural organization in the country', maintaining close links with the new administration despite the fact that many of its members regarded the settlement embodied in the Anglo-Irish Treaty of 1921 as falling short of nationalist expectations (Keogh, 1994: 34). In the subsequent 75 years since the setting up of the new state the GAA has become and remained a pillar of the new establishment, not only providing leaders for all three major political parties but also championing in the new era of professionalism and sponsorship by commercial interests, all aspects of cultural nationalism.

9

SPORTING ASSIMILATION AND CULTURAL CONFUSION IN BRITTANY

Philip Dine

INTRODUCTION

Since the publication of Eric Hobsbawm's seminal essay 'Mass-Producing Traditions: Europe, 1870–1914', a wide variety of cultural commentators have asserted the importance of organized sport as 'a medium for national identification and factitious community', and this particularly in so far as 'the rise of sport provided new expressions of nationalism through the choice or invention of nationally specific sports' (1983: 300–1). Hobsbawm's general principle has been applied to notably productive effect in the specific cases of the principal Celtic cultures of the British Isles: Ireland, Scotland, and Wales (Bairner and Sugden, 1993; Jarvie and Walker, 1994; Smith and Williams, 1980). In contrast, those cultures relegated to the periphery of this Celtic sporting centre have been less well served: the Isle of Man and Cornwall thus await their sports historians and sociologists, as, *a fortiori*, do those of the modern Spanish province of Galicia and the modern French region of Brittany. Of these seven Celtic cultures, it is the last named which will provide the focus for the present chapter.

The link between the belligerently nationalistic ideology of the French Third Republic (1870–1940) and the growth of the first of that country's modern physical recreations – military-style gymnastics – has been well documented (Holt, 1981: 39–60; Arnaud, 1987; Holt, 1995). Also numerous are those works examining the role played by modern sports spectacles such as the annual Tour de France cycle race in the establishment of a French national consciousness (Holt, 1981: 81–103; Vigarello, 1992; Greaves, 1993). Less common are those studies devoted to the role of sport in the construction of regional identities in France, with the obvious exception of the mass of material devoted to the link between rugby union and its heartland in the south-west of the country. More specifically, a serious analysis of the role of sport in the making of Breton culture remains to be conducted, and it is the intention here simply to outline some of the areas which such a study might usefully address. To that end, the discussion begins by situating Breton sport against the broader background of the economic, political, social, and, above all, cultural transformation of Brittany since 1870.

THE NATURE OF BRETON CULTURAL IDENTITY

In his autobiographical account of the impact of modernization on the hitherto rigidly traditional society of rural Brittany, Pierre-Jakez Hélias, the leading Breton-language writer of the twentieth century, looks to the advent of modern forms of physical recreation for an appropriate symbol of profound social transformation. The lasting shock produced in the 1920s by the sight of the first local woman daring to swim in the sea – her black bathing costume incongruously combined with the high white-lace head-dress famously worn by the women of the ultra-conservative Bigouden region – was such that 'I don't know why, but at least as far as I was concerned, it was on that very day that ... the modern era first dawned' (1975: 491–2; cf. Hubscher, 1992: 188). In order to understand the engagement of Hélias's traditionalist Brittany with the sporting practices so characteristic of the condition of modernity, it is necessary briefly to consider the nature of Breton cultural identity as a whole.

The slogan 'seven nations with one soul' is a neat encapsulation of the belief of Breton particularists in both Brittany's cultural identity and the continued existence of an ancient Celtic supernation, despite the general absence of local political self-determination (with the obvious, and major, exception of the twenty-six counties of the Irish Republic). However, Brittany's Celtic specificity is deeply problematic, for a variety of reasons. On the one hand, Brittany undoubtedly shares in the relative geographical isolation, and associated economic, political, and cultural marginalization, central to the experience of 'the Celtic fringe' in the modern period. Yet, on the other hand, the formal union with France which the duchy of Brittany entered into in 1532 meant that this particular Celtic culture would ultimately be the victim of an almost total assimilation by its infinitely more powerful neighbour. So while a large degree of Breton autonomy may have been retained under the monarchical *ancien régime*, the full-scale incorporation of Brittany into the main body of the nation state which emerged in the wake of the French Revolution of 1789 was inevitable in the longer term. Arguably still the most highly centralized and culturally aggressive state in western Europe, the new Republic was so determined to overcome the hostility of the traditionalist west of the country to enforced unification and homogenization that it embarked on a series of bloody military campaigns against the Catholic and monarchist counter-revolution in Brittany, together with the Vendée region on its southern border.

However, prior to the historical watershed of the Franco-Prussian war (1870), the Republican ideal of national unity was still strikingly at odds with the reality of extreme diversity to be found in the French countryside (Weber, 1977: 95–114). It thus fell to the Paris-based governments of the nascent Third Republic (1870–1940) to embark on a determined imposition of a unitary national consciousness. Basic to the Third Republic's project was a process of linguistic homogenization rooted in a centrally controlled network of state schools which dispensed free, secular, and compulsory education to all French children from the early 1880s onwards. Breton, one of the most important of the non-French mother tongues still used by a quarter of French citizens in 1870, was, predictably, gravely affected by this rapid and radical marginalization of traditional languages (Weber, 1977: 45–6). Indeed, so successful has been the state's campaign against the use of Brittany's Celtic tongue, even in its far western heartland, the so-called *Bretagne bretonnante*, that in the early 1980s no more than 700,000 Breton-speakers were estimated to exist out of a total population of some three and a half million (O'Callaghan, 1983: 151). Given that many of these speakers were old people, and that the language is not being effectively perpetuated – specifically in spite of belated government initiatives – it is hardly surprising that figures for 1992 (the latest available) indicate that less than 300,000 people now speak Breton as their mother tongue (Frémy, 1995: 922).

This is a doubly serious blow for those (overwhelmingly French-speaking) Bretons who seek nowadays to preserve Brittany's cultural identity: for not only is their 'own' traditional language in a decline which may well turn out to be terminal, but they are obliged to deal with the (overwhelmingly English-speaking) representatives of their fellow Celtic nations through the medium of a second 'colonial' language. The nature of Brittany's cultural identity, and thus Breton 'nationality', must consequently be very different in the modern era from that associated with the strongly regionally differentiated France of 1870. A key figure in the post-war reinvention of *bretonnitude*, the musician Alan Stivell, usefully draws attention to the paradox at the heart of contemporary Breton nationalism when he states that 'the Bretons who display a real Breton national feeling (subjective nationality) are those of my generation, for whom Breton is not their mother tongue: they are objectively of French nationality' (1979: 24). Underlying Stivell's telling observation is the recognition not only of the seemingly irreversible decline of the Breton language, but also of the extent of Brittany's cultural assimilation by the modern French nation state.

As a region made up of four *départements* (Côtes-du-Nord, Finistère, Ille-et-Vilaine, and Morbihan), the bulk of historical Brittany has, since 1941, been administratively isolated from its ancient capital of Nantes, now a part of the otherwise non-Breton Loire-Atlantique *département*. In spite of continuing opposition by Breton militants to this amputation (Valo, 1997), the modern administrative entity has effectively been legitimated as the appropriate location for the expression of Breton aspirations in the post-war period. Indeed, so thorough has been the cultural assimilation conducted by France since 1945 that, in so far as modern Brittany does retain a distinctively Celtic identity, that cultural specificity may properly be said to be rooted in a regionalist rather than a nationalist project. The contemporary primacy of the modern French-speaking region of *Bretagne* over the ancient Breton-speaking 'nation' of *Breizh* has its roots in the transformation of the Breton economy since 1945, which may usefully be considered in conjunction with the evolution of separatist political sentiment in this period.

From its origins in the Celtic revivalism of the nineteenth-century Romantics, the Breton nationalist movement – generally known as *Breizh Atao* or 'Brittany Forever' – has been characterized by organizational fragmentation and ideological division. Given a major boost, as was Celtic nationalism as a whole, by the accession to independence in 1922 of the Irish Free State, the autonomists' political stock was to suffer irreparable damage as a result of the decision by the movement's most extreme element to embark upon a military campaign against the 'colonial' French state in the 1930s. The age-old cleavage between *la Bretagne rouge* (the republican, anti-clerical, and left-leaning urban centres) and *la Bretagne blanche* (the monarchist, Catholic, and generally reactionary rural hinterland) became an unbridgeable gulf as the most militant of the separatists embraced the fascist movements which emerged to challenge parliamentary democracy in France as elsewhere. The pro-German line taken by *Breizh Atao* from 1937 onwards may briefly have furthered the armed struggle against France – the Germans' supply of weapons to the clandestine *Gwenn ha Du* (White and Black, the colours of the Breton flag) was apparently facilitated by the IRA's willingness to act as an intermediary (O'Callaghan, 1983: 61) – but was deemed to be unacceptable by the mass of Bretons, and even by most members of the nationalist movement. As the balance of the war swung towards the Allies in the autumn of 1943, the home-based Resistance began to make its presence felt, with leading Breton nationalists becoming targets for assassination.

These clandestine shootings were replaced by public executions as part of
the purges which followed the Liberation of France in the summer of 1944.
Such was the strength of the anti-Breton reaction in the immediate post-
war period that open political activity by the autonomist movement was
virtually non-existent before 1950.

In consequence, the first post-war attempt to give expression to Breton
aspirations would constitute a qualitative change in the region's politics.
The Comité d'Etudes et de Liaison des Intérêts Bretons (CELIB) was an
all-party pressure group committed to getting the best for Brittany out of
les trente glorieuses: the thirty glorious years of unprecedented French
economic growth and social transformation which followed the war. The
post-war era was thus characterized by a desire on the part of all those
Breton politicians not discredited by wartime collaboration to bring what
was widely regarded as a 'retarded' province into line with the rest of
France. This broad political consensus made possible a rapid and radical
transformation which saw a rural society founded on family-based
agricultural production move from an autarchic system of local economic
relations to full integration with French markets, and thus, through the
project of Europeanization, the international capitalist economy. Major
state investment in rural development and transport infrastructures –
including support for inter-Celtic initiatives such as Brittany Ferries
(establishing links with Cornwall and Ireland) – was accompanied by a
significant measure of administrative decentralization designed to encourage the industrial and tertiary sectors. The consequent rise in general
living standards was a major factor in the slowing down, if not the
complete halting, of the region's traditional demographic haemorrhaging,
with the young population henceforth seeking employment in Brittany's
urban centres. While agriculture, in a reorganized and more efficient form,
is still very significant to the region's economy – as are such traditional
employers as the fishing industry and the military (such as the navy in
Brest and the air force in Landivisiau), it is perhaps the rise of the Breton
tourist industry which epitomizes its transformation from an inward-
looking traditional society into an export-oriented free-market economy.

Political nationalism was generally unable to keep pace with this
thoroughgoing economic and social change, and has been hamstrung by its
inherent ideological confusion and organizational fragmentation. While
the 1950s did see a revival of interest in the Breton language, it was only in
the later 1960s and early 1970s that serious unrest revealed the existence of
a new 'Breton problem'. This was particularly true of the agricultural
sector, where the full impact of Brittany's integration into the French and
European economic systems finally made itself felt in milk and artichoke

'wars' sparked by reductions in the prices paid to the region's producers. If the violence of Breton farmers was sometimes suggestive of the *jacqueries* (peasant revolts) which had characterized agricultural protest in the later medieval period, it was the thoroughly modern bombing campaign waged against state targets by the Armée Républicaine Bretonne (ARB) between the mid-1960s and the late 1980s that most concerned successive French governments. Clearly inspired by the IRA, and part of a broader wave of autonomist violence which was – and continues to be – most marked in Corsica, this campaign was effectively countered, if not totally halted, by a wave of arrests and convictions in the late 1970s (O'Callaghan 1983: 87–93). With the coming to power of François Mitterrand's socialists, on a platform which included significant decentralization measures implemented in 1984, the more extreme separatists were effectively undermined. Now living lives which are typically every bit as urbanized, industrialized and/or tertiarized, and technologically mediated as those of their counterparts in other areas of metropolitan France – thanks essentially to the undeniable advances made in the period 1945–75 – the mass of the Breton population appears to be broadly satisfied with Brittany's economic and political status as a thoroughly integrated French region.

Where does this leave all those who wish to assert Brittany's Celtic specificity? More particularly, what role has sport played thus far in the cultural life of this problematic nation-*cum*-region? Will sport have a meaningful role to play in the construction of Breton identity in the future? In an attempt to answer these and related questions, we might usefully begin by considering Brittany's most traditional sport: wrestling.

BRETON WRESTLING

Breton wrestling or *ar gouren* is the most obviously 'Celtic' of the three sports which may readily be identified as sites of Breton cultural identity. A truly ancient sport, evidence for its existence dates back to the arrival of Celts in the Armorican peninsula as they sought refuge from the Anglo-Saxon invasion of the British Isles between the fourth and seventh centuries AD. The sport was certainly popular throughout the Middle Ages, when it became firmly established as a focus for and symbol of Breton specificity. So, for instance, when Pierre II, Duke of Brittany, went to pay his respects to the French king in Bourges in 1455, he was accompanied by a group of famous wrestlers (Le Joncour *et al.*, 1984: 12). However, under the combined pressures of the Third Republic's campaign against traditional (and thus regionally differentiated) cultural values, the social upheavals of the Great War, and the rapid popularization of such distinctively modern recreations as cycling and football, *ar gouren* was to retreat into the rugged westernmost district known as *Kerne* or *Cornouaille* (Kernow or Cornwall). Ominously, wrestling ceased to be a quasi-obligatory part of local church-based festivity – as had the Breton language, banned from Catholic rituals in 1903 – and particularly the age-old *pardons*: unique to Brittany, these celebrations, usually including a formal procession around the parish of the local patron saint, are still an important focus for Breton specificity to this day (Le Bris du Rest, 1976: 31–3). The decline in wrestling's importance after World War I was particularly noted by Pierre-Jakez Hélias, who comments on the sport's falling from favour with the young men of his native Bigouden region, to be replaced by 'a new game, called football' (Hélias, 1975: 436).

It was in reaction to this marked decline in wrestling's fortunes that Dr Charles Cotonnec established the Fédération des Amis des Luttes et Sports Athlétiques Bretons (FALSAB). Although other traditional sports – usually involving agriculturally based contests of weight-lifting or weight-throwing akin to those typical of the Scottish Highland games and the Basque feats of strength – undoubtedly interested Cotonnec, it was Breton wrestling which preoccupied him. A meeting in 1927 with Dr Tregoning Hooper, secretary of the Cornwall County Wrestling Association (later Cornish Wrestling Association) proved crucial in this regard. The CCWA had been founded in 1923, precisely in order to prevent the disappearance of the Cornish variety of traditional Celtic wrestling (the two versions are virtually identical, with the goal being to throw one's opponent from a standing position – an outcome known as *lamm* – and holds or moves on the ground forbidden). With Hooper's encouragement, Cotonnec organized in 1928 an inter-Celtic wrestling tournament in his home town of Quimperlé. This innovation proved highly successful, attracting 6,000 spectators and the attention of the local press. The first of many such encounters between Breton and Cornish wrestlers, the day was understandably hailed as a 'resurrection of Breton wrestling' (Le Joncour *et al.*, 1984: 15–18).

Encouraged by this success, FALSAB set about codifying and regulating the traditional sport, introducing a number of significant innovations: time limits on matches; weight categories; registered referees; licences for competitors; intermediate results decided on a points system; and the imposition of penalties for foul or dangerous play. In this modernized form, the sport was relaunched throughout Brittany. Demonstration competitions were even organized in the French capital in the early 1930s by the wrestling section of the 'Bretons de Paris' organization: an exiles' association which might well be compared with its

London Irish, Scottish, Welsh, and, indeed, Cornish counterparts. Under Cotonnec's guidance, wrestling became an obvious focus for particularist tendencies. For instance, it continued to act as a repository for the area's Celtic language, in that technical terms – such as the names of throws or the reasons given for awarding points – were kept in Breton. The *serment du lutteur* personally introduced by Cotonnec was also of considerable symbolic importance in this regard: in itself a straightforward pledge to play fair and uphold the values of the game, the *serment* was, and is still, given in Breton first and then in a French translation. However, whatever success the partisans of *ar gouren* may have had in Paris or nearer home in the interwar years was effectively undone by the onset of World War II.

In the wake of the fall of France and the German invasion in the summer of 1940, the collaborationist administration of Maréchal Philippe Pétain would favour a 'return to the soil' as part of its fascistic programme of 'National Revolution'. As far as sport was concerned, this Vichy-based regime became the first French administration – with the partial exception of the pre-war Popular Front – to seek a leading role for the state. While professional sports were either banned (in the case of rugby league) or severely restricted (in the cases of cycling and football), amateur sport was encouraged at all levels and, together with the lack of alternative forms of recreation in the dark years of the war, led to an unprecedented expansion of interest in sports of all kinds. Local and regional sports were particularly favoured at this time, both for ideological reasons and more mundanely as a result of the severe limitations on travel within an occupied and partitioned France (Gay-Lescot, 1991: 166–76). However, with the notable exception of the Basque sport of pelota (championed by Vichy's first Minister for Sport, the 'Bounding Basque' himself, former tennis champion Jean Borotra), traditional sports were not able to generate much in the way of durable public interest.

For all its encouragement of traditional games, Vichy's moral and financial investment in sport was to encourage the tendency to massification around the major modern sports that had become visible in the pre-war period. Paradoxically, the attempts made to preserve Breton traditions during the war years may actually have contributed to their post-war demise. In particular, the efforts of ethnographers like Anthony (1942) and Creston (1943) to catalogue Breton wrestling as part of a broader survey of the disappearing *folklore* of Breton-speaking Brittany may have reinforced the widespread perception, regularly bemoaned by its supporters, of the sport as essentially outmoded and fit only for survival as a museum piece. The general antipathy to Breton separatism in the immediate post-war period was, as we have seen, prompted by the pro-

German stance of a significant section of the nationalist movement. Traditional sports would be tarnished by association with the forces of political reaction before being condemned to folkloric marginality in the frenetically modernizing France of the Fourth and, especially, the Fifth Republics (respectively 1944-58 and 1958-present).

Intriguingly, Breton music and dance, local cuisine, and popular festivals such as the *fest noz* (the Breton equivalent of the *ceilidh*) would not, for their part, be condemned to archaic obscurity. On the contrary, the post-war period was marked by the founding throughout Brittany of *cercles celtiques* which sought to stimulate interest in traditional Breton costumes, songs, dances, and even games such as local varieties of bowls and skittles. The highlight of this renewed interest in Breton traditions was to become the annual Grandes Fêtes de Cornouaille, first held in Quimper in 1948, and still a major focus for Celtic culture within Brittany and beyond. The post-war reinvention of 'traditional' Breton identity would continue throughout the 1950s and 1960s just as the region's insertion into mainstream French economic, social, and political life made the cultural order which had given rise to those traditions increasingly a thing of the past. This movement undoubtedly helped to rehabilitate and rejuvenate traditional Breton culture. However, as an 'aesthetic' recuperation of what was, for all practical purposes, a dead local folklore, it was largely confined to the transplanted urban young; this as part of a character-istically modern quest for an 'authentic' cultural identity (Morin, 1967: 333–4). As such, the revival was extremely selective, and would have little time for traditional sports like wrestling. So, while the young Alan Stivell may have preferred copying out lists of related words in Breton, Gaelic, and Welsh to playing football (1979: 19), the presence even in the heart of the ultra-conservative Bigouden region of the archetypally French Café des Sports, complete with noticeboards giving the results of the region's football matches (Morin, 1967: 24), is an unmistakable indication of even this most traditional area's assimilation into the sporting mainstream by the later 1960s.

Against this background, Breton wrestling's chances of survival as anything other than a strictly minority interest were severely limited. Undoubtedly, some of the sport's administrators did still look to it as a vector for nationalist sentiment in the 1960s (Le Bris du Rest, 1976: 47); while the work done by a new generation of ethnographers based at the Musée de Bretagne (1976) and the Institut Culturel de Bretagne (1984) may have helped to publicize the ancient sport's continued existence. However, their combined proselytizing efforts were hampered by the organizational fragmentation of the sport as Cotonnec's FALSAB split into three groups all claiming responsibility for *ar gouren* in the mid-1970s. Excluded from the music-led Celtic revival of the 1960s and 1970s, traditional wrestling would number no more than 1,000 practitioners by 1976; as opposed to the 11,500 Breton *judoka*, to take only the most obviously compatible Olympic discipline (Le Bris du Rest, 1976: 46). The inter-Celtic championships may still continue, as may the traditional summer tournaments conducted *mod kozh* – 'in the old style', on sawdust rings with the fighters issuing ritual challenges as they compete for a sheep or similar prize – but this ancient sport now looks doomed to extinction. By the same token, Breton wrestling may even have its own Internet website (http://www.bretagne.com/doc/culture/lutte.htm), but today's matches are merely residual demonstrations of past cultural glories rather than genuine sporting events with anything like a mass base in the modern Breton population. For that, we have to look to the adopted 'Breton sports' of football and, above all, cycle road-racing.

BRETON FOOTBALL

Although sometimes cited as a precursor of rugby in the south-west of France, the violent traditional football known as *soule* was principally played in the north-west of the country, with Brittany one of its bastions (Lacouture, 1979: 24–6; Cadiou, 1982: 13–21). Like the ritualized, but no less vicious, gang-fights between the youths of neighbouring villages which also constituted a prominent feature of nineteenth-century Breton 'sport' (Holt, 1981: 132–4), *soule* was a profoundly serious 'game': it was closely associated with the calendar of the Catholic Church and provided a relatively controlled outlet for deep-rooted intercommunal antagonisms (Weber, 1977: 383). The codified and 'civilized' modern version of football introduced to Brittany around the turn of the century may have been markedly less violent than the traditional variety, but it would be scarcely less serious, at least as far as its intimate relationship with the Catholic Church was concerned.

As elsewhere in France, the association game was, like rugby and the rest of the athletic sports imported from Great Britain in the 1880s, initially the preserve of the privileged classes, with a leading role being played in its dissemination by school and university students, together with key institutions such as the *écoles normales* (teacher-training colleges) in major urban centres like Rennes and Nantes. As the region most strongly associated with the ancient handling game of *soule*, and, moreover, the one geographically and (at least theoretically) culturally closest to the Celtic rugby-playing nations of the British Isles – Ireland, Scotland, Wales, and even Cornwall – Brittany might have seemed an ideal base for the union code. Wrestling and other such indigenous celebrations of agricultural strength may also have been expected to produce suitable players, much as they have undoubtedly done in other parts of France with a strongly regionalized sporting culture, such as the Basque country. The early indications were that the game would, indeed, do well in Brittany: the *lycée* in Brest had a rugby team as early as 1893, one of the first school sides in France; while the Nantes rugby club actually became champions of France in 1917 (beating the great Stade Toulousain 8–3 in the Paris final). However, it was to be football which established itself durably as Brittany's principal team game, both as a participant activity and as a commercial spectacle, which explains why Jean Lacouture should refer ironically to Bretons as 'Celts with their hands cut off' (1979: 40–1).

As one of France's most traditional regions, Brittany was to be particularly affected by the antagonisms which brought Catholicism into conflict with the French state in the lead up to the disestablishment of the Church in 1905, and, indeed, until the *Union Sacrée* was forced upon a deeply divided French nation by the onset of World War I. Following the encyclical *Rerum Novarum* of 1891, which launched Pope Leo XIII's project of building a 'social Catholicism', sport in general and football in particular were to constitute privileged sites for the ideological conflict between Church and state (Holt, 1981: 190–211). Central to this process was the battle for primacy between the secular Union des Sociétés Françaises des Sports Athlétiques (USFSA) – the umbrella body established in 1887 as the sole guardian of French athletic sport, under the watchful eye of the pioneer of the modern Olympic games, Baron Pierre de Coubertin – and the Church's rival body, the Fédération Gymnastique et Sportive des Patronages de France (FGSPF). Several commentators have drawn attention to the particular success enjoyed by this youth organization in the traditionalist west of the country. As Georges Cadiou puts it, 'the FGSPF was at home in Brittany' (1995: 19), where, as Richard Holt has explained 'in general, [sports] clubs were based on the parish unit and were run by priests themselves ... [and] played a notable part in the processions and rituals of Catholicism' (1981: 197). The phenomenal recruitment of the *patronages* (Catholic youth clubs) in Brittany was initially marked by the regular organization of large gymnastics and athletics festivals throughout the region. However, football was the sport in which the Church made the principal investment of its resources, running a championship for the Breton *patronages* from the 1905–6 season onwards (Cadiou, 1995: 19). Such was the strength nationwide of the FGSPF's challenge to French football's established (and secular) authorities that not only would France have rival national football leagues in this period, but also two international football teams; a situation which was only resolved when the Catholics eventually gained control of a single united league in 1913 (Holt, 1981: 201; Wahl, 1990: 85–6).

The first Breton football clubs emerged in the early years of this century, led by Stade Rennais (known in its early days as the Stade Rennais Université Club) in 1901. The *doyen* of Breton football was joined by two more clubs in Rennes by 1903, followed by clubs in Quimper and Saint-Brieuc in 1904, and many more throughout the region by 1914. Stade Rennais's early name was an accurate indication of the club's student origins, while others such as 'les Old Boys de Dinard' and 'La Laïque d'Ernée' reflected the climate of aristocratic anglophilia and popular sectarianism of the day (Cadiou, 1982: 22–7). The leading Breton club prior to the establishment of FC Nantes in 1943, Stade Rennais would be particularly active in the campaign for a professional championship in the later 1920s and early 1930s, and was involved in clandestine payments to players before professionalism was approved by the unitary football authority, the Fédération Française de Football (FFF), in 1932 (Cadiou, 1982: 37–8). The 'red-and-blacks' first came to national prominence in 1922 when they lost the final of the French knock-out cup competition 2–0 to the prestigious Red Star club from Saint-Ouen in the Paris suburbs. In the 1930s they became a major force in the French game, although the open and attacking style with which the club became associated promised rather more than it actually delivered, with another defeat in the 1935 cup final – this time 3–0 to Olympique de Marseille – all that Stade Rennais had to show for its efforts in the interwar period. Indeed, it was only in the 1960s and early 1970s that the club would fleetingly taste national success, beginning with a 3–1 victory against US Sedan in the 1965 cup final.

The extent to which this victory, the first ever major title won by a Breton club, was perceived as a distinctively Celtic achievement is hinted at in contemporary newspaper coverage which includes photographs of Rennes supporters at the 1965 cup final with *biniou* bagpipes and *gwenn ha du* (white and black) Breton flags (Cadiou, 1982: 72). While the Rennes team sheet for the final reads much like those of many other French professional sides then and now – with 'indigenous' French names juxtaposed with those reflecting Spanish, Italian, or other Mediterranean (and thus immigrant) ancestry – the presence of a key playmaker like Marcel Loncle, a French international from nearby Saint-Malo, and Louis Cardiet, a fellow international born in Quimperlé and brought up in Lorient, ensured that the Stade Rennais team did have a significant 'home-grown' element. Even the hero of the replay, Parisian-born striker Daniel

Rodighiero chose to describe himself in 1971 as 'an adopted Breton' when recalling the club's 1965 success on the eve of their 1971 final against Lyon, which they went on to win 1–0 (Ollivier, 1980: 139). Here too there was a significant indigenous Breton presence with an old hand like Cardiet, the captain, being joined by rising star Raymond Kéruzoré from Châteauneuf-du-Faou (Finistère). Above all, the key to the club's success at this time was undoubtedly the inspirational guidance of manager Jean Prouff, a native of the Morbihan *département* and a former player for the Rennes club both as a schoolboy and as a professional (Ollivier, 1980: 235–40). The 50, 000-plus supporters (over a quarter of the city's population) who welcomed Prouff and his players home to the (modern) Breton capital in 1965, and again in 1971, are also an indication of the high level of local identification achieved by the club at this time, which, it will be recalled, was a key one both as regards the political reassertion and the cultural reinvention of Brittany's Celtic identity. The success which they came to applaud would prove to be short-lived, however, with Rennes unable to make an impact either in Europe or in subsequent domestic competitions.

The year 1965 undoubtedly marked a high point for Breton football, for not only did Stade Rennais lift the French cup, but FC Nantes became national league champions for the first of their seven times. Formed in 1943, *les canaris* (the canaries) gained promotion to the first division in 1963, alongside the great Saint-Etienne, and with *les verts* (the greens) would dominate French football for the next fifteen years. League champions in 1965, 1966, 1973, 1977, 1980, 1983, and 1995, and rarely out of the top five, Nantes were also cup-winners in 1979 (and runners-up in 1966, 1970, 1973, 1983, and 1993). They also enjoyed some rare French success in Europe, as cup-winners' cup semi-finalists in 1979–80, going out to the eventual winners of the competition, the Spanish side Valencia, trained by the legendary Alfredo Di Stefano and led by Argentinian World Cup star Mario Kempes. The management between 1960 and 1976 of José Arribas, a former docker and civil war refugee from the Spanish Basque country, was central to this development, while more recently a leading role has been played by inspirational players such as Henri Michel and Maxime Bossis, the latter a key member of the outstanding national side led to European championship success and a classic World Cup semi-final by Michel Platini in the mid-1980s.

However, if the success of *les canaris* over the past three decades cannot be denied, it is far from obvious that this performance has made any significant contribution to the construction of Breton cultural identity. To begin with, and as was discussed above, the administrative status of Nantes as the principal city of the Loire-Atlantique *département* means that it is by no means automatically to be considered a Breton city. The at best marginal Breton identity of modern Nantes is all the more apparent in the case of the city's football club, which has made no obvious attempt to assert a Celtic specificity. Moreover, the very nature of success in such an increasingly 'delocalized' sport as modern football has meant that Nantes, as a typical professional team, has had to become a nationally, and even internationally, based organization, rather than a regionally focused entity. Dominated by ever more mobile players and administrators, the club had a Spanish coach as early as 1960, and was henceforth to have fewer and fewer locally recruited players. This pattern would be significantly reinforced by the consistent signing from the mid-1960s onwards of non-French players: from the Argentinian playmaker Ramon Muller (signed in 1964) to the Yugoslavian striker Vahid Halilhodzic, France's leading scorer in 1983 and 1985; not forgetting, in more recent times, the controversial Scottish star of both Celtic and Rangers, Maurice Johnston. All of which explains why one chronicler of Breton football should open his account of FC Nantes's success with the question: 'Is Nantes a Breton city?' (Ollivier 1980: 180). If Jean-Paul Ollivier's response is, for obvious marketing reasons, in the affirmative, there nevertheless remain solid grounds for believing that the most glamorous of Brittany's footballing representatives are actually its least 'Celtic'.

As will be confirmed in the final section of this discussion, devoted to cycling, Brittany is perhaps most remarkable for the constant migration of its sporting talent to other parts of France; a pattern which mirrors the region's enduring status as a net exporter of the professionally active young (INSEE, 1993: 42). Football is no exception to this pattern, with Breton players most noteworthy as members of teams based outside the region: from Alex Thépot (Red Star), the goalkeeping hero of the French national team's campaign in the first ever World Cup competition in 1930 in Uruguay; via Jean Prouff and Raymond Kéruzoré, lost to the 'big guns' of Reims (in the 1940s) and Olympique de Marseille (in the 1970s) respectively; to contemporary stars like Paul Le Guen of Paris Saint-Germain, the 1996 European cup-winners' cup-winning side (and 1997 runners-up), and the French national side. The experience will be a not wholly unfamiliar one to followers of Irish, Welsh, and even Scottish football.

BRETON CYCLING

For all the obvious local significance of football, it is cycle road-racing, that most national of French sports, that the Bretons have chosen to invest in as the primary signifier of a regional sporting identity. With the mass commercialization of the modern bicycle in the later 1880s, France's still predominantly rural society was effectively transformed, both in terms of the new technology's general impact on personal communications, and as regards the very specific development of 'France's first national spectator sport' (Holt, 1981: 82). As ideally suited to a demography of scattered, and frequently impecunious, rural communes as association football was in this period to the English and Scottish industrial centres, cycle road-racing was rapidly and durably to capture the French popular imagination.

The first leisure cycling clubs to be established in Brittany, such as the Véloce-Club Rennais in 1869 and the Véloce Vannetais in 1870, were among the earliest in France. However, it was the organization by the Parisian *Petit-Journal* newspaper of a 1,200-kilometre race between Paris and the Breton naval base of Brest, and back, which marked the real beginning of competitive cycling in the region. The involvement, and victory, of Charles Terront, the thoroughly professional champion of the Paris tracks and the first of a new breed of national sports stars (Holt, 1981: 92–3) was of great importance to the race's success. However, so was the high profile of Breton competitors such as Ludovic Morin, Gabriel Poulain, and, especially, Corentin Corre. Corre would go on to become Terront's great rival on track and road, famously issuing a challenge to him over 1,000 kilometres on the brand new Vélodrome d'Hiver in Paris in February 1893. Terront won, but the event made headlines in all the Paris papers and ensured Corre's notoriety. The news of the Breton's successful completion in September 1895 of a solo tour of France totalling 5,012 kilometres in 25 days on a revolutionary aluminium machine – a full eight years before Henri Desgrange's celebrated launching of *Le Tour* proper – was similarly reported, and particularly well received by the press in his native Brittany (Cadiou, 1990: 11–15).

Such publicity boosted the new sport's appeal both as a participant activity and as a commercial spectacle in the 1890s. The founding of the first proletarian clubs, such as the Pédale Ouvrière Morlaisienne (1894) and the Pédale Ouvrière Brestoise (1895), was one indication of this upsurge of interest, while the rapid building of *vélodromes* throughout Brittany was another (Cadiou, 1990: 18–20). The subsequent development of local road races, such as the Circuit de l'Ouest and the Circuit du Morbihan, and major national events, including the Paris–Rennes and the Paris–Nantes, should also be noted as important aspects of cycling's implantation in Brittany. However, it is the involvement of the region in the premier national cycling event, the annual Tour de France, which is of greatest significance in the present context.

From the outset, Brittany, as one of France's most geographically and culturally distinctive regions, was a logical inclusion in *la grande boucle*'s mobile celebration of the nation's unitary geography and history. Nantes was selected as a staging-post in the very first race, in 1903, with Rennes featuring similarly in 1905 and Brest in 1906; this is a pattern which has been repeated up to the present day. Moreover, local competitors were prominent early on, their first major success coming in 1907–8, when Lucien Mazan, better known by his nickname of 'Petit-Breton', became the first competitor to win the race in successive years. Such was the difficulty of finishing, let alone winning, the event in these heroic early days of *touristes-routiers* (wholly unassisted lone competitors) that the successful completion of the race in 1907 and 1909 by Alfred Le Bars, the first Breton-speaker to distinguish himself in the Tour, is worthy of note in itself. Indeed, the symbolic importance attached by the local press to the completion of the circuit by Breton competitors would continue to be indicative both of the harshness of the event and of the way in which Brittany perceived its sporting representatives. As *La Dépêche de Brest* wrote on 25 July 1923 in a tribute to 'local boy' Félix Richard, who had just finished 37th overall in the Tour:

> Your success, after the misfortunes of [so many other competitors], comes just at the right time to demonstrate to sporting France, and come to that to France as a whole, that the will to win of the 'pig-headed Bretons' ... as they like to call us in their lofty and disdainful way, remains unshakeable. You wanted to succeed, and you did succeed. You are a real and modest apostle of Breton sport. (Cited in Cadiou, 1990: 22)

Breton success in the Tour would continue after World War II with victories for Jean Robic (1947), Louison Bobet (1953–5), and Bernard Hinault (1978–9, 1981–2, 1985). An important breeding-ground for these great names, but also less celebrated Breton talent, would be the *courses de pardon* which increasingly replaced traditional sports as part of the secular accompaniment to the region's distinctive religious festivals. Where peasants would once come into town to wrestle or compete in horse races on beasts normally used as draught animals, they took increasingly to competing for prize money on what Breton-speakers called *ar marc'h houarn* (the iron horse). Particularly remembered in this context are the Breton-speaking Le Drogo brothers from Pontivy, who graduated from *courses de pardon* to national prominence: Ferdinand as road-racing champion of France in 1927; and Paul as the victor in the Paris–Rennes in 1930 (Cadiou, 1981: 40–5). A legendary Breton figure such as the farmer Joseph 'Job' Morvan, active in the 1950s, was even reckoned to be able to increase his livestock in direct proportion to his success in the region's cycle races. Never beaten in the region's premier time trial, the Manche-Océan (run over 130 kilometres from Binic on the English Channel to Auray on the Atlantic coast), Morvan also won the last running of its greatest stage race, Le Tour de l'Ouest, in 1959. Disdaining competitions outside Brittany, Morvan was very much a local campaigner who specialized in taking on all comers on the Breton roads which he knew so well (Cadiou, 1990: 187).

Jean Robic, the winner of the 1947 Tour de France, was a very different breed of competitor. A very competent cyclo-cross racer – he was champion of France and of the world in 1950 – Robic was later identified by the celebrated critic and cultural theorist Roland Barthes as the incarnation of ethnic Celtic virtues in his pioneering analysis of the Tour's functioning as a national myth-system (1957: 111). A key member of the Ouest team in the Tour de France when it was run as an inter-regional competition between 1939 and 1961, he was also regularly selected for the French team which competed in the international competition also run at this time. Indeed, his avowed preference for racing in the national colours rather than those of the west (Cadiou, 1981: 80) are an indication of the limitations which he himself imposed on his identity as a sporting hero of the Breton 'nation'.

For Louison Bobet, as for Jean Robic, success as a cyclist was to bring about a social promotion which both men signalled by purchasing houses in the Paris suburbs (Cadiou, 1981: 80, 89). Like Robic a specialist mountain-climber, Bobet would become his fellow Breton's greatest rival in a private battle which fascinated journalists and spectators alike; and this well beyond the confines of the two men's home region. An outstanding performer in a period of major talents such as the Frenchman Jacques Anquetil and the Italian Fausto Coppi, Bobet would settle the score finally with his unprecedented three successive Tour victories between 1953 and 1955. An important innovator both as regards dietary regimes and training strategies, the Breton was additionally crowned world champion in 1954. A talented middle-distance runner and footballer in his youth, Bobet was as effective in one-day events as he was in stage races, winning several of French cycling's 'classic' road races (Cadiou, 1990: 41–6).

If the 1950s represented the golden age of Breton cycling, the 1960s were destined to be a period of disappointment. Of particular note in this period was the region's reaction to the disqualification of its rising star, Désiré Letort, in the 1967 French national road-racing championships. Having recently been the revelation of that year's Tour de France, which he finished in a highly creditable fourth place, Letort dominated the domestic event with a solo breakaway of 55 kilometres to emerge as the clear winner. However, he subsequently failed a drug test and was disqualified by the national authorities. The outraged reaction of the Breton cycling public – which included a poster campaign hailing Letort as Brittany's national champion – is primarily to be understood as a reaction to several very lean years for Breton cycling. However, it may also be usefully set against a broader background of serious Breton – and, indeed, French – unrest in the late 1960s and early 1970s (Cadiou, 1981: 124–5).

It was in the mid-1970s that Breton cycling finally discovered the new star that it had been searching for ever since the glory days of Robic and Bobet. Born in 1954 in Yffiniac near Saint-Brieuc, into the large family of a railway worker, Bernard Hinault was very much in the popular tradition of Breton cycling heroes. Second only in cycling's hall of fame to the great Belgian champion Eddy Merckx, whom he effectively replaced as the sport's leading figure, Hinault dominated the Tour de France for the better part of a decade. His five victories between 1978 and 1985 made him a member of an élite club of five-time winners with Merckx and the leading French rider of the 1950s and 1960s, Jacques Anquetil, together with the Basque Miguel Indurain, the first cyclist to win Le Tour five times in succession (1991–5). World road-racing champion in 1980, *le blaireau* (the badger) excelled in the one-day 'classics' – such as the Liège–Bastogne–Liège (1977, 1980), the Flèche wallonne (1979, 1983), and the Paris–Roubaix (1981) – as much as in the great stage-races. Yet, paradoxically, and although regarded by the historian of Breton cycling Georges Cadiou as a product and an incarnation of his homeland's traditional virtues, it may be that Hinault was more highly regarded outside Brittany than within it. For, as Cadiou concludes, 'the Bretons sometimes find it difficult to accept their greatest talents' (1981: 142). If this is true, then it is tempting to compare Bernard Hinault with other Celtic 'prophets without honour in their own land' – Scottish footballer Denis Law would be an obvious case in point (Holt, 1994) – and to wonder whether this phenomenon might not in itself be a feature of the sporting identity of Celtic cultures more at ease with the self-image of the valiant (local) underdog than that of the all-conquering (national and/or international) superstar.

CONCLUSION

As part of a highly centralized nation-state, Brittany must be reckoned to have achieved only a very limited sporting expression of its Celtic specificity. The Bretons certainly cut a poor figure when compared with the Celtic nations of the British Isles: with no investment by political nationalists in reinvented games to compare with the success of the Gaelic Athletic Association (GAA) in Ireland; no separate football league or international football team to compare with Scotland; and no national rugby side to compare with the Welsh (or even the very successful Cornish sides in recent English county championships). Where a cultural investment has been made in sports, it is either in those such as wrestling which, like the Breton language, seem doomed to extinction, or those which are primarily remarkable for their role in the construction of French national identities, such as football and cycling, and which are consequently weak sporting symbols of Breton aspirations. With the majority of Bretons apparently resigned (if no more than this) to the thorough assimilation of their Celtic specificity by a partially decentralized French state, then this is perhaps only to be expected. Indeed, it may even be that in an age characterized by the technology-led globalization of leisure, as of so much else in public and private life, the consciously constructed and systematically reasserted national sporting mythology of France will prove more of a bastion against the forces of cultural dissolution than Brittany's weak Celtic sporting identity.

10

MORE THAN A GAME: PHYSICAL CULTURE, IDENTITY AND CITIZENSHIP IN WALES

John Evans, Brian Davies and Di Bass

INTRODUCTION

In this chapter, as elsewhere (Davies *et al.*, 1997; Evans *et al.*, 1997), we use the concepts both of 'national identity' and 'personal identity' with great caution. Conceptually, 'identity' denotes distinction, uniqueness, difference from 'another'; also coherence and consistency of attitude, aspiration, outlook and behaviour where often none, or very few, of these attributes 'in reality' are to be found. Much recent post-modern social theory is at pains to point out that our identities are not distinct, unified, coherent, intransient, non-contradictory sets of attributes, interests and aspirations. They are complex, heterogeneous, contradictory, conceptual entities drawn from discursive regimes which are themselves not 'closed' in time and space or unique. It is not possible to ring fence a discursive regime.

To acknowledge this is to accept that in talking of Welsh or English (or any other) identity, either as an individual or a national construct or phenomenon, we are addressing an abstract entity, an artificial ideal, constructed both historically and contemporaneously within a framework of values and aspirations that are ever changing, always contested, reflecting the diversity of cultures within the geographical domain. In his brilliant penetration of the history of Wales, Gwyn Williams (1985: 2) reminded us that

> the first point to grasp about the history of its people is that Wales is impossible. A country called Wales exists only because the Welsh constructed it. The Welsh exist only because they invented themselves and will continually have to re invent themselves. They had no choice.

They will have to continue remaking themselves if they are to survive and meet the challenges of a post-industrial world. Echoes of this standpoint are found in Caitlin Matthews' reminder that the Celts did not call themselves this, nor did they speak 'Celtic'. 'They thought of themselves as Bretons, Irish, British or Gaels. Earlier than the Roman invasion, they probably thought of themselves as 'the people of such-and-such tribe' (Matthews, 1989: viii). She goes on, 'the Celts are a family of people continually moving through time and adapting to new parameters. The use of the word "Celtic" is therefore merely convenient, used to describe a confederacy of very different peoples, embraced in a Europe wide Celtic language family' (ibid.).

What interests us here, in particular, is how certain attributes and relations come to be defined as quintessentially 'Welsh', generating real and imaginary divisions and distinctions between insider and outsider, the 'other', 'them' and 'us', given that both the concept and the practice of establishing national identity depends on exclusion as much as on inclusion: 'the "foreigner" whose expulsion is a precondition of national independence, or the ethnic minority whose pretensions threaten national unity, are the functional counterpart to the symbolic and material mechanisms of forging national cohesion, present in most historical processes of nation building' (Woolf, 1996: 32).

Is it inevitable that only by defining ourselves as 'Welsh' either in relation to or excluding 'the other' can we feel that we belong? Woolf also noted that

> the definitions of who should be included and who excluded are fundamentally arbitrary, dependant on the very myths that underpin nationalist ideology (history, language, race, religion, territory...) expressed and sometimes imposed ruthlessly by elites in control of the state. (ibid.)

More specifically, how has sport generally and recent education policies in particular, positioned certain forms of physical culture in processes such as these? (Evans *et al.*, 1997; Evans and Davies, 1997; Andrews, 1996). Are they implicated in practices of inclusion and exclusion, the creation of 'the other' as a negative, oppositional cultural form? We ask, whose voices are heard in official and popular discourses on sport and PE? Alternatively, can they play a part in the cultural production of forms of identity, citizenship and 'Celtic culture' sensitive to diversity, cohesive, and productive of collaborative associations at many social levels? These questions are difficult to frame, let alone answer.

SETTING THE SCENE

We cannot here offer either a detailed social history of Wales, or an account of the development of sport and education in the principality (see, for example, Williams, G. A. 1985; Morris Jones and Singh Ghuman, 1995; Andrews, 1996; G. E. Jones, 1997; Davies *et al.*, 1997). But we cannot appreciate what goes on in PE in schools in Wales unless we have at least some basic understanding of its socio-cultural and historical contexts of sport and education that have shaped the curriculum for the last hundred years and which continue to influence practice in its schools.

Wales 'enjoys' the status of a principality, within the unitary British state, dominated by England, suffered by Scotland and clung to by Northern Ireland. It has always been 'a patchwork of cultures'. It is, as Gwyn Williams (1996: 201) stated, 'a land of diversity often amounting to division', a divided society, its most familiar and obvious divisions are between town and country and between Welsh and English speakers, which, 'despite heroic efforts seems to be getting worse', and is 'itself the product of the selfishly seductive, destructive, globalising tendencies of earlier corporate capitalism'. Others depict it as a plural society characterized by a unilingual majority and a bilingual minority, though 'In comparative multilingual terms, it is a very simple society with fairly stable social conditions and only moderate degrees of social tension and economic differentiation' (Williams, 1995: 48–9).

Even a cursory glance at the pages of the *Western Mail*, the national daily paper, reveals how persistently the 'language issue' pervades the politics, cultural fabric and outlook of life in Wales. The celebration of the Welsh language and literature as the most noble, influential and precious cultural forms has often been as brilliantly prosaic and passionately polemical as it is pernicious and divisive to those who do not share narrow Welsh nationalist ideals. For example, a different language, wrote Ned Thomas (1971: 32–3)

> does not assert one's total difference from that of other groups of the human race, but it registers the degree of difference that in fact exists; it is from the recognition of this that all worthwhile efforts at understanding between groups must start...

> In the first place, by its existence, the language tells us we are Welsh. All the feeling of nationality that is supported for the Englishmen by the Queen, the House of Parliament, the London policemen, the bewigged judges, the customs officer at Dover and a whole range of political, cultural and popular institutions, rests for the Welshman on the language and literature,

and on a few cultural phenomena such as the eisteddfod which are closely linked with the language.

Such a view has served as much a powerful rallying cry to those who cherish separatist ideals as it stands as a distortion of the complexities of cultural life in Wales, an espousal of a form of Welsh Nationalism and Welsh identity, a 'Cymry fach', the equal or more of John Major's (in early 1997 leader of the Conservative party) little Englander ideals. By 1971, the Welsh language seemed to be in terminal decline. Welsh speakers were down to a bare 20 per cent. Yet, as Gwyn Williams (1985: 293) reminded us, in response to a militant campaign, driven by sentiments of a kind alluded to above, 'the British state, ruling a largely indifferent or hostile Welsh population, has in a manner which has few parallels outside the Soviet Union, countenanced and indeed subsidised cultural Welsh Nationalism.'

Although the number of Welsh speakers remains around one fifth of the population,

> Wales is now officially, visibly and audibly a bilingual country.... Whole Welsh-language structures, serviced by an effective training and supply apparatus, exist in education, administrative life and the media. The issue of the Welsh language, in many fields of Welsh action, blots out all other political considerations.

The consequences of this, as Williams (1985: 293) pointed out, have been contradictory.

> There has been a wave of support for the enterprise from English-speakers, the heaviest demands for Welsh schools has come from English-speaking Glamorgan, the language courses are full. On the other hand there has been a growing resentment, impatience and anger which at times and in places has become a kind of hatred. An English-speaking working class, neglected and treated with shoddiness, its necessities, not only social but cultural, scorned not least by some leaders of the Welsh language movement, sees a British state subsidising the Welsh language production of what is to them a middle-class minority. They see bilingual language qualification shutting off areas of employment for their children. They perceive Welsh-language schools as nurseries of a new order of privileged beings who employ Welsh and particularly the new language of Cymraeg Byw much as the Irish middle class has used official Gaelic and the medieval clergy used Latin, to manufacture a new oligarchy. They see subsidies going everywhere except to their culture.

Although it is perhaps some over-exaggeration of the divisions and conflicts within the principality to state that Wales 'has been fortunate to have escaped a rebellion by English speakers' (*Western Mail*, 24 April 96), this sentiment is evidence, Williams contended, of a much deeper malaise

> which is more ominous: the denial of Welshness to the English-speaking Welsh, an exclusion which is becoming rapidly and increasingly, and inevitably a bitter self-exclusion of the English-speaking Welsh from the Welsh people and nation. The adjective 'Welsh' is increasingly applied, outside and inside Wales, only to the Welsh-speaking component of the people, which is one-fifth of the actual numbers. A new shadow line runs across the face of Wales. (1985: 293)

It has to be said that the brilliance of Williams' visionary analysis is matched only and equally by the depth of its pessimism. For some, his observation that 'Whom the Gods wish to destroy, they first afflict with a language problem' (1996: 294), goes too far. Devotion to the development of bilingualism in Wales, others claim, is no longer exclusively concerned with the needs and interests of Welsh speakers, but rather the concerns and involvement of second language learners and non-Welsh-speakers, 'thereby extending the bi-cultural nature of society from both ends of the spectrum' (Williams, 1995: 65).

Acknowledging the socio-economic and cultural divisions within the principality is a vital first step towards understanding the nature of the forces and pressures, including the career aspirations that parents hold for their offspring and the school choices they make for them, at play within and upon schools and PE and sport in Wales.

MORE THAN 'THE GAME'

Sport has long been used to symbolize the distinctive characteristics of Celtic Welsh culture and to help define what the good citizen and the Nation state, ideally, ought to be. As one form of socio-cultural practice it is therefore deeply and inextricably implicated in the production and reproduction of popular and official fable and mythology, about 'the nation', the individual and what 'the appropriate body' ought to be; providing narratives that not only help frame and give meaning to people's lives but also position them in relation to others in the immediate community and wider nation state. For this reason sport in Wales, as elsewhere, deserves critical scrutiny. Its practices are inevitably hierarchical. They celebrate and elevate certain forms of physical culture and attendant attributes and predispositions while either excluding or silencing others, positioning them on the margins, or the 'lower echelons', of the nation's cultural terrain. In this there is nothing new. David Andrews' (1996) critical analysis of the masculinization of national identity in Wales from the end of the eighteenth century until 1914, for example, incisively reveals how rugby, defined as expressing all the virtues of Celtic culture, played a significant role both in gendering Wales as a modern nation state and in placing masculinity at the centre of a unified Welsh national identity (Chandler and Nauright, 1996: 8). He pointed out that at the turn of the century the new industrial middle class, confidence burgeoning from their economic successes 'immersed the game into the masculine discourse of Cambrian Celticism, which explained national progress in terms of the supremacy of the Celtic race (and by association the Celtic males).... Through linking contemporary progress with Celtic virtuosity, there emerged an immediate line of descent to a successful and celebrated past' (ibid: 55). As the *Western Mail* put it, celebrating victory in 1905 against the undefeated New Zealanders, 'The prestige of Wales has been enhanced tremendously as a nation possessed of those splendid (Celtic) qualities – pluck and determination' (ibid.: 56). Commentators deployed the full range of Darwinian logic to the comparative cultural qualities of different races to extol this great Welsh success. 'Here at last, in the view of some sentimental observers, Matthew Arnold's analysis of the superior intuitive qualities of the Celt, in contrast to the more prosaic virtues of the steadier Saxon, had found its ultimate fulfilment' (Morgan, 1981: 123). It is Andrews' (1996: 67) contention that during 'the period 1890–1914 bonds were resolutely strengthened between Wales – the male dominated industrial nation – and rugby – its masculine national pastime – through immersing rugby into the (momentarily) complementing patriarchal discourses associated with dualistic membership of both the modern Welsh nation and the British nation state'. The reputation of 'the Welsh' as having 'unique' Celtic qualities of strength, tenacity, resilience, cunning, expressed in industry as on the rugby field, and in the latter especially in the finer points of attacking, open half-back and three-quarter play, was regarded as firmly established, despite the fact that economic wealth was no more evenly distributed amongst the peoples of Wales than was the following of rugby. As Morgan pointed out, rugby was very much 'only' a South Wales game: 'Most of Wales was not a rugby territory at all but took pride from the success of Welsh soccer players'. He goes on, however, 'the success of Welsh club sides, and above all, the triumphs of the Welsh international fifteen made rugby in South Wales a game apart' (Morgan, 1981: 134). This caricature endures[1] despite dramatically altered economic conditions requiring a different 'habitus', new forms of social relation and attitudes between women and men, cerebral rather than physical skills in the work place and the changing fortunes of the nation's rugby team.

What is of particular interest is not just the way in which sport has been used in popular and official mythology to 'speak for' the nation and represent its defining characteristic qualities but the selective investment/embodying of the nation's attributes and ideals in mainly one form of physical culture, rugby, historically and contemporaneously in Wales predominantly 'a men's game' (see Andrews, 1996). As Andrews points out, 'given the masculine hegemony of the modern nation state, it is hardly surprising that the preponderance of the images of nationhood, and the cultural practices associated with the burgeoning national identities were articulated to the dominant discourses of male supremacy and masculinity' (ibid.: 53) and that, from being an emergent popular pastime, the game was transformed in the early twentieth century into a high profile symbol of a vibrant, and self-confident, male-oriented Welsh national ideology. Social histories of Wales almost invariably talk (though not at any length) about its diverse physical cultures in terms of the development and achievement of a single, men's game, leaving the analysis of other forms of cultural embodiment relatively untouched. At one level it is no accident that rugby is privileged in social histories of Wales. History does not write itself, but is continuously made and remade in the imaginations of those who claim to have discovered its patterns and ways. Maybe it is because the providers of such narratives have (with recent notable exceptions; see Aaron, S. *et al.*, 1994; Betts, S., 1996) been mainly white, middle-class men that their attentions have centred predominantly on the achievements of 'the game'. For example, in the brilliantly prosaic writing of Gwyn Williams (1985), 'the game' is used to mark out, describe, and distinguish, the embodied characteristics, the qualities, achievements and aspirations of 'the people' of Wales. Williams, like Morgan, characterizes the vibrancy and confidence of 'Welsh culture' of early twentieth-century Wales, as embodied in the actions of significant males, most notably, David Lloyd George, Prime Minister of Britain in 1916.

> The Wales he came from, and particularly its Southern metropolis, was no less simultaneously Welsh-national and British-imperial. Ruin would have been in no one's mind in 1913, or even in 1921. These men, with most, if not all their women dutifully behind, strutted like fighting cocks through an economy which was perhaps the most buoyant and expansive in Britain. It found its most memorable human expression in what, after an initial struggle, had become its national game, rugby, the only field where it was possible to be simultaneously Welsh and a gentleman (normally a difficult

undertaking), where doctor and lawyer could ruck happily shoulder to shoulder with miner and where Wales, safely lodged as a major directive element within imperial Britain, could hope to express its now self-confident identity in a continuous eisteddfod of Grand Slams and a continuous rugby-dinner chorus of God Bless the Prince of Wales (duly invested at Caernarfon by a Lloyd George who was as inventive of Welsh traditions as any Lady Lanover or Iolo Morganwg). How much more Welsh was this than boxing, distressingly full of aliens and as brutal an escape route out of the poverty of South Wales as it was for blacks in the USA! How preferable to soccer, so irredeemably proletarian and English! (Williams, 1985: 221)

Here, then, vividly described, all that was good about the developing socio-economic order and culture of Wales, represented/embodied in what, by the turn of the century, had become 'the nation's game'. Welsh culture in microcosm, systemically patriarchal, but otherwise proudly egalitarian, passionately meritocratic, and, at least on the playing surface, classless to boot, a culture which simultaneously lifted, mixed and separated the worthwhile from the worthless, the valued from the valueless cultural form, while pitting the posh and the proletariat together against the English/Anglo-Saxon and 'other' nation states. But as both Gwyn Williams' and Kenneth Morgan's narratives indicate, it is a caricature, a mythology, that barely disguised the cracks beneath the socio-cultural terrain, or the economic divisions existing within Wales, the expression of 'a Celtic culture' that was always essentially derivative and inescapably heterogeneous. Beneath the carapace of this mythologized consensus and uniformity of sporting ideal, unmentioned but ever present, were the English 'other', the less worthy boxers, football players, followers of other sporting pursuits, and women, barely mentioned, positioned either on the margins in sport or as followers of men. This is men's talk of men and, as such, seldom are the achievements of women to be heard. As Andrews pointed out, consequently,

To the popular Welsh imagination, the re-birth of modern Wales was realised by an almost exclusively male cast (be it the men who worked down the mines and in the factories, those managers and administrators who oversaw Wales' great industrial leap forward, or those popular heroes who donned the scarlet jersey of the national rugby XV) who were widely thought to have created a nation in their own image; it was as the national anthem affirmed, the Land of My Fathers. (Andrews, 1996: 66)

This discursive representation and reduction of the physical culture of Wales to male sport, is not, however, confined only to the writing of men.

It has also framed the perspective of women historians in Wales. Consider here, for example, Kate Olwen Pritchard's (1973) little known, wonderfully vivid but grossly romanticized social history of life after the industrial revolution, through the post-war depression years, in the small South Wales Ogwr Valley town of Gilfach Goch. The writer lived in Gilfach Goch for most of her life and for 32 years served as headteacher at a local infants school. In the preface, Brynmor John, Member of Parliament for Pontypridd in 1973, recounts that Gilfach Goch was a typical product of the nineteenth-century industrial revolution in South Wales. The scene of the fictional *How Green Was My Valley*, it became, as well as a product, a symbol of this time to many who did not live in or even know the valley. Pritchard, in common with the other writers mentioned above, colourfully portrayed sport as a prominent and important part of the life of the community in early industrial Wales. It was the only diversion afforded to the men from sweat and toil. Because of 'the nature of the geography of the valley, its steepness, with its basin and flat areas dominated by slag heaps – sport was mainly confined to physical prowess' (Pritchard, 1973: 184). Here, as elsewhere in industrialized Wales in the early twentieth century, it seems, the physical culture was both vibrant and diverse, despite enormous economic and social hardship. Pritchard pointed out that wrestling, boxing, quoits, throwball and walking and running contests were popular, as was tennis, bowling and cricket, at one time the valley boasting three separate clubs. It also produced many notable top-class performers, most notably in soccer, rugby and boxing. The scene, then, is of valley life grounded in economic hardships, but with a vibrant culture enriched with music, theatre and sport. A physical culture, profoundly patriarchal, dominated by men, celebrating the then required qualities of masculinity, the physical strength and character needed to endure hard and dangerous physical labour. Women were positioned either as less serious participants in sport or not mentioned at all. Indeed, this makes the pictorial imagery of valley life presented in Pritchard's book all the more intriguing. Amongst the pictures of 'the men's Gilfach Goch Rugby Football Club', 'Gifach Goch Cricket Club' and 'schoolboys off to the international', unmentioned, defying words but compelling further investigation, is a picture of Gilfach Goch Ladies football team – a glimpse, perhaps, of a defiant substratum of women's aspirations and involvement in sport – rarely seen or heard of in male-centred histories of sport.

The hierarchies evident and developing within the physical culture of Wales, no doubt, both reflected the male hegemonic, socio-economic and cultural conditions of industrialization of the Edwardian and Victorian age and helped contribute to the creation and perpetuation of an imagined community of the nation. The idea was and is that there exists consensuality and homogeneity of cultural practice, aspiration and ideal. By the late nineteenth century the 'game' had become 'the Nation's game', a rich cultural resource, rallying point, and powerful binding force for those espousing nationalistic ideals. It may also have become a corrosive force, not only because it functioned as palliative for economic hardship, 'a harmless safety valve for national sentiment, rugby and investitures, the bread and circuses of the populace, ... a peaceful therapy to suppress embarrassing political aspirations' (Morgan, 1981: 134). It certainly also reduced and occluded other cultural forms of significance and interest in the lives of many people, positioning them marginally, so that their interests and the voices they represent were either silenced or had continually to struggle to survive, making it difficult to catch glimpses of the many other physical forms that historically have found expression in the routine lives of the people of Wales, that are as much a part of the cultural fabric of Wales as rugby, but because of the privileging of 'the game' have had to struggle to survive or have died. Perhaps it is indicative, for example, that Olwen Pritchard notes, by 1972 all Gifach Goch's cricket teams had been disbanded.

What we see here is that in the gender ideologies of the state,

> nationalism is constituted, from its origins, as a highly gendered relation-ship, dependent upon the marking on women's and men's bodies and in their identities, of the ideologies of national difference. Women are not 'imagined' in Anderson's (1991) suggestive phrase, to be national citizens. (Radcliffe and Westwood, 1996: 135)

The model of 'masculinity' and 'machismo' in Wales, as in the Latin American contexts described by Radcliffe and Westwood, initially founded on a profound religiosity, revolved around the idea of specific family social relations and gendered relations,

> based on openly heterosexual and controlled, aggressive male behaviour, and on meek and self-abnegating female behaviour and chaste female bodies.... The interaction between male and female in nationhood was grounded on assumptions of heterosexuality, and nationally beneficial reproductive behaviours. Broadly speaking, women function as dominated reproducers of national citizens while male sexuality is channelled into reproductive forms, and homosexuality is curtailed. (ibid.: 145)

National attributes of physicality, sexuality and fraternity all came to the fore in male leisure activities in early twentieth-century Wales. Rugby and football, the more physical and invasive forms of sport and physical culture practised in Wales, were the bodily practices which,

> although carried out by highly specific and markedly sexed/gendered bodies, were embedded within wider social notions about bodies per se and the appropriate practices to display national belonging, sexuality and pride. (ibid.: 144)

Rugby in particular offered a robust and physical masculinity through which socio-cultural differences, between men and women and different class factions, could be announced, and national pride could be reasserted, especially in opposition to other nationals.

Given rapidly changing family structures, social relations and economic circumstances, and the behaviours and expectations of women and men, the impropriety of this positioning is writ large, not least because women have entered the labour market in Wales, as elsewhere, on a grand scale. No longer are they simply domestic and maternal figures not reflected in physical cultures of leisure and sport.

At a time when Wales seeks and needs to remake itself, facing the forces of globalization, nationalism and the changing socio-economic requirements of a post-modern age, this narrow cultural specialization, the hegemony of 'the male game', the social relations it reflects and reproduces, the failure to both recognize and nurture other cultural forms and the voices they represent, may be profoundly damaging not only to the development of more robust and liberal forms of citizenship but to the literal and metaphorical health of the nation state. If nothing else it has meant that with the 'failure' of 'the Game' on the national stage, there is in place no other cultural form, to readily take its place. With its death goes the erosion of the nation's identity and pride.

'MODERN TIMES' – STILL PLAYING THE GAME

The more immediate backdrop to the connections between physical education, sport, nationalism and citizenship in England and Wales is provided by their recently invented National Curricula (NC) and the switch to Local Management of Schools (LMS) (Davies *et al.*, 1997). On the surface, the 1988 Education Reform Act (ERA), with its origins and ideology infused with the intentions of English Conservative restorationist ideals, had very little to offer a curriculum for Wales. Yet, according to G. E. Jones (1987) and G. E. Jones and Lewis (1995), the Act presented Wales with a new opportunity to review its educational policy and reemphasize its unique needs. It may also be an opportunity to rethink and help redefine what 'Welsh culture' ought to be, given the changing socio-economic circumstances of a post-modern age. ERA legislation legally established the Welsh language as a 'core subject' in Welsh medium schools and a 'foundation subject' in all other maintained schools in Wales. It also legislated for the establishment of a Curriculum Council for Wales (CCW) with a brief similar to the National Curriculum Council (NCC) which was to serve England. On the surface, the ERA presented Wales with the opportunity 'to create, for the first time ever, a state school curriculum which was unique to Wales in content and context' (Jones and Lewis, 1995). Richard Daugherty, chair of the CCW in 1993, stated that 'just being there has been a means of giving expression to Welsh views which differ from those in England' (1993: 4).

In the context of PE and sport, in a letter sent in 1993 to John Redwood, the Secretary of State for Wales, Rudi Plaut, the Chairman of the CCW, expressed concern about the order for physical education that made games a compulsory area of activity for all pupils aged 14–16. He wrote

> In the Council's view, the interests of pupils at this age are best served by giving them an unrestricted choice as to which two activities they choose from the six Areas of Activity mentioned in the proposals, namely: games, gymnastics, dance, athletics, swimming and outdoor and adventurous activities.

It would be equally inappropriate, however, to overstate the autonomy afforded to schools and teachers in Wales to reconstruct and modify the texts of the NC and institute a curriculum reflecting the goals and aspirations of more than a marginally different curriculum Cymreig. As the CCW (1994: 2) noted, there could be no blueprint for a CC, nor therefore, concomitantly, for forms of Welsh identity, as every school situation is unique. Each school community and the curriculum which it provides, is characterized by Welshness, albeit in differing ways, and in different geographical and cultural settings.

Thus 'schools will need to establish clear aims and policies to ensure that pupils are helped to explore the concepts of Wales and Welshness *from their own particular standpoints*' (CCW, 1991: 5, our emphasis). These worthy aspirations of a curriculum Cymreig require assessing in terms of PE and sport.

RECONSTRUCTING PHYSICAL CULTURE: TOWARDS A CURRICULUM CYMREIG?

The issue of sport in schools has rarely been out of the public domain in the last decade as Conservative central government committed itself to romanticized notions of ideal states achieved through it and PE. The noises of the New Labour government which swept to power in 1997 give no indication that these sentiments are abating. The argument has run that competitive team games, purportedly in decline and taught badly in schools, should be reinstated at the heart of the PE curriculum because of their capacity to both socialize and skill pupils, create good (elite) sports men (and women) and disciplined citizens of good character, simultaneously helping to ameliorate society's contemporary social and economic ills. The publication in 1995 of a key policy document, *Sport – Raising the Game* (Department of National Heritage, 1995) made clear the then Conservative government's intent to rebuild the British Nation through success and involvement in competitive sport and PE in schools. In John Major's inimitable chauvinistic words,

> Some people say that sport is a peripheral and minor concern. I profoundly disagree. It enriches the lives of the thousands of millions of people of all ages around the world who know and enjoy it. Sport is a central part of Britain's National Heritage. We invented the majority of the world's great sports. and most of those we did not invent, we codified and helped to popularise throughout the world. It could be argued that nineteenth century Britain was the cradle of a leisure revolution every bit as significant as the agricultural and industrial revolutions we launched in the century before. (DNH, 1995: 2)

Leaving aside the accuracy of such claims about the global status and significance of 'British sport', we see here the expression *par excellence* of a view of sport as social cement, 'a binding force between generations and across borders'.

> But, by a miraculous paradox, it is at the same time one of the defining characteristics of nationhood and of local pride. We should cherish it for both those reasons. (DNH, 1995: 2)

Following the publication of *Raising the Game* Wales, Scotland and Northern Ireland were asked to publish documents setting out its aims in their contexts. The sentiments of the PM were echoed and endorsed by the Welsh Secretary of State, William Hague (now leader of the Opposition) in the text of *Young People and Sport in Wales* (Sports Council for Wales,

1995: 2), the Welsh equivalent of *Raising the Game*.

> A thriving Wales is a Wales that raises great sportsmen and sportswomen,
> that produces golfers, athletes, and cricketers of world quality. It is a Wales
> where many enjoy sport at their own level of success and enjoy the reflected
> glory of the international success of others. May we all enjoy sport even
> more as new talent comes from our schools and colleges.

Sport now, as it has done so historically, is to act simultaneously as a
Welsh and as a populist, British, imperialist ideal (Williams, G. A., 1996:
202; Andrews, 1996). Although the 'Welsh text' is subtly different in
significant respects, as its title implies, centring attention more on the child
and the young person than on performance in sport, it too announced its
commitment to ensuring that 'competitive sport is at the centre of PE in
schools' (SCW, 1996: 15). Indeed, their shared platform is clearly the
positioning of competitive team games in both England and Wales as the
dominant form of activity in the PE curriculum in all state sector schools,
with all 5–7 and 7–11 year olds being taught the skills of competitive games
and how to play them, the latter also enjoying mini-versions of recognized
adult games, while all 11–14 year olds play the fully recognized versions of
team games and 14–16 year olds play a competitive game, alongside other
sports and physical activities of their choice (DNH, 1995: 7). Changes to
Initial Teacher Training (ITT), Ofsted (England) and OHMCI (Wales)
inspections are to combine to ensure the institutionalisation of this state of
affairs.

MAKING A DIFFERENCE? THE PRACTICE OF PE

What kind of citizenship, 'celtic culture', nationalism and Welsh identity are,
then, being currently nurtured in the curriculum and pedagogy of sport and
PE in schools in Wales? To answer these questions we have turned to three
secondary schools set within an education market in one Local Education
Authority (LEA) in Wales, reported in detail in Evans *et al.* (1997). In that
report we document how PE and sport, as currently constructed, rarely
express the explicit intentions of a curriculum Cymreig, but rather the
residues of history and the 'effects' of the interplay of market principles
combined with the constraints of National Curriculum PE requirements,
limited resourcing and the traditions of what teachers consider to be the
aspirations of parents. The case study research suggested that teachers'
views concurred with those expressed by the Welsh Inspectorate referred to
above and found that, as in England, extra-curricular PE is dominated by a
narrow range of competitive team sports. We may also put alongside this

the view of one senior educationalist in Wales (interview data) who felt that Initial teacher training was effectively defining the shape of the National Curriculum for PE (NCPE) in Wales and that the single most important influence on both male and female PE teachers was that the 'vast majority' of specialists were trained at an institute that in her/his view, offers a 'narrow experience'. It is, she/he suggested, a 'rugby stable'.

None of our case study schools make anything other than a passing reference to the aspirations of a curriculum Cymreig as outlined in CCW texts. There appears to be little evidence in these schools that there is anything particularly/explicitly Welsh about the PE lessons, except the emphasis on rugby, the fact that some children occasionally took part in the events of Urdd, the national youth movement, and in the occasional use of Welsh music for dance. Yet what we see in these contexts is unmistakably 'Welsh'. In a very real sense they express some of the cultural divisions and tensions that define contemporary Wales. The content of PE in these contexts is constructed not with reference to the nationalistic aspirations of any Welsh Office, or CCW text, but to market forces, levels of resourcing, including the limits of staff expertise, and the economic aspirations of parents and the choices they make. Together such forces are played out in the 'hidden curriculum' of PE. In Llanwerin and, to a lesser degree, Ponteg (both coeducational 'Welsh medium' schools) we witness a powerful sense of distinctiveness and difference being generated. In the former, teachers convey the view that they and their pupils are guardians of the language, thus of Welsh heritage and tradition, of standards best expressed in sport and PE by playing and offering allegiance to the nation's major team games. PE is to play its part in the restoration of 'a monoglot Welsh *gaeltacht* in a Western *bro* (or Welsh heartland)', a movement which, as Williams points out, seems to see Welsh-speaking Cymry as the only truly Welsh (Williams, 1985: 300). The hierarchies created are as evident and potentially as destructive within the institution as they are in the wider cultural field.

In all three schools, girls are positioned as the 'other' in relation to boys and men and considered often as less active than them. 'Ability' seems to be constructed, firstly, with reference to the needs of the nation and the national game, rather than those of the children who are thus imbued with a sense of ownership of a game that they do not necessarily have an ability to play. The narrowness of this perspective, set on the restoration of 'how Wales used to be', driven and endorsed by the requirements of the NCPE and the sentiments of *Raising the Game* is consolidated by very limited resources. Ponteg, by contrast, dipping its toe into different forms of practice, toys with new orientations in provision, not least through the empowerment of a female head of PE. Here the endeavour is to nurture the possibilities of new social and educational horizons, to reconstruct PE around excellence, the interests of the pupils and the aspirations of 'sport for all'. Facilitated by access to new sport facilities, a renewed emphasis on breadth and balance and a rejection of any desire to only/simply reproduce and restore a golden age of sporting achievements, children learn something of their own and others' potential for involvement in sport and PE in the local and wider community, as well as of their own distinctiveness as Welsh-speaking Welsh.

With parents viewing bilingual education as opening up areas of employment for their children, seeing Welsh language schools 'as nurseries of a new order of privileged beings' (Williams, 1985: 293) and buying into the economic and cultural capital offered by Ponteg and Llanwerin, the response of Heddfan (a coeducational 'English medium' school), understandably, is not to offer a distinctive and different form of education, a real choice of images of being Welsh, but to copy the restorationist aspirations of Llanwerin.

In this respect the 'concessions' made to Wales to construct a curriculum Cymreig seem insignificant when set against the effects of other ERA (Education Reform Act) legislation, namely LMS and the devolution of budgets to schools, the powerful play of market principles within the community, and the residues of history which continue to define what games are of value and what 'good' Welsh citizens ought to be. Ironically, we see competition between schools, far from producing choice for the consumer, as the rhetoric of the market promises, presaging homogeneity and increasing momentum towards narrow conservative restorationist ideals.

CONCLUSION

Who recognizes themselves as of value in the overt and hidden curriculum of PE and sport in schools such as these? All children, in each of these schools? We think not. A school, says Bernstein (1996: 7)

> metaphorically holds up a mirror in which an image is reflected. There may be several images, positive and negative. A school's ideology may be seen as a construction in a mirror through which images are reflected. The question is: who recognizes themselves as of value? What other images are excluded by the dominant image of value so that some students are unable to recognize themselves? In the same way, we can ask about the acoustic of the school. Whose voice is heard? Who is speaking? Who is hailed by this voice?

For whom is it familiar? In this sense there are visual and temporal features to the images the school reflects and these images are projections of a hierarchy of values, of class values.

What forms of physical culture and images of physical activity are valued, included and excluded in the PE curriculum in schools in Wales? Our case studies provided, we suggest, are not atypical. PE in the principality remains dominated by the traditional teaching of 'traditional games'. But what kind of Physical Education should be found in Wales if it is to avoid reproducing and even amplifying its current socio-cultural divisions and tensions? What kind of PE we want in schools is going to depend greatly on what we envisage Welsh society to be. In a Wales bristling with confidence, anticipating devolution and new powers of self-government, there is a very serious need to ask whether our institutions are to reflect the diversity of the 'Celtic' cultures that already define our communities or the narrow aspirations of politicians and their pernicious imagery of how little England or little Wales used to be. Certainly, if a curriculum Cymreig in PE is to materialize then it will need to rest on the aspirations and interests of teachers, parents and pupils and be grounded in the physical cultures of the communities they serve. A PE curriculum expressing a curriculum Cymreig would, then, as the CCW (1991, 1994) suggested, start from an analysis of people as they are and be sensitive to existing forms of physical culture and wider behaviour, not to what they might become. Whatever particular vision of the world teachers adopt, their first step has to be to involve pupils in linking the world of physical culture and pleasure as they find it with the world as they would like it to be through the curriculum of sport and PE. This must be to give people a stake in their communities and the wider societies that they serve.

We have muddles and myths in abundance about the invidious differences that mark ourselves. Crick reminded us that the UK is 'not only a multi-national state practising, contrary to what was in the old textbooks, a kind of quasi-federalism, but a state in which many people have real sense of dual nationality. Most Scots see themselves, clearly enough, as Scottish and British. Similarly most Welsh, and so do a majority in Northern Ireland (not just Protestants, but also, a growing number – about 20 per cent – of Catholics)'. Only the English, it seems, 'confuse English with British' (*Times Higher Education Supplement*, 2 May 1997: 15). 'The Welsh' also continue to confuse nationality with language and rugby with life, thus privileging minorities of competence and interest at the expense of the wider talents and desires of the many.

NOTE AND ACKNOWLEDGEMENTS

1. Such attitudes prevail. We are reminded that recent press coverage of the home international rugby tournament often collectively talked of 'Celtic flair' when referring to anything other than English.
2. We are extremely grateful to Nonn Evans of Hengoed and to Leslie Worthing-Evans, Frank Rowe and Professor Richard Daugherty at the University of Wales, Aberystwyth for their invaluable assistance with this research. We also extend our gratitude to the teachers and pupils of the schools involved in the study for their time and cooperation. We are grateful to Loughborough University for the financial support to conduct this research.

11

HURLING: AN OLD GAME IN A NEW WORLD

Art Ó Maolfabhail

Sport encompasses an immense spectrum, ranging from occasional pastime to commercial industry, and incorporates vital physical and aesthetic elements. The particular sport referred to in this chapter is the traditional Irish game of hurling, which is a stick-and-ball game played, in the modern male version, in a physical-contact manner between two teams of fifteen. The game is regulated by Cumann Lúthchleas Gael, the Gaelic Athletic Association, which was founded in 1884. The female version, with no previous tradition, was devised early in this century. It is basically the same game with some variation in the rules, and is regulated by Cumann Camógaíochta na nGael, which was founded in 1904. The basic unit of organization is the club, which usually corresponds to the parish. The club/parish is the unit within the county and there are 32 historical counties in Ireland. Hurling, at all levels, is an amateur sport, although in recent decades it has had commercial sponsorship for some competitions and for some teams.

The earliest recorded use of the term 'hurling' with reference to the game can be found in a statute of 1366 in the French language addressed to the English colonists in Ireland. It resembles similar orders issued in the same century in England, Lowland Scotland and France. The general intention was to suppress so-called 'useless games' in favour of archery for military purposes. In Ireland the statute, one of those known as the Statutes of Kilkenny, makes reference to '*Les jues que home appelle horlinges oue graunds bastons a pillot sur la terre*' (the games which men call hurlings with great clubs of a ball on the ground) (Berry, 1907: 439). The traditional Irish language term *iomáin* (var. *iománaíocht*) means 'driving', and its earliest known occurrence in the context of the game is in a manuscript made around AD 1100, although the text is probably older.

CELTIC CULTURES

Taken as an entity, the term 'Celtic cultures' is no easier to define than the term 'sport' and it may be useful to observe the work of the International Committee for the Study of Celtic Cultures. This group came into existence as a result of a resolution unanimously adopted at the twenty-first General Conference of the United Nations Educational, Scientific and Cultural Organization (UNESCO), held in Belgrade in 1980. In accordance with this resolution it was agreed to add Celtic cultures to the programme of activities of the Organization. The following year a group of experts on Celtic culture from sixteen countries met in Dublin and drew up a list of projects for inclusion in the programme. These projects included the compilation of a thesaurus of living speech 'in those countries where the Celtic languages are still spoken'; the compilation of a comprehensive survey, *History and Culture of the Celts*; an exchange of information about archaeological research on Celtic history and culture; study of the influences of the Celts on the Germanic tribes; and a comparative investigation of the musical traditions of the Celtic countries (*Celtic Cultures Newsletter*, 1983: 8–9). In all, fifteen subjects were listed but there was no mention of sport.

The ever-controversial term 'culture' can be left to fend for itself in the world of semantics but the term 'Celtic' requires some clarification. On the modern global scale there are many difficult terms, such as 'African', 'American', and 'English'. Terms on the more local scale, like 'Celtic', are not usually known to the wider world and so may be difficult only to themselves and to their immediate neighbours. As to being 'Celtic' today, who is entitled to claim to possess this rather subjective attribute? Which are the marks of Celticity in time and space? Blood, apparel, games may not be intrinsically 'Celtic', although to some people any of them might appear to be 'Celtic' at a given point in time.

Properly, the term 'Celtic' refers to a group of languages in the Indo-European family of languages, but this clearcut and practical definition is viewed with reservation by some who are well-qualified to make comment (see Chapter 1). For instance, Professor Ellis Evans (1995: 9) states 'The term "Celtic" is at best vague and it has been too easily, but improperly, claimed by some scholars that it should, strictly speaking, have a linguistic connotation.'

Naturally when boundaries are not clearly defined there is vagueness, but surely it is not improper to set some clearly defined boundary in order to stabilize perception. To interpret 'Celtic' as 'language-related' is a narrow definition but it fixes a point from which to begin. It may be that having to deal with a timespan which reaches from the prehistoric to the present day is the source of the diffidence which leads to describing the term 'Celtic' as being 'vague'. To describe 'Celtic' as 'vague' is merely to deal in vagueness. Terms like 'Celtic' continue in use when they adapt, or are adapted, to current circumstances.

For instance, the term 'Irish' could, with some justification, be described as 'vague' even when used in a specific context. A 'history' of the Welsh Britons was written by Nennius in the eighth century. A version of the 'history' was made into a long poem in Norman French in the twelfth century. The French was almost immediately turned into English by a priest whose name, Lagmann, may be Norse. In the twentieth century Lagmann, apparently from his literary composition, has been described as having an 'Irish character and atmosphere', whatever that means in the context of the twelfth century (Tatlock, 1950: 529). Ireland and the Irish have changed somewhat since the twelfth century. In some non-Celtic languages of Western Europe the broad meaning of 'Celtic' may contain such well known elements as noble, naïve, childlike, dreamy, romantic, fiery, irascible, troublesome, difficult, insubordinate, unruly, misguided, etc. A degree of irrationality or instability in things and people Celtic seems to be suggested, if not mythologized.

The earliest written references

In the fifth century before Christ Herodotus, the Greek historian, could say of the Celts only that the River Danube rose in Celtic territory, although, of course, it is unlikely that he had an accurate geographical knowledge of the source of the Danube (Tierney, 1960: 194). In the next century Plato, another Greek, described the Celts as hard-drinking belligerent people. In 390 BC Celts captured Rome and thereafter Rome feared Celtic peoples. In 55 BC Julius Caesar, having subdued the Gallic Celts of the area corresponding to modern France, crossed the English Channel and commenced the invasion of Britain purportedly in order to prevent the Britons from supporting their continental neighbours.

At that time most of Britain was Celtic-speaking (i.e. the inhabitants spoke British, the ancestor of modern Welsh) and Ireland also was Celtic-speaking, the language being Gaelic from which derives modern Irish. It is possible that these two strains of language were not strictly confined to their respective islands. Roman power ruled most of Britain during the following five hundred years but did not extend to Highland Scotland, nor to Ireland.

The Antonine Wall was built in AD 142 to protect the northern border of Roman Britain and extended for nearly 60 kilometres from Dumbarton, near Glasgow on the Firth of Clyde, to Bo'ness, near Edinburgh on the Firth of Forth. The northern boundary of the Roman Empire in the second century extended from Dumbarton 'the fort of the Britons' to the Roman town of Aquincum, in the territory of the Celtic Eravisci people, near the modern Hungarian capital Budapest. (The Emperor Hadrianus whose name is commemorated in the name of Britain's major Roman fortification, Hadrian's Wall, was the first Governor of Aquincum.) Between this northern boundary and the Atlantic Ocean and the Mediterranean Sea, people speaking Celtic languages had occupied a large part of the European Continent during the previous five centuries. This is borne out by the wide distribution of placenames accepted as originating in Celtic languages. Obviously Celtic Europe was a significant historic fact.

It appears that the 'Celts' have been moving across the stage of history for the last three thousand years, but it also appears true that for one third of that period they are invisible, or more precisely, that the view of them has been obstructed. From the sixth until the sixteenth century the Celts go unnoticed. The history of the Celts is covered by the moss of time. A less romantic and more factual way to describe what happened would be to say that Imperial Rome conquered most of the Celtic population on the European continent, and that literate Roman Christianity was not entirely averse to writing the Celts out of history. Those who write the history have the advantage.

Scientific enquiry

When the question of surviving Celtic languages and emerging archae-ological remains began to come together in scientific enquiry following the thousand-year gap in continuity, a dichotomy developed whereby some enquirers considered 'Celtic' in terms of archaeological remains while others, who accepted that Celtic speech still survived (alive if not well), turned their attention to the linguistic context. Despite some misguided effort both groups eventually made sensible progress. As clearly pointed out recently by John Collis (Collis, 1997: 197), the printed works of George Buchanan (1594), of Paul-Yves Pezron, who popularized the term 'Celte' in modern times (1703), and of Edward Lhuyd (1707) are significant milestones in the linguistic field, where theories of the prehistoric gradually adjusted to understanding of the contemporary. To these I would add Le Pelletier (1752) and Kaspar Zeuss (1853). Publications of other sorts stimulated interest in the 'noble' Celt; for example, the compositions of

James MacPherson (1760), which introduced Ossian, Oscar etc. first to readers of English, and through them to a wider world.

The archaeological enquiry did not always work in cooperation with the linguistic enquiry. However, political awareness came to draw on the work of both disciplines, at first with appreciative delight in finding technical skill among 'Celtic' forebears, and later with intellectual satisfaction in the independent identity of living Celtic speech with its long literary tradition. The word 'Celtic' was soon to become a word of great potential, capable of being used in a multitude of creative contexts: literary, musical, spiritual and, especially, political. This development, cultivated mostly in good faith, and sometimes by opposing interests, can easily provoke bitterness and dissension. For instance, in discussing the definition of 'Celt' and 'Celtic', one modern author writes in French of 'these terms greatly abused by authors and politically-minded people with few scruples who have used them, and who continue to use them, as an anchoring-point for their cultural and racial obsessions' (Galliou, 1994: 25–6).

Fellow Celts

Just as I begin to assemble these thoughts, an 'international' game of rugby is taking place in Dublin between Ireland and Wales. There will be some Welsh-speakers rambling the streets of the city tonight. Will they feel 'Celtic' in this environment? Will they feel that they are among 'Celts'? The number of Irish persons who can communicate in Welsh is small and the number of Welsh who can communicate in Irish is probably smaller. Will sport in the form of an oval ball make 'fellow-Celts' of all those who are that way inclined, irrespective of the common non-Celtic language, the *lingua Anglica*? Will this help to make more 'Celtic culture'?

HURLING IN HISTORY: A PERSPECTIVE

At this point I would like to put the game of hurling into my historical perspective. Hurling in Ireland seems to go back to prehistoric times (Ó Maolfabhail, 1973). Some evidence exists for games of the type in other parts of the world but the origin of hurling in Ireland has not been established. It is not necessarily Celtic. The word *camán* (which means 'curved thing') is the traditional Gaelic name for the playing-stick, both in Ireland and in Scotland, and is the basis of the Gaelic name of the Scottish game of *camanachd* or shinty (see Chapter 7).

If complete Celtic culture ever existed in Ireland, then it must have been before the beginning of the seventeenth century, when Ireland as a Celtic-speaking nation lost its effective sovereignty consequent on the defeat of the Irish and their Spanish allies by the English at the Battle of Kinsale in County Cork in 1602. Subsequently Ireland became less and less Celtic-speaking so that by 1922, when some sovereignty was redeemed through the setting up of the modern Irish state, the restoration of the not-quite-extinct Irish Celtic language was adopted as a fundamental aim of the new state. This policy had been actively promoted by the Gaelic League which was founded in 1893 by Douglas Hyde, first President of Ireland (1938–45), and might be described as an attempt to 'make' a modern Celtic culture. It was, and is, observed with varying degrees of interest and sympathy, particularly by the non-Irish who have Celtic aspirations.

Hurling an old game

The earliest Irish records show that the stick-and-ball game, in whatever form, had a romantic, heroic character in Ireland. Early references to the *camán* (hurley), which is also referred to as *lorg* (shaft) and *lorg ána* (driving shaft), together with *liathróid* (ball) occur in legal texts in the Irish language which are believed to have been written down in the seventh or eighth centuries, and which may descend from pre-Christian times. Some of the legal texts are obscure as to meaning but the context shows the seriousness of the subjects mentioned. In one particular text on the laws of fosterage it is stated that it is proper for a king's son to have 'silver on his scabbards and bronze on his *camáin* (the plural of *camán*), and tin on scabbards and copper on *camáin* for those of lesser degree'. Clearly the *camán* was held in high esteem. In the literary references to hurling it is the sons of kings and other important persons who are the players. Probably the most famed hurler of the literature is Cú Chulainn, warrior hero of the saga named *Táin Bó Chuaille* (the *Cattle Raid of Cooley*) which survives in manuscripts written in the twelfth century. In this and other tales the game is referred to as *iomáin* (driving) and is a vigorous game requiring skill and physical prowess. Conall Gulban and Diarmaid are other famous mythical figures who excel at hurling.

Apart from the sagas and tales, there is actual contemporary reference to hurling in the classical poetry. For example, in 1366 in County Cork a young leader is urged to exchange the *camán* for the sword; this echoes the Statutes of Kilkenny. About 1425 a poet recalls nostalgically watching the hurling near the harbour of Carrickfergus in County Antrim. A poet who died in 1487 refers to the Virgin Mary as 'the winning stroke of women'; in a poem written about 1550 three young men of County Clare are called 'the three hurleys which won the game'. And the most impressive visual representation of a *camán* is on a fifteenth-century stone graveslab in northern County Donegal. On this stone the *camán* resembles closely the modern Scottish *camán* and is accompanied by a ball and a sword. Having this solid historical, as well as romantic, background it was quite logical for the *camán* to take its place beside other symbols of Ireland's former glory during the national resurgence in the nineteenth century. Firstly, however, we must consider how the *camán* developed its recent political character.

Ireland's changed world

It is only since the seventeenth century, when Ireland no longer had sovereign power, that hurling became a mark of Irishness, especially of that kind of Irishness which refutes and opposes English claims to sovereign authority in Ireland. The following extract is from a letter written by Lord Orrery (Roger Boyle), who at the time was styled President of Munster under the Restoration Parliament in Ireland. The letter is dated 9 July 1667 and has a pronounced political and religious bias.

> I hear out of Tipperary, that there is a view taken of Irish Papists, and several are enlisted, both horse and foot, and buying arms and fixing old ones. Since the enlisting, the priests have great meetings, one at Knock-graffan of about 800 men, whereof many armed: their presence was for consecrating a priest. Another great meeting in Clanwilliam, on the edge of Kilnamanagh, under pretence of a match at hurling. (Kelly, 1848: 23)

The idea of using sporting gatherings as a camouflage for other activities can hardly have been a new one, even in the seventeenth century, and Orrery's statement may not have been particularly adverse to the 'match at hurling'. Indeed there is ample evidence in newspaper notices during the eighteenth century that some, at least, of the landed gentry of Ireland promoted hurling events which seem to have been modelled on challenges at cricket in England. For example, in June 1708 advance notice in a newspaper announced that on the next St Swithin's Day, the 15th of July, on the Curragh of Kildare (the modern horse-racing venue), in conjunction with a fair, there would be a hurling match between thirty men from each side of the River Liffey for thirty shillings, and that a barrel of ale, tobacco and pipes would be given to the hurlers (*Flying Post*, 28 June 1708). Perhaps the following deposition from 1726 refers to an equally pleasant occasion, but the official record shows it in a particularly political light:

there was a great assembly on the said 24th June (1726) to play at hurly which this examinant believes was contrived on purpose to bring persons together in order to be enlisted [ostensibly for Spain, but in reality for the Pretender, James Stuart, as stated in another paragraph of the deposition] and the rather for that there had not been any hurlyings suffered by the said Charles McCarthy [of Carrignavar, County Cork] on his lands on any 24th of June since the time of his turning, or pretending to turn, Protestant which was in 1720, except the said day. (PROSP 63/388)

The association with political unrest is again recorded later in the eighteenth century. In letters to a leading Dublin newspaper a correspondent deplores the barbarity and debauchery evident at hurling matches. Writing from Fethard in County Tipperary he says:

At these meetings all associations and midnight revels are hatched; and positively hurling matches were the first beginnings of the deluded unthinking people called White Boys, who are now rising again in a neighbouring county, in open defiance of the laws, though their wicked combustans have already been the occasion of so much blood spilt; of so many women bereft of their husbands and sons and so many helpless orphans of the source of their beings; and which has caused the Government to much uneasiness, expence and trouble. (*Freeman's Journal*, 16–19 September 1766)

The White Boys were an agrarian organization in the south of the country which often used violent means in seeking to redress grievances. Other groups, such as the Hearts of Oak and the Hearts of Steel, which had similar aims and methods, existed at this time in the north of the country. Instead of achieving reform this movement brought about the introduction of coercion acts. However, the unedifying picture painted by this writer in his letters is in complete contrast to other accounts of matches in the late eighteenth and early nineteenth centuries.

Sabbath observance

Down the centuries Sundays, augmented by a number of feast days, had been the free days of the poorer people. It is difficult to determine whether the zeal of the Catholic clergy in promoting solemn observance of the sabbath in Ireland was inspired more by the desire to conform to the Protestant view of strict sabbath day observance, or by the desire that their flock should avoid all occasions which might encourage social or political unrest. Much reference is made to unbecoming behaviour at hurling matches and similar public gatherings, and this may, indeed, be well founded. However, it must also be borne in mind that during the period in question the Catholic Church in Ireland was striving to reach an accommodation with the Protestant English Government and would have been anxious to appear as amenable and as conformist as possible.

The following is an extract from a pastoral letter issued by the bishop of Ferns (County Wexford) to the priests of his diocese shortly after the 1798 Rising to which the bishop refers (*Spicilegium Ossoriensis*, 1884: 563):

Rev. Sir,
Being just now informed that numbers of people assemble for the apparent purpose of ball playing or other amusements on Sundays and Festivals; and whereas such public amusements on such days are and constantly have been attended with many scandalous breaches of the Law of God, and of his holy Church, being the occasion of drunkenness, quarrels, debauchery, and other excesses, besides being a glaring violation and profanation of the Sabbath, the Lord's Day, so repeatedly commanded to be sanctified, to be kept holy; and to be only employed in acts of devotion, piety and divine worship; and whereas the late heinous and glaring misconduct of alas! too many of the poor people of our communion, and the peculiar circumstances of the present times, make it highly improper and dangerous to themselves to have any unlawful or unnecessary meeting or assemblies; these are therefore to require you to renew to them from your altars the admonitions, instructions, and orders which you have heretofore repeatedly received from Us on that head. You are immediately to exhort them zealously, as they fear the just judgement of God, as they hope in his mercy, as they respect his holy law, as they regard their own eternal salvation and their personal safety here, by these and by the Passion of Jesus Christ and the bowels of his mercy, you are to conjure and warn them to desist and avoid all such unlawful, sinful meetings; you are to charge them strictly, that having heard Mass on Sundays and other Festivals, thay immediately depart and return direct to their respective homes, and continue to be there the remainder of the day and night, without offence to God or man.
I remain, Rev. Sir,
Your very faithful servant in Christ
James Caulfield

The same county of Wexford produced two long mock-heroic poems in the English language which give a different impression of hurling matches, as may be seen from the following short excerpts. The first, published in 1779, gives a sympathetic description in iambic pentameter of the teams, the spectators and the match; a barrel of beer and a piper complete the scene.

> Hurling, we may from gravest authors find,
> To be of two Olympian games combin'd.
> There strength of body, swiftness in the race,
> These qualities in hurling still take place:
> Alike in each th'athletic youth is crown'd,
> While with their praises the distant hills resound.
>
> (Devereux, 1779, lines 133–8)

The second poem, again in iambic pentameter, dates from February 1805 and refers to a match arranged for a Saturday

> Stern Mars inflames, and makes the Duff'ry rise;
> Their blood thus quicken'd, flashes in their eyes.
> Apollo sage, by long experience knew,
> That courage, without wisdom, will not do;
> Directs their ardour, regulates their will,
> That every blow is aim'd with art and skill.
>
> (Broadsheet, 1805, lines 69–74)

The Catholic Church in Ireland, however, while ministering to the vast majority of the population, including the majority of the transmitters of the hurling tradition, continued during the nineteenth century to distance itself from that tradition. The Catholic colleges which were established during that period for the further education of Irish Catholic boys, like their non-Catholic counterparts, adopted the games played in the public schools of England, and, in doing so, established a new modern Irish tradition. (Curiously, it can be argued that the greatest organized disregard of the puritan Sabbath observance in Ireland has come from the Gaelic Athletic Association, whose headquarters and principal stadium, Croke Park in Dublin, commemorate one of its first patrons, the Roman Catholic Archbishop Croke of Cashel, a Tipperaryman who died in 1902.)

The 'tithes hurlers'

If the seditious character associated with hurling is only slightly documented up to the end of the eighteenth century it soon became well documented. The tithes tax was one of the major causes of grievance during the eighteenth and the early nineteenth centuries. This was a compulsory tax levied on the entire population for the support of the officially established Protestant Church of Ireland. After the passing of the Catholic Emancipation Bill in 1829 public resistance to the tax became increasingly violent, not only among Catholics who formed the majority of the population, but also among the large Presbyterian community in the north of the country.

During 1829 and the years immediately following, public opposition to paying of tithes became intense and the large gatherings of men which met to demonstrate, and also to intimidate the tithe-proctors, came to be known as 'hurlers', apparently from the fact that they often carried hurleys. The hurleys may have been carried in order to disguise proscribed meetings, but often the numbers involved must have appeared suspiciously large and the hurley itself must have acquired an undeniably seditious character. Various well documented pitched battles took place between the people and the authorities with many fatal casualties. One such 'battle' which occurred at Carrickshock in County Kilkenny on 16 December 1831, resulted in about twenty-five civilian deaths or serious injuries and the death of the process-server and twelve policemen. The incident is commemorated in what probably was the last song composed in the traditional Irish language of the region (O'Hanrahan, 1990: 491).

An account of an incident at Burnchurch in County Kilkenny in 1830 mentions a crowd of between 1000 and 1500 (*Kilkenny Journal*, 30 July 1831). 'The crowd was shouting and flourishing sticks and hurls, and calling out "No tithes". One of those present, and one who had consulted the Catholic Bishop of the area the previous day, addressed the crowd and he later stated in court that "... in consequence of my address, telling them it was wrong to cut timber, as had been done at previous meetings, they threw hundreds of sticks into the river" ' (O'Donoghue, 1966: 70).

In considering whether the sticks carried by the anti-tithes 'hurlers' were indeed hurleys or merely sticks it must be borne in mind that at the time suitable sticks, freshly cut and with little modification, may have been adequate for hurling.

While the age-old stick-and-ball game continued, as ever, to keep its sporting character, its political association seems to have been openly accepted, not particularly because of the nature of the game, but because the gatherings would be naturally convenient for political activity, whether open or clandestine. On 24 June 1848 a correspondent of *The Nation*, the nationalist Dublin newspaper, suggested (p. 408) that 'if a hurling club, or cricket club was got up with its regular place and hour of meeting, and mixing of amusement and politics which would be an additional attraction', it could serve also as a Confederate Club of the Young Ireland Movement. The reference to cricket may indicate an attempt to attract a broad spectrum of Irish society to the Movement.

Trinity College, Dublin, Hurling Club

In 1870 a set of rules entitled *Laws of Hurling* was drawn up and published by the Dublin University Hurley Club (*Handbook*, 1870) and a revised set was published in 1879 (*Handbook*, 1879), which was the year in which the Irish Hurley Union was founded. In 1884 the Gaelic Athletic Association was founded and in the following year the Association undertook the organizing of the game, seeking the allegiance of all those interested. However, by 1892 the Irish Hurley Union had become the Irish Hockey Union and had adopted the rules of the English Hockey Association.

The Gaelic Athletic Association can be regarded as an expression of the strong nationalist feeling which was pervading Ireland at the time and which was centring largely on a campaign in support of tenant farmers. In 1879 the Irish National Land League had been founded by Michael Davitt with Charles Stewart Parnell as its president. In 1870 Davitt, the son of an evicted small tenant, had been sentenced to fifteen years penal servitude for his part in the Fenian Movement and had served seven years. Parnell, the son of an Anglo-Irish country gentleman, was an elected Member of the British House of Commons and a leading figure in the Irish Home Rule Party.

In the General Election of 1885 the vast majority of the members of Parliament returned in Ireland were in favour of Home Rule for Ireland, and in Britain the leader of the victorious Liberal Party, William Gladstone, also declared in favour of Home Rule for Ireland. In 1888 two leading Liberals arrived in Dublin to address a public meeting in favour of Home Rule and were met by a tremendous organized procession of welcome, representative of many societies. The following is part of the report in one of the daily newspapers (*Freeman's Journal*, 2 February 1888: 5):

> It may be safely said without fear of raising any trade jealousy that far and away the finest section of the procession were the members of the Gaelic Athletic Association. About a thousand strapping young men clad in jerseys and bearing their *camáns* on their shoulders marched under the banners of their respective branches.

Parnell died in London in 1891. His body was brought to Dublin on Sunday, morning 11 October, and lay in state for some time in the City Hall.

> At two o'clock the funeral procession began. Drenching rain still fell, but no one remembered the rain. Two thousand Gaels, each carrying a *camán* draped with black, appeared in a formation of six abreast, and made a

pathway through the thick, swaying crowd. There was noise and confusion until an uncovered man appeared on the high steps of the balcony and cried out, 'Hush! Hush!' and instantly there was a deep silence and heads were uncovered, and what before was a black, indistinguishable mass became a sea of white, anxious faces. The body was brought out. The Gaels raised their *camáns* in salutation, and a deep wail rose from the assembled Irish. At a quarter-past two, when all was ready, the procession moved off. Forty bands with muffled drums, played Chopin's *Funeral March* or *Adeste Fideles* along the road to Glasnevin. It was nearly half-past six when at last, in the wet dusk, he was buried. A hundred and fifty thousand men and women had trudged through the drenching rain to bid farewell to their only chief. 'Farewell, our chief, our dear chief! Farewell! Farewell!' (Irvine, 1925: 318)

And in 1903, on the occasion of the commemoration of the public execution of Robert Emmet in 1803 for plotting to break the recently enacted union with Britain, the procession to the spot in Thomas Street in Dublin where Emmet met his death consisted solely of young men carrying hurleys on their shoulders. Thenceforth the *camán*, the hurley, was regarded as a symbol of defiance of British rule in Ireland. In August 1917 Éamonn De Valera, survivor of the 1916 Rising, future Taoiseach (Premier), future President of Ireland, and future President of the Council of the League of Nations was greeted in Tipperary Town with a defiant display of hurleys (Breen, 1924: 7–9). A special proclamation had just been issued prohibiting the carrying of any 'weapon of offence or article capable of being used as such'. The immediate cause of this prohibition was the death of a police inspector from a blow of a hurley received in an attempt by police to break up a public meeting held in protest against the treatment of nationalists in prison in England.

In 1971 young women demonstrating outside courts of law in Belfast carried hurleys. They were arrested, charged with possessing the sticks, and with wearing military-type uniforms, and were sentenced to six months imprisonment (national newspapers, 1 January 1971).

The Gaelic Athletic Association

When the Gaelic Athletic Association was founded by Michael Cusack in 1884, organized field and track sports were generally the preserve of the socially better off – gentlemen amateurs – and these did not welcome competition from an association which, if successful, was likely to have great potential while possibly in sympathy with Nationalism.

'The Association swept the country like a prairie fire,' wrote Cusack, years later, regarding the first two years of the GAA. This is how Marcus de Búrca sums up the progress of those first two years (de Búrca, 1980: 23):

Indeed in rural Ireland the founding of the GAA caused something approaching a social revolution. Many sports meetings were held in places that had not seen such contests for half-a-century (since before the Great Famine of the late 1840s); they drew crowds of sizes that had not been seen since [Daniel] O'Connell's repeal meetings of the 1840s. In conjunction with many of these meetings hurling and (to a lesser extent initially) football games were organised, mostly in places where one or both games had survived the Famine. As a result hurling was saved from almost certain extinction. Its position where it was still played was greatly strengthened, and often a revival of the game in adjoining areas occurred.

On several occasions, including one when under oath in court, Cusack asserted that his dual object in starting the GAA was to open athletics to the ordinary citizen and to halt and reverse the decline in Irish games. While frankly admitting that 'every social movement in Ireland is to a certain extent necessarily political', he swore that the GAA was 'not in any way connected with politics'. (ibid.: 29)

The huge support which the Association drew to itself identified it clearly with the separatist Home Rule movement. Its opponents could neither defeat it nor join it. In short, polarization occurred. The main strength of the GAA was in the independent-mindedness of its members, the determination to manage their own affairs. Without that philosophy it was most likely, at the height of the British Empire's power, that their energy would be channelled into organizations with headquarters outside Ireland, and with little inclination to preserve, let alone encourage, Irish traditions.

The significance of the hurling game is twofold. Firstly, historical evidence shows it to be undeniably Irish (while having close relatives in Britain in the form of *camanachd*/shinty and hockey/bandy). Secondly, it is a vigorous sport, played between two teams, in which a two-handed implement is used to contest for a ball at close quarters. It is the use of this implement, the *camán*/hurley, by each player throughout the game, which ensures that each player carries his personal *camán*, an obvious and distinct indicator of his purpose. Such an implement necessitates physical and mental discipline on the part of its user. Furthermore, it clearly distinguishes the active from the passive participant. In short, to carry a hurley is to make an unequivocal statement.

Even had the Gaelic Athletic Association never come into existence it is quite likely that the *camán* would have joined the imagery of resurgent Irishness in the nineteenth century alongside the shamrock, the round tower, the harp, the wolfhound, the uncanonized native saint, even the shillelagh. These all played their part in the search for an independent national identity and were probably more influential than the concept of Celticity. Ironically, when the early GAA stabilized and concentrated on promoting the two field games, hurling and Gaelic football, it was the football which made most progress, becoming the most popular and the most widely practised game in twentieth-century Ireland.

Football

There are no references to football of any kind in Irish language sources before the end of the seventeenth century and it seems that all the earliest substantial references to football in Ireland are from the eighteenth century onwards in areas on the east coast of the country. These areas were probably subject to influence from Britain, where there is definite mention of football from the early fourteenth century (Ó Caithnia, 1984: 1, 5). In 1841 travel writers from England state, 'But the great game in Kerry, and indeed throughout the South, is the game of "Hurley" – a game rather rare, although not unknown in England' (Hall, 1843: 288). County Kerry won its first All-Ireland Senior Championship in 1891 – for hurling, yet has never repeated that success in hurling although winning thirty annual All-Ireland Senior Football Championships since then.

Since the early years of the Gaelic Athletic Association about ten of the thirty-two counties have been considered strong traditional hurling areas while the game is considered to have been virtually extinct in the other counties in those early years. (Incidentally, there is not sufficient evidence extant to show that games of the hurling nature were ever universal in Ireland at any one time before the advent of the Gaelic Athletic Association.) Today Gaelic Football is the most popular game of all throughout Ireland, yet due to policy and due also, perhaps, to the intrinsic attraction of the game, all counties in Ireland, as well as, on occasion, teams from outside Ireland, participate in the annual National Hurling League, which is graded for an annual promotion and relegation system.

The National Hurling League for counties was instituted in 1925 and provides matches for all counties at a suitable level. The annual All-Ireland Senior Hurling Championship Competition has been in existence since 1884 and is a more intense competition than the National League. It is contested on a knock-out basis and over the years has been won by just thirteen counties, with more than half the total held by three counties (Counties Cork, Kilkenny and Tipperary). The annual All Ireland Club Championship (Hurling) was instituted in 1972 and is a very popular knock-out competition contested by the champion club of each county. There are many other hurling competitions. Of course Gaelic football has a similar range of competitions.

A small number of noted players excel in both hurling and football; usually where counties and clubs can maintain a high standard in both. It is sometimes evident, as would be expected, that rivalry exists between the two games, especially when both make demands on individual players. However, the cohabitation is generally fruitful, evidenced by the steady spread of modern hurling, while football continues as popular as ever. It should be pointed out that both games, each with teams of fifteen players, are played on the same field with the same scoring system.

CONCLUSION

There is an obvious parallel between the fortunes of hurling and the fortunes of the Irish (Celtic) language. Each indigenous in Ireland but virtually extinct at the end of the nineteenth century; each neglected, and in effect repressed, by the temporal and spiritual powers of the land; each revived deliberately and seen as a very distinctive badge of Irish identity. In each case the revival adopted a policy and a political agenda which, due to the enthusiasm of idealists and the force of popular support, renewed the vigour of two of the more ancient elements of European culture. Such a revival today, if sympathetically viewed, might end up under the wing of a Heritage Council with no great prospect of lift-off.

Languages may become extinct and survive only in fossilized form. Ball games, on the other hand, may flourish or fail like seasonal vegetation in its various forms with the seed lying dormant until favourable conditions return. Hurling, I believe, and as I have tried to show, is a good example of a social activity which consumes and generates energy. The growth of the Gaelic Athletic Association to its present stature as a 'national' umbrella for 'national' games probably owes more to the hurling tradition than is generally acknowledged. Equally the recognition of a perceived Irish identity in the modern world owes much to the hurling tradition. The extent to which the term 'Celtic culture' can honestly be applied to that identity may be a matter of opinion (Dowling, 1997).

This is my reading of the story. Like the Gaelic storyteller I finish with the words '*Má tá bréag ann, bíodh; ní mise a chum ná a cheap*'. (If falsehood be there, so be it; it is not I who invented or fabricated.) As to the game, and the spirit of the game, I believe that the pure attraction and beauty of playing the ball with the stick in the face of physical opposition will outlast transient politics and cultures.

12

HERITAGE, CULTURE AND IDENTITY: THE GAELIC ATHLETIC ASSOCIATION IN SCOTLAND

Joseph M. Bradley

In societies which have a Celtic as well as a non-Celtic heritage, sport has contributed considerably to ideas about identity, in particular in relation to images and conceptions which inform and concern community, nation and culture. For over one hundred years identity in much of Ireland has often been defined with a significant strain of passion for Gaelic sports. This passion has invoked nationalist, political, cultural as well as purely sporting sensibilities. For 'Gaels', these passions came together in Gaelic sport with the formation of the Gaelic Athletic Association (GAA) in 1884. Thus, any study of the GAA is also a consideration of the sociology, history, culture and political nature of Ireland. It forms part of the story of the people of Ireland and it reflects on activities which run deep in Irish consciousness.

This can also be considered to be applicable to the Irish diaspora, historically part of the Irish people and an important concern linked to interpretations of Ireland. This work focuses on those migrated to Scotland, in particular, those who have created, sustained and become part of one of the most significant institutions in modern Irish society, the GAA. The GAA has seen its influence spread among the Irish in the USA and Britain, and its games have been played in almost every country which has experienced a sizeable Irish presence. Although there are reports of hurling being played in London in 1775 (on a field where the British Museum now stands), presumably amongst early Irish immigrants, such occurrences seemed to have been occasional (*Irish Post*, 3 November 1884). By 1885 the first GAA club in Britain had been founded in Wallsend near Newcastle upon Tyne, an area of high Irish migration. In a more formal sense, the Gaelic Athletic Association was founded in London in 1895, though it would be around 1903 before Central Council in Dublin began reporting on Gaelic activities in Britain.

In 1984 the Gaelic Athletic Association celebrated its centenary. It was by then a complex organization which, without losing its essential character, was continually adapting to the ways and practices of the mass media and sponsorship. By this time also, Gaelic games had either been played or continued to be played in countries which traditionally hosted Irish ex-patriot communities: Rhodesia, Argentina, the USA, Canada, England, Wales, New Zealand and Scotland. The centenary celebrations of 1984 were to provide a landmark for Gaelic sports in Scotland.

Scotland has been home to an immigrant Irish population since the early nineteenth century, but particularly since the years of the exodus from Ireland during *an Gorta Mor* (the Great Hunger) of 1845–9. Handley (1964), estimates that of those million or more who departed Ireland during the Famine years, 100, 000 came to Scotland. Over the remaining part of the nineteenth and for much of the twentieth century, hundreds of thousands more arrived, invariably settling among the previous generations.

Although 1984 was significant for the Association in Scotland, or more accurately, for the Association in Glasgow, it was not really a celebration of the GAA's place in Irish culture in west central Scotland or amongst the Irish diaspora there. Indeed, not only was the Gaelic Athletic Association of little relevance to most members of that community, so also were Gaelic sports. In 1984, the GAA in Scotland was a tiny moribund organization which had little bearing on the Irishness of the wider community. By far the dominant sport in Scotland and indeed Britain, was football, or soccer as it is more often called among the Gaelic fraternity. Nonetheless, Gaelic sporting history in Scotland remains a rich one.

Of course, the GAA had taken many decades before it finally began to make a major impact upon Irish life. It is important to recognize that part of the explanation for the weakness of the Association in Scotland is that the Irish had a presence in Scotland before the Gaelic Athletic Association in Ireland was founded and before it had established its place even in Irish society. This is crucial to understanding why it was to soccer that many Irish in Scotland turned for expressing themselves culturally, especially through sport.

Although all the counties of Ireland's provinces are represented among Irish immigrants coming to Scotland, most observers relate that a majority of these immigrants, certainly in later waves of migration, originated in the Ulster counties, north Leinster, or Mayo and other northerly areas from the province of Connacht: generally the northern half of the country. Many of these places were the very areas in which the Association struggled most in Ireland. In addition, the masses of Ireland had been demoralized throughout the years of colonialism and particularly as a consequence of the Great Famine. Kinealy believes that the price paid by the Irish for the Famine was 'privation, disease, emigration, mortality and an enduring legacy of disenchantment' (Kinealy, 1994: 359). Dr Douglas Hyde, later to become the first President of Ireland, concluded:

> The Famine destroyed everything. Poetry, music and dancing stopped. Sport and pastimes disappeared. And when times improved, those things never returned as they were. (*Irish Post*, 2 September 1895)

Immigrants from Ireland were often wholly concerned with surviving in an alien and hostile environment and not drawing attention to themselves. Many had left Ireland some years before the new era of confidence in Irish cultural activities had began to make an impact. Nevertheless, towards the end of the nineteenth century the GAA began to make progress amongst the Irish abroad. By the mid-1890s, New York, for example, had some twenty Gaelic clubs operating. In England, in 1896 the GAA was founded by the ex-patriot community. This was followed in 1900 by the organization of a provincial council. Reflecting the sense of patriotism often felt by Gaelic-minded people, one of the first clubs affiliated to the growing GAA in London was the Robert Emmet's Club of Marylebone. The idea of calling a club after a perceived patriot has been a hallmark of GAA clubs since the founding of the Association. Indeed, when the Tuam Krugers Club was founded in County Galway around 1900 (Central Council Minutes, 1900: 31–2), that club's name amounted to a clear statement with regards 'British colonialism' and the Boer War then underway in South Africa.

In 1895, the main Irish Catholic newspaper of the time, the *Glasgow Examiner*, printed a letter on 20 April which complained at the lack of Irish cultural activity reflecting the Gaelic revival in Ireland. A positive response was forthcoming. The same year, the William O'Brien Gaelic Class was formed and had become a branch of the Gaelic League before the year was out (*Glasgow Examiner*, 24 August 1895). This year thus marks the establishment of the Gaelic League in Glasgow, only two years after its founding in Dublin. Over the next few years the Gaelic League underwent a significant growth among the Irish communities of greater Glasgow and Lanarkshire.

The first record of a GAA club in Scotland is to be found in 1897. The *Glasgow Examiner* carried news that 'a large and enthusiastic meeting of young Irishmen of the city was held in the Young Ireland Hall ... for the purpose of forming a branch of the Gaelic Athletic Association in Glasgow.'

It was agreed by those present that the Red Hugh O'Neill Gaelic Athletic Club be set up to include all branches of Irish national pastime – hurling, football, running, jumping, boxing, dumb-bell and Indian club exercises, etc, (*Glasgow Examiner*, 11 September 1897). The club was to be non-sectarian but membership was restricted to respectable young men of Irish birth or parentage, and of good moral character. The emphasis on such a strong Irish lineage probably reflected that most people in that community came into this category. Noticeably, there was no reference to the religion of potential members, though it would be inevitable that almost all would be Catholic by faith.

Again, it was likely that it was the politically active amongst the Irish community who gave birth to the 'Red Hugh' Club. After all, the location for engagements was well established as a place for nationalist meetings, and there seems to have been some overlap in membership of those of the Irish National League and the new club: John Brolly and Joseph McFaulds (or McFalls) being involved in both bodies. Tom Fergie of the Ormond Club was designated trainer and Mr P. Honeyman became president. Although the club was reported as being in regular training and preparing for a match against a London side, reports of hurling activity in Glasgow quickly died.

Among the immigrant community, Irish political and cultural activities were plentiful. The Irish National League, the Irish Independent League, the Ancient Order of Hibernians and the Irish National Foresters, added to the plethora of Catholic bodies, and Celtic Football Club, meant that by the end of the nineteenth century being Irish in Scotland had an array of outlets. The first signs of the impact of the Gaelic revival in Ireland appear in the regular Gaelic League columns of *The Examiner* from August 1896 onwards. By 1897 there was seventeen branches of the League in Ireland, four in England and the one in Glasgow: the latter based in St Francis Parish in the east of the city.

Although Irish political and cultural activities in west central Scotland were both plentiful and vibrant until the 1920s, with the advent of 'the Great War' and the gradual unfolding of a pivotal stage in Ireland's struggle against British rule (particularly the 1916 Rising, the War of Independence and the Irish Civil War), the cultural and political landscape which the Irish in Scotland experienced was on the verge of change. With morale low and the unenviable depression of losing family and friends, many local organizations never again regained their vibrancy.

Little Gaelic sporting activity in Scotland can be detected during the 1920s. Certainly some clubs were playing the occasional game, as is evidenced in a Pearse Harps – Patrick Sarsfields football match in 1920

(*The Examiner*, 28 February 1920), as well as the founding of another hurling club in Coatbridge in the same year (*The Examiner*, 17 July 1920). However, there seem to have been few formal GAA activities at this time.

By the 1930s the Gaelic Athletic Association in Scotland was facing its lowest ebb. It had long struggled to be recognized even amongst its own community in Scotland but with the changing environment its chances for survival, never mind vibrancy, were severely restricted. In the decades prior to the Second World War, the Irish in Scotland were the focus for much antagonism on the part of religious, political and popular organizations, as well as a number of significant individuals (see Bradley, 1996). This period can be characterized as one where to be seen to be Irish was to court fewer life chances.

Nevertheless, some activity on the part of Irish Gaels remained. In early 1933, after initial contacts between representatives of the Irish National Association and the Southern Shinty League, an advertisement in the *Glasgow Observer* appealed for support for a new initiative:

> that the Irish people in Glasgow will give ... the support it would receive in Ireland by turning out in large numbers to give the Irish team a hearty welcome and show that the exiles still hold dear the National games of Ireland. (From 1984 centenary brochure of Glasgow GAA)

The result of the meeting was the arrangement of a fixture between an Irish University hurling team playing a compromise rules game against a selection of players from the Scottish Shinty League at Shieldhall Park, Hardgate Road in south Govan, Glasgow. The hurling team was composed of players from the University Colleges of Dublin, Cork and Galway. The Glasgow Southern Shinty League selection were all of Highland birth and descent. The hurlers won the match by the only goal of the game (*Glasgow Observer*, 13 May 1933: 8). Nonetheless, according to one report (1984 centenary brochure): 'the result was of secondary importance to the fact that this essentially Gaelic game was shown to have a large following in the West of Scotland and the possibilities for its development are attractive.'

The GAA in Scotland was clearly looking anxiously for revival. In October of the same year, Rev. Daniel O'Keeffe of St Charles Kelvinside, Glasgow, Rev. Daniel Horgan, Irish National Association, acting as an intermediary for the GAA in Dublin, along with Mr P. O'Keeffe, secretary of the GAA in Ireland and Mr P. McNamee, secretary of the Ulster Council, met with officials of the Camanachd Association in Scotland: 'with a view to unifying the rules of hurling and shinty' (*Glasgow Star and Examiner*, 9 September 1933). Among the camanachd representatives were ex-provost Skinner from Oban and Messrs Fletcher (Glasgow) and Patterson (Beauly). The result of the meeting was that future games between hurling and shinty representatives would be directed by the attending members at this meeting. They would 'settle points of divergence in the unified game' (*Glasgow Star and Examiner*, 21 October 1933). Despite the plans and expectations, nothing appears to have been done during the rest of the year.

According to Hutchinson (1989), at various junctures during the twentieth century efforts were made to substantiate competition between hurlers in Ireland and shinty players in Scotland. However, the Scottish shinty authorities did not welcome the Irish competition and in 1964 the Camanachd Association pronounced itself to be 'firmly against any links' with Gaelic sports in Ireland. Nonetheless, in 1971, Blessed Oliver Plunkett School from Dublin travelled to play Oban High School and according to Hutchinson, 'the ice was broken'. Since then, a number of clubs in both countries have played each other and 'international' matches have also been held (Hutchinson, 1989). Despite the existence of committed Gaelic enthusiasts and continued attempts on the part of the Irish National Association, who were at the forefront of Gaelic Irish activities, to revive Gaelic games and other Irish pursuits and pastimes, a revival was still a long way off.

Irishness was still important within the immigrant community, as was partly reflected in the thousands who followed Celtic Football Club and the 40,000 who turned out for a march by the Ancient Order of Hibernians at Carfin in Lanarkshire in August 1937 (*Glasgow Star and Examiner*, 28 August 1937), but Gaelic sports struggled to rise above 'minority' status. Few families who were Irish, Irish-minded or of Irish antecedents, had any affinity for these uniquely Irish sports. By the 1940s other 'Irish Ireland' cultural activities, and Gaelic sports in particular, were at a low point in the west of Scotland. It would be some years before Gaelic enthusiasts recognized that if Irish sporting activities were to survive and become popular, there would have to be a concerted effort to recruit young people of Irish antecedents. Indeed, Gaelic activity, as integral aspects of being Irish in Scotland, would virtually require to be introduced as new sports to many of those with Irish forebears.

A few years after the Second World War a Gaelic sporting revival did take place, 'chiefly attributable to the post World War II situation when Irish immigrants found a great demand for their labour in Scotland in vast building and construction developments' (centenary brochure, 1984). By the late 1940s, as a result of the efforts of a few Gaelic enthusiasts amongst the new wave of immigrants, GAA activities began to re-emerge in west central Scotland.

In June 1950 the Central Council in Dublin sponsored an exhibition game of hurling at Moore Park, Govan, the home of St Anthony's Junior Soccer Club, between two senior county teams from Ulster, Derry and Antrim. The match ended Antrim 3:11, Derry 2:8. In 1954 Glasgow played Antrim in Casement Park and later travelled to Clones to meet Monaghan. In 1963 Glasgow played and defeated Lancashire Champions, John Mitchells' from Liverpool, in a challenge match in the English city. The following year a Scottish-based side were well beaten by London in the British Provincial Championship. In 1970 and 1971 the Glasgow Champions were accepted to play in the Ulster 'Club' championship. Around this time Glasgow played Clan na Gael of Armagh in the tournament. Although beaten 2:12 to 3:7 at Eastfield Park, Glasgow took great store from the fact that the winning club subsequently went on to become beaten finalists in the All-Ireland Club Championship.

By this time clubs in Glasgow were again experiencing a demise and subsequent reorganizing. Much of this was to be the result of players and activists moving on to new employment, either to some other place in Britain or back to Ireland. The St Brendan's Club was one example of this reorganization, soon becoming Mulroy Gaels, called after the bay of the same name in County Donegal. Other St Brendan's players formed Rosses Rovers (again called after a Donegal location) whilst they also drew other players from the Clan na Gael club. During this time clubs struggled to field regular sides and it was in fact the case that many games were played with teams lacking in numbers. In 1970, the *Irish Weekly* (19 December 1970) included an article attempting to revive the Association in Scotland.

> As far as the clubs were concerned during 1970 the efforts of St Eunan's and St Patrick's as effective units were almost nil. Some individuals make token efforts, but no more. St Brendan's found themselves with no opposition. . . . The GAA in Glasgow hope to have a social centre at Eastfield Park before the end of 1971. The presence of such a centre would ensure regular football as well as providing the very necessary social amenities.

Little GAA activity took place in Glasgow during most of the 1970s and into the early 1980s. During the barren years, priests such as Eamonn Sweeney of Ballycroy, Dominic Towey from Kilmovee in County Mayo and James Shiels of Derry tried to keep matters Gaelic alive in Glasgow. Father Sweeney in particular was to become a crucial figure in the latest regeneration of the Association in Scotland. Few second and third generation Irish who esteemed their Irish identity were aware of the GAA in Glasgow or even that there existed such a way to express Irishness, distinct from or complementary to, supporting Celtic Football Club.

Although a small group of Gaels had maintained Gaelic games throughout the 1960s and 1970s, the GAA in Glasgow was unorganized and lacked a development plan. The organization was limited by paucity of numbers and little publicity, and were an unrepresentative group in that many of them were Gaelic activists of latter Donegal origins.

In 1984 the small existent GAA in Glasgow decided to celebrate the centenary of the Association by holding a special function. This was held in Moodiesburn, outside Glasgow. For some members of the tiny group this event presented both an opportunity as well as an inspiration to attract more individuals to Gaelic sport. Along with Eamonn Sweeney, successful Glasgow-based Donegal building and demolition contractor Seamus Sweeney, and fellow countyman Eamonn Cullen, these GAA enthusiasts decided to attempt to try to form football teams in their respective areas of Lanarkshire, Glasgow and Dumbarton.

Advertising began and a handful of young people responded: training and coaching under the auspices of Father Eamonn Sweeney and Michael Moran got under way. By the following year the first competitions started and Gaelic football was reborn in the west of Scotland. By early 1985 four clubs, Pearse Harps and Mulroy Gaels from Glasgow, St Patrick's Dumbarton and Clann na Gael from Hamilton were competing in the first competitive league and championship set up for a generation. Over the course of the next ten years or more almost twenty senior and minor clubs participated in GAA activities in Scotland: Ayrshire Gaels Saltcoats, Beltane Shamrock's Wishaw, Coatbridge Gaels, Clann na Gael Hamilton, Cuchulains Glasgow, Derryvale Glasgow, Dundee Dalriada, Dunedin Connolly's Edinburgh, Glasgow Gaels, Glencovitt Rovers Clydebank, Michael Davitts Glasgow, Mulroy Gaels Glasgow, Paisley Gaels, Pearse Harps Glasgow, Sands MacSwiney's Coatbridge, Shotts Gaels, St Malachy's Calderbank and Chapelhall, St Patrick's Dumbarton, and, Tir Conaill Harps Glasgow.

In the 1990s a high point for the County Board of Scotland (formed from the old Glasgow County Board), was reached with participation of a representative side in an international Gaelic football competition held in Dublin under the auspices of the GAA authorities at Croke Park. Taking part in the 1996 tournament for the Dr Dermot Clifford Cup, and held at the grounds of Dublin-based St Enda's of Ballyboden, were Gaelic football sides from Australasia, Canada, London, New York, North America and the Rest of Britain, as well as from Scotland. The County Board of Scotland lost both matches against the North American Board and the London County, but participation in both the inaugural tournament in 1994 and the subsequent competition in 1996, reflected the progress of Gaelic football in Scotland since 1984.

In addition, the promotion of such a tournament resonated with a recognition of the place which the diaspora has in the progress of Gaelic games. An increasing recognition of the Irish beyond the shores of Ireland by Irish President Mary Robinson also characterized her office during the 1990s. Jack Boothman, president of the GAA during 1996, also recognized what the Irish have given to other lands as well as what Ireland has contributed to a sense of self and community for those who have had to leave the country:

> when one considers the tragedy of emigration and the great haemorrhage of our people to foreign lands. They brought with them to those lands their music, their culture and above all the legacy that is the GAA and Gaelic Games. In turn, the GAA provided them with a focus, a link with their homeland and a medium that stimulated togetherness and a sense of identity. (From the programme for *Irish Holidays International Football Tournament*, 9–13 September 1996)

Although there has been a series of falls, steady and sometimes dramatic progress has been made since 1984. Hundreds of young Irish-born, hundreds more of second, third and fourth generation Irish offspring, as well as others from outside the community, have participated in Gaelic football in the west as well as in a few places in the east of Scotland. A number of Glasgow and Lanarkshire schools have adopted the game. By 1997 a women's football team existed as well as a camogie and hurling set up in Glasgow.

The visit to Glasgow of the Kilkenny hurling team in 1913 has been surpassed by the visits of Donegal, Derry, Mayo and Dublin during the 1990s, three of the four being recent winners of All-Ireland football titles. In 1993, in front of approximately 2,000 spectators at St Aloysius Rugby Ground in the Millerston area of Glasgow, Donegal beat Mayo; in 1994 they defeated Derry; and in 1995 it was Dublin's turn to be vanquished by the west Ulster side. In 1996 the challenge was between Tyrone and Dublin, the latter winning the Willie Dowds Trophy in front of 1000 people. An inter-county Celtic challenge cup was also played for by a number of minor teams prior to each of these inter-county games. At a variety of Glasgow hotels, successful banquets were also held on the evening of the respective matches.

During April 1997, as a contribution to the celebration of its centenary year, the County Board of Scotland requested the visit to Glasgow of County Sligo. Subsequently a Gaelic football match took place at St Aloysius Rugby Ground in Glasgow, between the Scotland County and Sligo. The match finished with a convincing victory by the visitors of 7:21

to 1:4, Sligo winning the Willie Dowds Cup, until then played for between counties from Ireland visiting Glasgow. By mid-1997, Sligo continued their own improvements by reaching the final of the Conaught Championship, only to be beaten by Mayo by the odd point.

By the 1990s there emerged a new confidence and articulation in relation to Irish identity in Scotland and Britain amongst those of the Irish diaspora. The re-emergence of the GAA in Scotland links with the resurfacing and new articulation of Irish identity in many parts of Britain. The Association and its members retain a unique identity amidst a growing emphasis on globalization and 'world sports'. Gaelic sports remain a forum through which cultural, national and, for some members, political identities are projected, maintained and celebrated. Nonetheless, many things which today give life to the GAA in Ireland, particularly parishes and counties, local tradition, history and bloodlines, added to coaching as a part of the modern educational curriculum, are not the same or are non-existent in Scotland. The sociology of Gaelic sports which exists in Ireland does not constitute any real influence amongst the diaspora.

In Scotland, over the course of the late nineteenth and twentieth centuries, a unique form of sporting activity and affinity, quite distinct from the Gaelic revival in Ireland, developed within the Irish immigrant community. For many members of the consciously Irish Catholic community, or for those members of the immigrant community who retain a sense of 'Irishness', not the GAA, but Celtic Football Club is the greatest single 'ethno-cultural focus', because it provides the social setting and process through which the community's sense of its own identity and difference from the indigenous community is sustained in and through a set of symbolic processes and representations. In becoming a focus for displaying Irishness, Celtic has also become a unique soccer club in Scotland. Many emotions, sentiments and passions which might have been displayed elsewhere, or indeed were diminished in other contexts, became central to the character of the Celtic support. 'For many Irish immigrants in Scotland, supporting Celtic has been a powerful strategy of identity building' (see Rokkan and Urwin, 1983: 89).

To many Catholics in Scotland (as to the Catalans in Spain who identify with Barcelona Football Club), Celtic have become a metaphor for the whole Irish and Catholic immigrant tradition (*Independent on Sunday*, 28 June 1992). In Scotland, soccer is bound up with the process of individual socialization and community construction. The history of Irish–British relations has meant that for the Irish in Scotland, as well as for those of an anti-Catholic and anti-Irish disposition, Celtic Football Club has emerged as a definition of Irishness itself (see Bradley, 1996).

In Ireland, whilst 1984 was a year for celebrating one hundred years of the GAA, for the Irish and their offspring in Scotland the most important facet of their cultural identity, Celtic – runners-up in the league to Dundee United – lost the Scottish Cup Final to Aberdeen. The match was attended by 59, 000 and watched by millions as the game was televised live by both ITV and BBC. Less relevantly for most members of the diaspora in Scotland, in 1984 Kerry won the All-Ireland football title and Cork defeated Offaly in the hurling final at Croke Park in Dublin. The important centenary for most of the Irish in Scotland was that of 1987/88 which celebrated the founding of Celtic Football Club. Nonetheless, although a comparatively weak organization, the history of the GAA in Scottish society reflects that it has been a crucial focus of Irish identity for some members of the diaspora in Scotland. Since 1984, the GAA in Scotland has played a notable role in maintaining and introducing ideas and images of Irishness amongst those with Irish antecedents in Scotland. For some activists, it provides an authentic, uncontestable manifestation of their Irishness.

The myths of descent, historical memories, territorial association with Ireland, religion and a sense of solidarity provide many GAA activists in Scotland with their motivation. The GAA is for some of the Scottish-born Irish community, a way of keeping in contact with their heritage and culture and with Ireland itself. Ethnic and national consciousness is maintained through the GAA. With three quarters of a million adults in membership within Ireland and the diaspora, thousands of children and many more people tied simply by emotion or occasional experience, clearly the GAA forms an important dimension of the Irish 'family' or diaspora, in addition to old and new conceptions of Irish identity. It also helps gives 'Irishness' a heterogeneous quality and outlook.

Since the revival of the Gaelic Athletic Association in Scotland in 1984 almost 5000 individuals have experienced Gaelic sports, the vast majority being people born in Scotland of Irish forebears. Such Celtic distinctiveness is a primary reason for the survival of the Association in Scotland as well as the primary rationale and motivation for those who maintain its existence as a valuable aspect of Irish identity. The GAA in Scotland provides an organizational locale for the idea of a common descent, a shared history in Ireland and common experience in Scotland. It provides for a concrete link with the country of birth or origin. It is an expression of diversity and a symbol of identity.

REFERENCES

Aaron, J., Rees, T., Betts, S. and Vincentelli, M. (1994) *Our Sisters' Land*. Cardiff: University of Wales Press.

Abse, D. (1954) *Ash on a Young Man's Sleeve*. London: Hutchinson (Penguin edn, 1982).

Abse, D. (1974) *A Poet in the Family*. London: Hutchinson.

Abse, D. (1983) *A Strong Dose of Myself*. London: Hutchinson.

Albouy, G. (1975) 'Le Red Star, Rennes et Angers joueront la saison prochaine en deuxième division'. *Le Monde*, 5 June, 15.

Allison, L. (1986) *The Politics of Sport*. Manchester: Manchester University Press.

Andrews, D. (1996) 'Sport and the masculine hegemony of the modern nation: Welsh rugby, culture and society, 1890–1914', in J. Nauright and M. Chandler (eds), *Making Men: Rugby and Masculine Identity*. London: Frank Cass, 50–70.

Anthony, J. and Lloyd, G. (1942) *Contribution à l'étude du folklore bas-breton: danses, luttes, airs populaires*. Rennes: Société d'Editions Bretonnes.

Apple, M. (1993) *Official Knowledge*. Routledge: New York.

Arnaud, P. (ed.) (1987) *Les athlètes de la République: gymnastique, sport et idéologie républicaine*. Toulouse: Privat.

Aubour, M. (1972) *Moi le breton*. Rennes: Ouest-France.

Bairner, A. (1996a) 'Sportive nationalism and nationalist politics: a comparative analysis of Scotland, the Republic of Ireland and Sweden'. *Journal of Sport and Social Issues*, **20** (3), 314–34.

Bairner, A. (1996b) 'Ireland, sport and empire', in K. Jeffery (ed.), *An Irish Empire? Aspects of Ireland and the British*. Manchester: Manchester University Press, 57–76.

Bairner, A. and Darby, P. (1999) 'Divided sport in a divided society: Northern Ireland', in J. Sugden and A. Bairner (eds), *Sport in Divided Societies*. Aachen: Meyer and Meyer, 51–72.

Bairner, A. and Sugden, J. (1993) *Sport, Sectarianism and Society in a Divided Ireland*. London: Leicester University Press.

Bale, J. (1994) *Landscapes of Modern Sport*. Leicester: Leicester University Press.

Ballachulish and Glencoe Curling Club Minute Book 1897–1907, Argyll and Bute County Archive DR1 February 6.

Bannerman, J. (1974) *Studies in the History of Dalriada*. Edinburgh: Scottish Academic Press.

Barthes, R. (1957) 'Le Tour de France comme épopée', in R. Barthes (ed.) *Mythologies*. Paris: Seuil, 110–21.

Beckett, A. (1994) 'How clean was my valley?' *Independent on Sunday*, 28 August, 4–8.

Bernstein, B. (1990) *The Structuring of Pedagogic Discourse*. London: Routledge.

Bernstein, B. (1996) *Pedagogy, Symbolic Control and Identity: Theory, Research, Critique*. London: Taylor and Francis.

Berry, H. F. (1907) *Statutes and Ordinances and Acts of the Parliament of Ireland*. London.

Berry, R. (1960) *Hunter and Hunted*. London: Hutchinson.

Berry, R. (1964) *The Full-time Amateur*. London: W. H. Allen.

Berry, R. (1970) *So Long Hector Bebb*. London: W. H. Allen.

Bertho, C. (1980) 'L'invention de la Bretagne. Genèse sociale d'un stéréotype'. *Actes de la recherche en sciences sociales*, **35**, 45–62.

Betts, S. (1996) *Our Daughters' Land*. Cardiff: University of Wales Press.

Bouchet, C. (1988) *Les vrais patrons du football. Dans les secrets des présidents des clubs français*. Paris: Solar.

Boyle, R. and Haynes, R. (1996) 'The grand old game: football, media and identity in Scotland'. *Media, Culture and Society*, **18** (4), 549–64.

Bradley, J. M. (1995) *Ethnic and Religious Identity in Modern Scotland*. Aldershot: Avebury Press.

Bradley, J. M. (1996a) 'Profile of a Roman Catholic parish in Scotland'. *Scottish Affairs*, **14** (Winter), 123–39.

Bradley, J. M. (1996b) 'Facets of the Irish diaspora: "Irishness" in 20th century Scotland'. *Irish Journal of Sociology*, **6**, 22–34.

Braudeau, M. (1996) 'Lorient célèbre une "celtitude" européenne et l'antimondialisation'. *Le Monde*, (9), 16.

Breen, Dan (1924) *My Fight for Irish Freedom*. Dublin: Cliàth.

'Bretagne', 1993, *Encyclopedia universalis*, **4**, 521–30.

Bromberger, C. (1995) *Le match de football. Ethnologie d'une passion partisane à Marseille, Naples et Turin*. Paris: Maison des Sciences de l'Homme.

Brown, S. J. (1991) 'Outside the covenant: The Scottish Presbyterian churches and Irish immigration, 1922–38'. *Innes Review*, **42** (1), 19–45.

Buchanan, G. (Georgius Buchananus Scotus) (1594) Rerum Scoticarum Historia. Frankfurt am Main.

Burnett, J. (1995) *Sporting Scotland*. Edinburgh: National Museums of Scotland.

Cadiou, G. (1981) *Les grandes heures du cyclisme breton*. Rennes: Ouest-France.

Cadiou, G. (1982) *Les grandes heures du football breton*. Rennes: Ouest-France.

Cadiou, G. (1990) *Les Grands du cyclisme breton*. Spezed: Keltia Graphic.

Cadiou, G. (1995) *Les Origines des sports en Bretagne*. Morlaix: Skol Vreizh.

Caithnia, L. P. (1984) *Báirí Cos in Éirinn*. Dublin: Baile Átha Cliath.

Campbell, J. F. (1861) *Popular Tales of the West Highlands*. Edinburgh.

Campbell, J. F. (1868) *Personal notebook with newspaper cuttings 1865–1869.* National Library of Scotland, Adv. Ms. 50. 7.d.

Campbell, John L. (1990) *Songs Remembered in Exile.* Aberdeen: Aberdeen University Press.

Campbell, M. (1995) *Argyll, the Enduring Heartland.* Grantown-on-Spey: Colin Baxter Photography, 2nd edn.

Campbell, T. and Woods, P. (1986) *The Glory and the Dream: The History of Celtic FC, 1887–1986.* Edinburgh: Mainstream Publishing.

Campbeltown Curling Club accounts book and letters file 1881–1907, Argyll and Bute County Archive DR4 March 84.

Caro, G. (1997) *Les Supporteurs de 3 clubs de football de D1. Etude comparative FC Nantes-Atlantique, Stade Rennais FC, En-Avant de Guingamp.* Rennes: ARIA-Foot-Culture.

Castaing, M. (1971) 'La cinquante-quatrième finale de la Coupe de France ou les signes d'un renouveau'. *Le Monde,* 22 June, 24.

Celtic Cultures Newsletter (1983) University College, Dublin: **1,** 8–9.

Chandler, T. and Nauright, J. (1996) 'Introduction: Rugby, Manhood and Identity', in J. Nauright and T. Chandler (eds), *Making Men. Rugby and Masculine Identity.* London: Frank Cass, 1–13.

Chappé, F. (1995) 'Une certaine idée de la Bretagne sous la République'. *Annales de Bretagne et des Pays de l'Ouest,* **102** (4), 83–107.

Coadic, L. (1992) 'Introduction et diffusion du football en Bretagne (1890-1925). De l'histoire à l'anthropologie religieuse'. *Sport Histoire,* **3,** 27–50.

Coakley, J. J. (1990) *Sport in Society: Issues and Controversies.* St Louis: Mosby.

Collis, J. (1997) 'Celtic myths'. *Antiquity,* **71,** 8–15.

Corry, E. (1989) *Catch and Kick.* Dublin: Poolbeg.

Cregeen, E. (1964) *Argyll Estates Instructions 1771–1805.* Edinburgh: Scottish History Society.

Cregeen, E. (1970) 'The changing role of the House of Argyll in the Scottish Highlands', in N. Phillipson and R. Mitchison (eds), *Scotland in the Age of Improvement.* Edinburgh: Edinburgh University Press, 5–23.

Creston, R.-Y. (1943, reissued 1957) *La Lutte bretonne à Scaër.* Rennes: Editions BAS.

Crick, B. (1997) 'The English and the Others'. *The Times Higher Education Supplement,* 2 May, 15.

Cronin, M. (1994) 'Sport and a sense of Irishness'. *Irish Studies Review,* **9,** 13–17.

Curriculum Council for Wales (1989) *A Framework for the Whole Curriculum: A Discussion Paper.* Cardiff: Welsh Office.

Curriculum Council for Wales (1991) *The Whole Curriculum.* Cardiff: Welsh Office.

Curriculum Council for Wales (1993) *Developing a Curriculum Cymreig,* Advisory Paper 18. Cardiff: Welsh Office.

Curriculum Council for Wales (1994) *Developing a Whole School Approach to a Curriculum Cymreig.* Cardiff: Welsh Office.

Dagg, T. S. C. (1944) *Hockey in Ireland.* Tralee: Hamilton.

Dalrudinians Rules and Constitution. No date, watermark 1824. Argyll and Bute County Archive.

Darling, F. F. (1955) *West Highland Survey*. London: Oxford University Press.

Daugherty, R. (1993) *Curriculum Council Wales Newsletter No. 13*. Cardiff: Curriculum Council Wales.

Davies, B. (1996) 'Difference with Distinction: Education in Wales'. *Wales Review*, 1 August, 22–4.

Davies, B., Evans, J., Penney, D. and Bass, D. (1997) 'Physical Education and Nationalism in Wales'. *The Curriculum Journal*, **8** (2), 249–70.

Davies, J. (1991) 'Barry John', in *Flight Patterns*. Bridgend: Severn Books.

Davis, G. (1991) *The Irish in Britain 1815–1914*. Dublin: Gill and Macmillan.

Davitt, M. (1904) *The Fall of Feudalism in Ireland*. London.

de Búrca, M. (1980) *The Gaelic Athletic Association: A History*. Dublin: Cumann Lúthchleas Gael.

de Búrca, M. (1989) *Michael Cusack and the Gaelic Athletic Association*. Dublin: Anvil Books.

Department of National Heritage (1995) *Sport: Raising the Game*. London: Department of National Heritage.

Devereux, R. (1779) *Wexford Stones*. Wexford: Carrigmenan.

Devine, T. M. (1988) *The Great Highland Famine*. Edinburgh: John Donald.

Devine, T. M. (ed.) (1991) *Irish Immigrants and Scottish Society in the Nineteenth and Twentieth Centuries: Proceedings of the Scottish Historical Studies Seminar*. Edinburgh: John Donald.

Devine, T. M. (ed.) (1995) *St Mary's Hamilton: A Social History, 1846–1996*. Edinburgh: John Donald.

Donald, J. (1992) *Sentimental Education*. London: Verso.

Dowling, M. (1997) ' "The Ireland that I would have": De Valera and the creation of an Irish national image', *History Ireland*, **5** (2), 64–75..

Edwards, W. J. (1956) *From the Valley I Came*. London: Angus & Robertson.

Ellis, P. E. (1992) *Dictionary of Celtic Mythology*. London: Thames and Hudson.

Elwyn Jones, G. (1995) 'Bordering on the New Renaissance'. *The Times Educational Supplement*, **30** (9), 11–12.

Evans, D. E. (1995) 'The early Celts: the evidence of language', in Miranda J. Greene (ed.), *The Celtic World*. London and New York: Faber & Faber.

Evans, G. Ewart (1983) *The Strength of the Hills*. London: Faber & Faber.

Evans, J. (1988) 'Body matters: towards a socialist physical education', in H. Lauder, and P. Brown (eds), *Education in Search of a Future*. London: Falmer Press, 174–92.

Evans, J. and Davies, B. (1997) 'Editorial Introduction'. *Physical Education, Sport and the Curriculum*, special issue of *The Curriculum Journal*, **8** (2), 185–97.

Evans, J. and Penney, D. (1995a) 'Physical Education, restoration and the politics of sport'. *Curriculum Studies*, **3** (2), 183–96.

Evans, J. and Penney, D. (1995b) 'The politics of pedagogy: making a National Curriculum Physical Education'. *Journal of Education Policy*, **10** (1), 27–44.

Evans, J., Davies, B., Bass, D. and Penney, D. (1997) 'Playing for position: Physical Education and nationalism in Wales'. *Journal of Education Policy*, **4** (1), 70–83.

Evans, T. (1740) *Drych y Prif Oesoedd*, 2nd edn. Shrewsbury.

Faure, J. M. and Suaud, C. (1994) 'Un professionnalisme inachevé. Deux états du champ du football professionnel en France, 1963–1993'. *Actes de la recherche en sciences sociales*, **104**, 7–25.

Favereau, F. (1995) *Bretagne contemporaine: langue, culture, identité*. Morlaix: Skol vreizh.

Fenton, A. (1980) 'The traditional pastoral economy', in M. L. Parry and T. R. Slater (eds), *The Making of the Scottish Countryside*. London: Croom Helm, 93–113.

Finlay, R. J. (1991) 'Nationalism, race, religion and the Irish question in inter-war Scotland'. *Innes Review,* **42** (1), 46–67.

Finlay, R. J. (1994) *Independent and Free: Scottish Politics and the Origins of the Scottish National Party 1918–1945*. Edinburgh: John Donald.

Finn, G. P. T. (1991a) 'Racism, religion and social prejudice: Irish Catholic clubs, soccer and Scottish society. I. The historical roots of prejudice'. *International Journal of the History of Sport*, **8** (1), 72–95.

Finn, G. P. T. (1991b) 'Racism, religion and social prejudice: Irish Catholic clubs, soccer and Scottish society. II. Social identities and conspiracy theories'. *International Journal of the History of Sport*, **8** (3), 370–97.

Fitzgerald, F. S. (1990) *The Great Gatsby*. Harmondsworth: Penguin.

Fraser, W. H. and Morris, R. J. (eds) (1990) *People and Society in Scotland: II. 1830–1914*. Edinburgh: John Donald.

Frémy, D. and Frémy, M. (eds) (1995) *Quid 1996*. Paris: Robert Laffont.

Gaelic Athletic Association (1991) *Gaelic Athletic Association Rule Book*. Dublin: Cumann Lúthchleas Gael.

Gallagher, T. (1987) *Glasgow: the Uneasy Peace*. Manchester: Manchester University Press.

Gallagher, T. (1991) 'The Catholic Irish in Scotland: in search of identity', in T. M. Devine (ed.), *Irish Immigrants and Scottish Society in the Nineteenth and Twentieth Centuries*. Edinburgh: John Donald.

Galliou, P. (1994) *Le Monde Celtique*. Paris: Gallimard.

Garlick, R. (1986) *Collected Poems, 1946–1986*. Llandysul: Gomer Press.

Gay-Lescot, J.-L. (1991) *Sport et éducation sous Vichy: 1940–1944*. Lyon: Presses Universitaires de Lyon.

Gerald of Wales (1984) *The Journey through Wales*. Harmondsworth: Penguin.

Gilles, W. (1970) 'The National Question'. *Liberty*, July, 70.

Grant, Mrs E. (1898) *Memoirs of a Highland Lady*. London:

Grant, I. F. (1960) *Everyday Life of an Old Highland Farm. 1769–1782*. London: Routledge.

Graves-Brown, P., Jones, S. and Gamble, C. (1996) *Cultural Identity and Archeology*. London: Routledge.

Greaves, A. (1993) 'Sport in France', in Cook, M. (ed.), *French Culture since 1945*. London: Longman, 125–48.

Gregory, A. (1970) *Cù Chulainn of Muirthemne*. Gerrards Cross.

Grieve, S. (1923) *The Book of Colonsay and Oronsay*. London.

Gunn, D. and Murray, I. (1991) *Neil Gunn's Country*. Edinburgh: Chambers.

Gunn, N. (1931) 'Highland Games'. *Scots Magazine*, **15** (6), 412–16.

Hall, Mr and Mrs S. C. (1843) *Ireland, its Scenery, Character, etc.*, (3 vols), Vol. 1.

Hamilton, W. M. (1832) *The Wild Sports of the West*. London.

Handley, J. E. (1960) *The Celtic Story*. London: Stanley Paul.

Handley, J. E. (1964) *The Irish in Scotland*. Cork: Cork University Press.

Hargreaves, J. (ed.) (1982) *Sport, Culture and Ideology*. London: Routledge.

Hargreaves, J. (1986) *Sport, Power and Culture*. Cambridge: Polity Press.

Hargreaves, J. (1992) 'Olympism and nationalism: some preliminary considerations'. *International Review for the Sociology of Sport*, **27**, 119–37.

Harvie, C. (1994) 'Sport and the Scottish state', in G. Jarvie and G. Walker (eds), *Scottish Sport in the Making of the Nation: Ninety-minute Patriots?* London: Leicester University Press, 58–74.

Hélias, P.-J. (1975) *Le Cheval d'orgueil: mémoires d'un Breton du pays bigouden*. Paris: Plon.

Hickman, M. (1995) *Religion, Class and Identity: The State, the Catholic Church and the Education of the Irish in Britain*. Aldershot: Avebury.

Hoberman, J. (1984) *Sport and Political Ideology*. London: Heinemann.

Hoberman, J. (1993) 'Sport and ideology in the post-communist age', in L. Allison (ed.), *The Changing Politics of Sport*. Manchester: Manchester University Press, 15–36.

Hobsbawm, E. (1983) 'Mass-producing traditions: Europe, 1870–1914', in E. Hobsbawm and T. Ranger (eds), *The Invention of Tradition*. Cambridge: Cambridge University Press, 263–307.

Holmes, M. (1994) 'Symbols of national identity and sport: the case of the Irish football team'. *Irish Political Studies*, **9**, 81–98.

Holt, R. (1981) *Sport and Society in Modern France*. London: Macmillan.

Holt, R. (1989) *Sport and the British: A Modern History*. Oxford: Oxford University Press.

Holt, R. (1991) 'Les héros du football et les mythologies nationales', in *Anthropologie du sport. Perspectives critiques*, Actes du colloque de la Sorbonne, Afirse-Quel Corps?, Paris, 50–5.

Holt, R. (1994) 'The king over the border: Denis Law and Scottish football', in G. Jarvie and G. Walker (eds), *Scottish Sport in the Making of the Nation: Ninety-minute Patriots?* London: Leicester University Press, 58–74.

Holt, R. (1995) 'Contrasting nationalisms: sport, militarism and the unitary state in Britain and France before 1914'. *International Journal of the History of Sport*, **2**, August, 39–54.

Holt, R. (1996) 'Sport and history: the state of the subject in Britain'. *Twentieth Century British History*, **7** (2), 231–52.

Hooson, I. D. (1958) *Cerdd I a Baledi*. Denbigh: Gee.

Howe, I. (1961) *Politics and the Novel*. London: Stevens & Son (first published in New York, 1957).

HMI (1994) *Survey of Physical Education in Key Stages 1, 2 and 3*. Cardiff: Welsh Office.

Hubscher, R. (ed.) (1992) *L'Histoire en mouvements: Le sport dans la société française (XIXè-XXè siècle)*. Paris: Armand Colin.

Humphreys, E. (1968) *Natives*. London: Secker & Warburg.

Hunter, J. (1976) *The Making of the Crofting Community*. Edinburgh: John Donald.

Hutchinson, J. (1987) *The Dynamics of Cultural Nationalism: The Gaelic Revival and the Creation of the Irish Nation State*. London: Allen & Unwin.

Hutchinson, R. (1989) *Camanachd: The Story of Shinty*. Edinburgh: Mainstream.

Inglis, J. (1982) 'The Irish in Britain: A question of identity'. *Irish Studies in Britain*, **3**, 11–19.

Inglis, W. (1957) *A History of the Cowal Highland Gathering*. Dunoon: Dunoon Standard.

INSEE (Institut national de la statistique et des études économiques) (1993) *L'Espace breton*. Rennes: Direction Régionale de Bretagne de l'INSEE.

Inveraray Curling Club minute book transcription 1855–1864, Argyll and Bute County Archive AGN 588.

Inveraray Festivities 1842, Handbill, Argyll and Bute County Archive.

Irvine, St John (1925) *Charles Stewart Parnell and Irish Nationalism*. London: Heath Cranton.

Jackson, K. H. (ed.) (1971) *A Celtic Miscellany*, 2nd edn. Harmondsworth: Penguin.

Jackson, L. (1969) Education in Argyll 1800–1872, unpublished MEd thesis, University of Glasgow.

Jaouen, G. and J.-P. Le Joncour, P. (1984) *Ar gouren. La lutte bretonne des origines à nos jours*. Rennes: Institut Culturel de Bretagne.

Jarvie, G. (1991) *Highland Games: The Making of the Myth*. Edinburgh: Edinburgh University Press.

Jarvie, G. (1993) 'Sport, nationalism and cultural identity', in L. Allison (ed.), *The Changing Politics of Sport*. Manchester: Manchester University Press, 58–93.

Jarvie, G. and Walker, G. (eds) (1994) *Scottish Sport in the Making of the Nation*. London: Leicester University Press.

Jenkins, N. (1981) *Song and Dance*. Bridgend: Poetry Wales Press.

Jones, Revd A. E. (1959) *Cerdd i Cynan*. Liverpool: Hughes.

Jones, B. and Lewis, I. (1995) 'A Curriculum Cymreig', *Welsh Journal of Education*, **4** (2), 22–35.

Jones, D. G. (1951) *Eples*. Aberystwyth: Gwasg Aberystwyth Cardiff: University of Wales Press.

Jones, D. (1978a) *Storom Awst*. Llandysul: Gomer Press.

Jones, D. (1978b) *Cyfansodd iadau. Eisteddfod Genedlaethol cymru Caerdydd*. Llandysul: Gomer Press.

Jones G. E. (1987) 'Introduction', in G. E. Jones (ed.), *Perspectives on the History of Education in Wales*, a special issue of *Education for Development*, **10** (1), 2–12.

Jones, G. E. (1997) *The Education of a Nation*. Cardiff: University of Wales (Cardiff) Press.

Jones, G. R. (1975) *Y syrcas a cherddi eraill*. Bala: Faner.

Jones, J. (1934) *Rhondda Roundabout*. London: Faber & Faber.

Jones, J. (1935) *Black Parade*. London: Faber & Faber.

Jones, K. (1995) 'Across the Great Divide? Culture, economic life and the re-thinking of education policy'. *Curriculum Studies*, **3** (3), 227–43.

Jones, T. (1971) *Hen faledi ffair*. Talybont: Lolfa.

Jones, T. (1993) 'Rhagor o redwyr'. *Canu Gwerin*, **16**, 38–42.

Jones, T. Gwynn (ed.) (1926) *Gwaith Tudur Aled*. Cardiff: University of Wales Press.

Jones, T. Llew (ed.) (1994) *Cerddi Bardd Y Werin*. Llandysul: Gomer.

Jouneaux, M. (1994) *Le stade lavallois. une histoire*. Laval: Siloë.

Kahn, Roger (1972) *The Boys of Summer*. New York: Harper & Row.

Kellas, J. G. (1987) *The Politics of Nationalism and Ethnicity*. London: Macmillan.

Kellas, J. G. (1996) *The Scottish Political System*. Cambridge: Cambridge University Press.

Kelly, M. (1848) *Cambrensis eversus, seu potius historica fides in rebus hibernicis Giraldo Cambrensi abrogata, Gratianus Lucius* [John Lynch] hibernus, MDCLXII, edited with translation and notes by Rev. Kelly, M., for the Celtic Society, Dublin; Vol 1, 1848; Vol 2, 1850; Vol 3, 1851–2.

Keogh, D. (1994) *Twentieth-century Ireland Nation and State*. Dublin: Gill & Macmillan.

Kinealy, C. (1994) *This Great Calamity: The Irish Famine 1845–52*. Dublin: Gill & Macmillan.

King, S. J. (1996) *A History of Hurling*. Dublin: Gill & Macmillan.

Kinsella, T. (1969) *The Tàin*. Oxford: Oxford University Press.

Kintyre Club (1884) *Kintyre and the Kintyre Club: A Historical Sketch of the Peninsula*. Glasgow: Kintyre Club.

Kirk, D. (1992) *Defining Physical Education*. London: The Falmer Press.

Knox, C. (1989) *Local Government Leisure Services: Planning and Politics in Northern Ireland*, unpublished D. Phil. thesis, University of Ulster.

Laclau, E. and Mouffe, E. (1985) *Hegemony and Socialist Strategy: Towards a Radical Democratic Politics*. London: Verso.

Lacouture, J. (1979) *Le rugby, c'est un monde*. Paris: Seuil.

Lagrée, M. (1992) *Religion et cultures en Bretagne*. Paris: Fayard.

Lanfranchi, P. (1989) 'Les "footballeurs-étudiants" yougoslaves en Languedoc (1925–1935)'. *Sport Histoire*, **3**, 43–59.

Emmet Larkin, E. (1976) *Historical Dimensions of Irish Catholicism*. Dublin: University Press.

Lawrence, J. (1870) *Handbook of Cricket in Ireland*. Dublin.

Lawrence, J. (1879) *Handbook of Cricket in Ireland*. Dublin.

Le Boulanger, J. M. (1995) *En-Avant de Guingamp. 1912–1995 l'aventure.* Quimper: Alain Bargain.

Le Bris du Rest, E. (1976) *La Lutte bretonne: un sport traditionnel.* Rennes: Musée de Bretagne.

Le Bris, M. (1995) 'Pierre-Jakez Hélias. Un "quêteur de mémoire" '. *Le Monde,* **16,** 6.

Le Joncour, P. *et al.* (1984) *Ar Gouren: La lutte bretonne des origines à nos jours.* Rennes: Institut Culturel de Bretagne.

Le Pelletier, Louis (1752) *Dictionnaire etymologique de la langue bretonne.* Paris.

Lhuyd, Edward (1707) *Archaeologia Britannica.* Oxford.

Lile, E. (1994) *Athletic competition in pre-industrial Wales c. 1066 – c. 1880,* unpublished M. Phil thesis, Birmingham.

Lingard, B. (1993) 'The changing state of policy production in education: some Australian reflections on the state of policy sociology'. *International Studies in the Sociology of Education,* **3,** 25–49.

Littlejohn Album. Aberdeen: University of Aberdeen.

Loire, C. (1994) *Le Stade rennais fleuron du football breton 1901–1991.* Rennes: Apogée.

Lynch, M. (1991) *Scotland: A New History.* London: Century.

McCulloch, M. (1987) *Neil Gunn: The Man Who Came Back.* Edinburgh: Polygon.

MacDonald, A. (1922) 'Shinty, historical and traditional'. *Transactions of the Gaelic Society of Inverness,* XXX, 24.

MacDonald, C. (1950) *The History of Argyll.* Glasgow: Holmes.

MacDonald, C. (1961) *The Third Statistical Account of Scotland: County of Argyll.* Glasgow: Collins.

Macdonald, M. (1992) *Skye Camanachd: A Century Remembered.* Skye: Portree.

MacDonald, Rev. J. Ninian (1932) S*hinty: A Short History of the Ancient Highland Game.* Inverness: Gaelic Society of Inverness.

Macinnes, A. (1994) 'Landownership, land use and elite enterprise in Scottish Gaeldom: from clanship to clearance in Argyllshire 1688–1858', in T. Devine (ed.), *Scottish Elites.* Edinburgh: John Donald.

McIntosh, P. C. (1981) *Landmarks in the History of Physical Education.* London: Routledge & Kegan Paul.

MacIntyre, N. C. (1881) *Book of True Highlanders.* London.

MacKay, D. (1980) *Scotland Farewell. The People of the Hector.* Ontario: Queen's University Press.

McKerral, A. (1948) *Argyll in the Seventeenth Century.* Edinburgh: Oliver & Boyd.

MacLagan, R. C. (1901) *The games and diversions of Argyleshire.* London: Folklore Society.

MacLagan, R. C. (1910) *Occasional Papers.* H.2.86.1349:3–42. Edinburgh: National Library of Scotland.

Maclaine, M. G. (1871) Pre-printed letter. APS.2.87.121. Edinburgh: National Library of Scotland.

McLaren, P. (1995) *Critical Pedagogy and Predatory Culture.* London: Routledge.

MacLennan, H. D. (1993) *Shinty!* Nairn: Balnain.

MacLennan, H. D. (1995) *Not an Orchid*. Inverness: Kessock Commun-ications.

MacLennan, H. D. (1996) 'Shinty and the traditional celebrations of New Year: Part 1'. *West Highland Free Press*, 27 December.

MacLennan, H. D. (1997a) 'Shinty: some fact and fiction in the nineteenth century'. *Transactions of the Gaelic Society of Inverness*, LIX.

MacLennan, H. D. (1997b) 'Shinty and the traditional celebrations of New Year: Part II'. *West Highland Free Press*, 3 January.

MacNeacail, A. (1993) *Sgàthach the Warrior Queen*. Nairn: Balnain.

McNeil, P. and Nicholson, R. (1975) *An Historical Dictionary of Scotland*. St Andrews.

McNeill, F. Marian (1961) *The Silver Bough*, Vol 3. Glasgow: Cateye.

MacPherson, James (1760) *Fragments of Ancient Poetry Collected in the Highlands of Scotland and Translated from the Galic or Erse*. Edinburgh.

Mailer, N. (1968) *The Presidential Papers*. London: Penguin.

Mailer, N. (1975) *The Fight*. New York: Little, Brown (Penguin edn, 1991).

Malcolm, G. (1971) 'The History of the Argyllshire Gathering'. *Oban Times*.

Mandle, W. F. (1977) 'The Irish Republican brotherhood and the beginnings of the Gaelic Athletic Association'. *Irish Historical Studies*, **xx** (80), 418–38.

Mandle, W. F. (1987) *The Gaelic Athletic Association and Irish Nationalist Politics 1884–1924*. London: Christopher Helm.

Mangan, J. A. (1996) *Tribal Identities: Nationalism, Europe, Sport*. London: Frank Cass.

Marsden, J. (1991) *The Illustrated Life of Columba*. Harmondsworth: Penguin.

Matthews, C. (1989) *The Celtic Tradition*. Shaftsbury: Element Books.

Meek, D. (1992) 'Modern Celtic Christianity: the contemporary revival and its roots'. *Scottish Bulletin of Evangelical Theology*, **10** (1), 6–31.

Mémoires de la Société d'histoire et d'archéologie de Bretagne, Vol. LXXI (1994).

Messenger, C. K. (1981) *Sport and the Spirit of Play in American Fiction*. New York.

Meyer, J. (ed.) (1972) *Histoire de Rennes*. Toulouse: Privat.

Minhinnick, R. (1982) 'Lines considering the death of Johnny Owen'. *Poetry Wales*, Winter.

Mitchison, R. (1982) *A history of Scotland*, 2nd edn. London: Routledge.

Moody. J. and Byrne, R. (1982) *A New History of Ireland*, Vol. 8. Dublin: Gill & Macmillan.

Moorhouse, G. (1989) *At the George and other essays on rugby*. London: Hodder & Stoughton.

Moreau, M. L. (1995) *Stade Rennais FC 1974–1994: Supporter des Rouges et Noirs depuis vingt ans. Première partie: 1974–84*. Rennes.

Morgan, K. O. (1981) *Wales: Rebirth of a Nation 1880–1980*. London: Oxford University Press.

Morin, E. (1967) *Commune en France: La métamorphose de Plozevet*. Paris: Fayard.

Morris Jones, B. and Singh Ghuman, P. A. (1995) *Bilingualism, Education and Identity*. Cardiff: University of Wales Press.

Mullan, M. (1995) 'Opposition, social closure, and sport: The Gaelic Athletic Association in the 19th century'. *Sociology of Sport Journal*, **12** (3), 268–89.

Murray, W. H. (1981) *The Curling Companion*. Glasgow: Richard Drew.

Nauright, J. and Chandler, J. L. (1996) *Making Men: Rugby and Masculine Identity*. London: Frank Cass.

Nicolas, M. (1991) 'Les mutations politiques en Bretagne 1958/1990'. *Annales de Bretagne et des Pays de l'Ouest*, **98** (3), 313–23.

Norris, L. (1967) *Finding Gold*. Bridgend: Gomer.

Norris, L. (1986) *Selected Poems*. Bridgend: Gomer.

Oates, Joyce Carol (1987) *On Boxing*. London: Bloomsbury (Pan edn, 1988).

O'Brien, Flann (1960) *At Swim Two Birds* [Snàmh-da-eun]. Harmondsworth: Penguin Modern Classics.

Ó Caithnia, L. P. (1980) *Scéal na hIomána*. Dublin: Clóchomhar.

Ó Caithnia, L. P. (1984) *Micheál Cíosóg*. Dublin: Clóchomhar.

Ó Caithnia, L. P. (1986) 'Hurling in early Irish law', in *The Book of Gaelic Games*. Kilkenny: Cliàth.

O'Callaghan, M. (1983) *Separatism in Brittany*. Redruth: Dyllansow Truran.

Ó Ceallaigh, S. (1977) *Story of the GAA*. Limerick: Gaelic Athletic Publications.

Ó Ciosáin, Éamon (1997) 'Glór na ndeoraithe Éireannacha sa Fhrainc sa seachtú agus san ochtú aois déag', in *Irisleabhar Mhá Nuad*.

O'Conner, K. (1970) *The Irish in Britain*. Dublin: Torc.

O'Donoghue, Patrick (1966/67) 'Opposition to tithe payment in 1830–1831'. *Studia Hibernica*, **5** and **6**.

O'Hanrahan, Michael (1990) 'The tithe wars in County Kilkenny 1830–1834', in W. Nolan and K. Whelan (eds), *Kilkenny: History and Society*. Dublin: Geography Publications.

O Hehir, M. (1984) *The GAA 100 Years*. Dublin: Gill & MacMillan.

Ollivier, J.-P. (1980) *Histoire du football breton*. Paris: Picollec.

Ollivier, J.-P. (1981) *Histoire du cyclisme breton*. Paris: Picollec.

Ó Maolfabhail, A. (1973) *Caman: Two Thousand Years of Hurling in Ireland*. Dundalk: Tempest Press.

Oriard, M. (1982) *Dreaming of Heroes: American Sports Fiction 1868–1980*. Chicago: Chicago University Press.

O'Rahilly, C. (1984) *Tàin Bò Cuailnge*. Dublin: Clóchomhor.

Orr, W. (1982) *Deer Forests, Landlords and Crofters*. Edinburgh: John Donald.

Ó Tuathaigh, M. A. G. (1985) 'The Irish in nineteenth-century Britain: problems of integration', in G. Gilley and P. Swift (eds), *The Irish in the Victorian City*. Dublin: Gill & Macmillan, 13–36.

Owen, D. (1986) *I fyd y faled*. Denbigh: Gee.

Owen, H. (ed.) (1892) *The Description of Pembrokeshire*. London: Cymmrodorion Society.

Péru, F. (1985) 'Les jeux de pardon en Bretagne'. *Annales de Bretagne et des Pays de l'Ouest*, **97** (3), 309–26.

Peru, F. and Floc'h, M. (1987) *C'Hoariou Breizh: jeux traditionnels de Bretagne*. Rennes: Institut Culturel de Bretagne.

Pezron, Paul-Yves (1703) *L'Antiquité de la Nation et de la Langue des Celtes*. Paris: Fayard.

Pigot & Co. (1837) *National Commercial Directory*. Argyll and Bute County Archive.

Powell, T. G. E. (1963) *The Celts*. London: Thames and Hudson.

Prentis, M. (1987) *The Scottish in Australia*. Melbourne: Lynedoch.

Prichard, C. (1961) *Un nos ola leuad*. Denbigh: Gee. (Published in translation 1973 as *Full Moon*. London: Hodder & Stoughton.)

Pritchard, K. Olwen (1973) *The Story of Gilfach Goch*. Newport: Starling Press.

Pugh, S. (1993) *Sing for the Taxman*. Bridgend: Seren Books.

Puirseal, P. (1982) *The Gaelic Athletic Association in its Time*. Dublin: Purcell.

Quinn, J. (1993) *Ulster Football and Hurling: The Path of Champions*. Dublin: Wolfhound Press.

Radcliffe, S. and Westwood, S. (1996) *Remaking the Nation: Place, Identity and Politics in Latin America*. London: Routledge.

Rees, A. (1987) 'Cardiff Arms Park', in M. Stephens (ed.), *A Cardiff Anthology*. Bridgend: Poetry Wales Press.

Reynolds, D. (1995) 'Creating an educational system for Wales'. *Welsh Journal of Education*, **4** (2), 4–21.

Rhys, Grace (1927) *A Celtic Anthology*. London: Harrap.

Richards, A. (1973) *Dai Country*. London: Michael Joseph.

Richards, A. (1986) *Days of absence*. London: Michael Joseph.

Richards, E. (1982) *A History of the Highland Clearances*. London: Croom Helm.

Rokkan, S. and Urwin, D. (1983) *Economy, Territory and Identity: Politics of West European Peripheries*. London: Sage.

Ross, A. (1986) *The Pagan Celts*. London: Batsford.

Rouse, P. (1993) 'The politics of culture and sport in Ireland: A history of the GAA ban on foreign games 1884–1971. Part 1: 1884–1921. *International Journal of the History of Sport*, **10** (3), 333–60.

Rowe, W. and Schelling, V. (1991) *Memory and Modernity: Popular Culture in Latin America*. London: Verso.

Rowe, D. and Wood, N. (eds) (1996) 'Editorial'. *Media, Culture and Society*, **18** (4), i–iv.

Said, E. (1984) *The World, the Text and the Critic*. London: Macmillan.

Sainclivier, J. (1989) *La Bretagne de 1939 à nos jours*. Rennes: Ouest-France.

Sainclivier, J. (1996) 'Culture politique et pouvoirs locaux en Bretagne (1935–1953)'. *Annales de Bretagne et des Pays de l'Ouest*, **103** (3), 11–30.

Scannell, V. (ed.) (1987) *Sporting Literature: An Anthology*. Oxford: Oxford University Press.

Shaw, J. (1989) *Tales Until Dawn*. Edinburgh: McGill-Queens University Press.

Smith, A. D. (1996) *Nations and Nationalism in a Global Era*. Cambridge: Polity Press.

Smith, D. (1990) 'Focal heroes: a Welsh fighting class', in R. Holt (ed.), *Sport and the Working Class in Modern Britain*. Manchester: Manchester University Press, 198–217.

Smith, D. and Williams, G. (1980) *Fields of Praise: The Official History of the Welsh Rugby Union 1881–1981*. Cardiff: University of Wales Press.

Smith, Rev J. (1798) *General View of the Agriculture of the County of Argyle*. London: Phillips.

Smout, T. C. (1970) 'The landowner and the planned village in Scotland 1730–1830', in N. Phillipson and R. Mitchison (eds), *Scotland in the Age of Improvement*. Edinburgh: Edinburgh University Press, 73–106.

Smout, T. C. (1986) *A History of the Scottish People*, 2nd edn. London: Collins.

Southey, R. (1929) *Journal of a Tour in Scotland in 1819*. London: John Murray.

Spicilegium Ossoriensis, being a collection of letters and papers illustrative of the history of the Irish Church from the Reformation to the year 1800, by the Most Rev. Patrick Francis Moran, DD, Archbishop of Sydney, third series, Dublin, 1884.

Sports Council for Wales (1995a) *Learning to Play*. Sports Update No. 30. Cardiff: Sports Council for Wales.

Sports Council for Wales (1995b) *The Pattern of Play: Physical Education in Welsh Secondary Schools: 1990 to 1994*. Cardiff: Sports Council for Wales.

Sports Council for Wales (1996) *Young People and Sport in Wales*. Cardiff: Welsh Office.

Sproat, I. (1996) *Hansard*, 7 June 1996, 823.

Statistical Account (1845) *The New Statistical Account*, vol. VII. Edinburgh: William Blackwood.

Statistical Account (1983) *The Statistical Account of Scotland*, new edn, vols VIII and XX. Wakefield: EP Publishing.

Stewart, C. B. (1848) *The Loiterer in Argyllshire*. Edinburgh: John Johnstone.

Stivell, A. (1979) *Racines interdites: Gwriziad Difennet*, Paris: J.-C. Lattès.

Sugden, J. and Bairner, A. (1986) 'Northern Ireland: sport in a divided society', in L. Allison (ed.), *The Politics of Sport*. Manchester: Manchester University Press, 90-117.

Sugden, J. and Bairner, A. (1993) *Sport, Sectarianism and Society in a Divided Ireland*. London: Leicester University Press.

Sullivan, A. M. (1877) *New Ireland*. Dublin: Cliàth.

Tatlock, J. S. P. (1950) *The Legendary History of England*. San Francisco: University of California Press.

Telfer, H. (1994) 'Play, customs and popular culture of West Coast communities, 1840–1900', in G. Jarvie and G. Walker (eds), *Scottish Sport in the Making of the Nation*. London: Leicester University Press.

Terry, D. (1997) 'Sport and health of the ancient Celts'. Unpublished paper delivered at the 4th International ISHPES Congress, 16–22 July, Lyons, France.

The Welsh Office (1995) *Young People and Sport in Wales*. Cardiff: Central Office of Information.

Thomas, D. (1993) *Collected Poems, 1934–53*. London: Dent, Everyman edition.

Thomas, G. (1964) *A Welsh Eye*. London: Hutchinson.

Thomas, G. (1985) *High on Hope*. Bridgend: Fordridge Books.

Thomas, N. (1971) *The Welsh Extremist: A Culture in Crisis.* London: Victor Gollancz.

Thomson, D. S. (ed.) (1994) *The Companion to Gaelic Scotland.* Glasgow: Gairm Publications.

Tierney, J. J. (1960) 'The Celtic ethnography of Posidonius'. *Proceedings of the Royal Irish Academy*, **60**, C 5.

Tranter, N. (1989) 'Sport and the economy in nineteenth century and early twentieth-century Scotland'. *Scottish Historical Review*, LXVIII, 1: No. 185: 53–69.

Trotel, J. C. (1986) *Public du Stade Rennais qui es-tu?* Rennes: Université de Haute-Bretagne.

Turnock, D. (1995) *The Making of the Scottish Rural Landscape.* Aldershot: Scolar Press.

Updike, J. (1991) *A Rabbit Omnibus.* Harmondsworth: Penguin.

Valo, M. (1997) 'La Bretagne a toujours des vues sur la Loire-Atlantique'. *Le Monde*, 4 July, 11.

Vigarello, G. (1992) 'Le Tour de France', in Pierre Nora (ed.), *Les Lieux de mémoire: III. Les France: 2. Traditions.* Paris: Gallimard, 884–925.

Wahl, A. (1986) 'Le footballeur français de l'amateurisme au salariat (1890–1926)'. *Le Mouvement social*, **135**, 7–30.

Wahl, A. (1989) *Les archives du football: Sport et société en France (1880–1980).* Paris: Gallimard-Julliard.

Wahl, A. (1990) *La Balle au pied: histoire de football.* Paris: Gallimard.

Wahl, A. and Lanfranchi, P. (1995) *Les footballeurs professionnels des années trente à nos jours.* Paris: Hachette.

Walker, G. and Gallagher, T. (eds) (1990) *Sermons and Battle Hymns; Protestant Popular Culture in Modern Scotland.* Edinburgh: Edinburgh University Press.

Webb, H. (1970) *Rampage and Revel.* Llandysul: Gomer.

Weber, E. (1977) *Peasants into Frenchmen: The Modernisation of Rural France.* London: Chatto & Windus.

West, T. (1991) *The Bold Collegians. The Development of Sport in Trinity College, Dublin.* Dublin: Lilliput Press.

Western Mail (1996) [Wales] 'Fortunate to have escaped a rebellion by English speakers', 24 April, 1.

Williams, C. H. (1995) 'Questions concerning the development of bilingual Wales', in B. Morris Jones and P. A. Singh Ghuman (eds), *Bilingualism, Education and Identity.* Cardiff: University of Wales Press, 47–9.

Williams, D. J. (1959) *Yn Chwech ar Hugain Oed.* Aberystwyth: Gwasg Aberystwyth.

Williams, G. (1997) 'Postponing death: sport and literature in Wales'. *New Welsh Review*, **36**, 37–46.

Williams, G. A. (1985) *When Was Wales?* Harmondsworth: Penguin.

Williams, G. A. (1996) 'When Was Wales?', in S. Woolf (ed.), *Nationalism in Europe 1815 to Present.* London: Routledge, 192–205.

Wilson, B. (1988) *Celtic: A Century with Honour*, Glasgow: Collins.

Woolf, S. (ed.) (1996) *Nationalism in Europe 1815 to Present*. London: Routledge.

Young, I. M. (1990) *Justice and the Politics of Difference*. Princeton, NJ: Princeton University Press.

Zeuss, Kaspar (1853) *Grammatica Celtica*, Leipzig.

INDEX